Constitutional Law

DR. FERGUS RYAN
LL.B. (Hons.) (Dub.), Ph.D. (Dub.)

DUBLIN
ROUND HALL LTD
2001

Published in 2001 by
Round Hall Ltd.
43 Fitzwilliam Place
Dublin 2
Ireland

Typeset by
Devlin Editing, Dublin

Printed by
Techman, Dublin

A CIP catalogue record for this book is available from the British Library

ISBN 1-85800-257-5

© Round Hall 2001

BIOGRAPHY

Dr. Fergus Ryan, a graduate and former scholar of Trinity College Dublin, has been teaching Constitutional Law in various capacities for over five years. Presently a lecturer in law at the Dublin Institute of Technology, he has taught a variety of legal subjects at both undergraduate and postgraduate level as well as preparing students for professional legal examinations such as the FE 1 for entry to the Law Society of Ireland.

PREFACE

Despite being a comparatively young State, the 64 years since the enactment of the 1937 Constitution have seen the growth of an impressive, if sometimes rather complex, constitutional jurisprudence in Ireland. Particularly since the mid-1960s, the Constitution has been the subject of much litigation and debate in the Courts, and the subject of some considerable comment and controversy in the public arena generally. The task of completing a succinct constitutional text is thus made rather unenviable. In some respects writing such a text – enjoyable as it has been for me – is somewhat akin to squeezing an elephant into a telephone booth. It is no small wonder that students of Constitutional Law often feel overwhelmed by the subject.

A particular challenge is the dynamic nature of the Constitution. Surely President de Valera, its primary architect, could never have envisaged that his Constitution would be used to establish a right to import contraception (*McGee v. Attorney General* (1973))? Or that the document would be altered so as to commit the State to a settlement of the argument over Partition (the Nineteenth Amendment of the Constitution Act, 1999)? Yet within the space even of a mere ten years the constitutional landscape of Ireland can change beyond recognition.

It is suggested, however, that it is this very dynamism that makes Constitutional Law so exciting and rewarding to study. A day does not go by when the evening news or broadsheet newspapers do not touch upon an issue that concerns an aspect of constitutional law. Constitutional Law thus enjoys that very rare privilege, of being perpetually topical and relevant.

It has to be said, however, that when compared to the United States, for instance, the public consciousness of constitutional norms and rights in this State is not as robust as it could be. This may simply reflect the fact that the Irish Constitution is considerably longer and more detailed than its U.S. counterpart, not to mention the fact that the latter has had over 200 years to settle into the public psyche. It may be that as a State, we have never made much of an effort to explain to the general public what the Constitution is about. It is suggested, however, that with the relatively homogenous nature of Irish society in former times we had less to argue about than in the more diverse and eclectic United States. Whether this will change in the more pluralist Ireland that is now emerging from the twentieth century is yet to be seen.

It is my hope then, that this text will go some small way towards informing the reader about this most important and fundamental of laws in a manner that dispels as much constitutional mystery as possible. The text is designed primarily with the student in mind, although practitioners and the general public alike should also find it useful and informative. It endeavours to explain the key principles and concepts of an often demanding subject in a manner that is easily comprehensible to the student. Particular emphasis is placed on the need to establish and identify the points most relevant to a study of what is an often densely layered subject.

It would be remiss of me to finish this preface without acknowledging the support of a number of people. This book would not have been possible without the support and assistance of several persons. My sincere thanks go out to Therese Carrick and all at Round Hall, to Eoin O'Dell of Trinity College Dublin, to my colleagues and friends at the Dublin Institute of Technology, particularly Bruce Carolan, most of all to my family, especially Chris Roufs and Raymund and Catherine Ryan, for their continued encouragement and support.

I have endeavoured to state the law as best I can as it stands as of August 1, 2001.

Fergus Ryan, Dublin, August 1, 2001.

For my parents, Raymund and Catherine and my partner, Chris

CONTENTS

Biography v
Preface vii
Table of Cases xvii
Table of Statutes xxvii
Treaties xxxv

Part I
General Issues

1. **A Brief History of the Constitution** 1

2. **The Purpose of a Constitution** 5
   2.1 Defining the jurisdiction of the State 5
   2.2 Establishing a framework for governing the State 5
   2.3 Regulating the relationship between the State and
        its inhabitants 6
   2.4 The "Rule of Law" 6

3. **Constitutional Interpretation** 7
   3.1 In the case of conflict between texts, the Irish text
        prevails 7
   3.2 Literal interpretation 7
   3.3 Broad interpretation 8
   3.4 Harmonious interpretation 9
   3.5 Hierarchical interpretation 10
   3.6 Historical approach 11
   3.7 Natural law approach 13
   3.8 The presumption of constitutionality 14
   3.9 The double construction rule 15

4. **Judicial Review: Challenging the Constitutionality
   of State Conduct** 16
   4.1 Acts of the Oireachtas enacted after 1937 16
   4.2 Article 50 — laws created prior to 1937 17
   4.3 Article 26 — reference of Bills to the Supreme
        Court 18
   4.4 Who may take a case — "locus standi" 18
   4.5 Retrospectivity of a finding of unconstitutionality 20
   4.6 Are certain matters beyond judicial review? 21

5. **Article 26 — Reference of Bills by the President** 25
    5.1   Who may make a reference? 25
    5.2   What measures may be referred? 25
    5.3   Can a part of a Bill be referred? 26
    5.4   To whom is the reference sent? 26
    5.5   What happens when a reference is made? 26
    5.6   Presumption of Constitutionality 26
    5.7   The "One Judgment" Rule 27
    5.8   The consequences of the decision 27
    5.9   Bills and parts of Bills referred 28
    5.10 Is Article 26 a good idea? 29

Part II
The Nation, the State and the Outside World

6. **The Preamble to the Constitution** 33
    6.1   Judicial comment on the Preamble 34

7. **The Nation and the Position of Northern Ireland**
    (Articles 1-3) 37
    7.1   The concept of a nation 37
    7.2   Articles 2 and 3 — The position of Northern Ireland 38
    7.3   The old Articles 2 and 3 38
    7.4   Recognising Northern Ireland 40
    7.5   The Good Friday Agreements, 1998 40
    7.6   The new Articles 2 and 3 41

8. **The Irish State (Articles 4-11)** 44
    8.1   The independence of the State 44
    8.2   The State as a legal person 45
    8.3   Is the State a "Sovereign" State? 45
    8.4   The national flag 47
    8.5   The languages of the State 48
    8.6   Citizenship 50

9. **Ireland in the International Order (Article 29)** 52
    9.1   International relations 52
    9.2   How does Ireland become a party to international
          agreements? 53
    9.3   Dualism v. monism 53
    9.4   The impact of International Law in the Irish courts 55
    9.5   Extra-territoriality 55

10. **Ireland in the European Union** 57

10.1 The Supremacy of European Law 58
10.2 Article 29.4.7 58
10.3 The direct effect of E.U. Law 59
10.4 Implementing Directives 60
10.5 Is a referendum required every time there is a new E.U. Treaty? 61

Part III
The Institutions of State

11. **The Separation of Powers** 65
    11.1 The exclusivity of roles 66
    11.2 Some blurring of the lines of separation 67
    11.3 Summary 68

12. **The President (Articles 12-14)** 69
    12.1 Electing the President 69
    12.2 The powers of the President 70
    12.3 The Council of State (Articles 31-32) 73
    12.4 Article 14 and the Presidential Commission 74
    12.5 Dismissing the President 75

13. **The Oireachtas (Article 15)** 76
    13.1 Sole and exclusive right to legislate 76
    13.2 The Oireachtas cannot pass certain laws 77
    13.3 The Oireachtas' exclusive powers within Ireland 77
    13.4 Delegated legislation 78
    13.5 Only the Oireachtas can change or repeal legislation 80
    13.6 The Oireachtas cannot delegate the right to make policy 81
    13.7 The *Sheehan* principle 81
    13.8 Parliamentary privilege 82
    13.9 Summary 83

14. **The Dáil and the Seanad (Articles 16-24)** 85
    14.1 The Dáil 85
    14.2 The Seanad 86
    14.3 The Dáil is the more powerful house 87
    14.4 Summary of voting rights 89

15. **Government (Article 28)** 91
    15.1 Membership of the Government 91
    15.2 An Taoiseach 92

15.3 The Tánaiste 94
15.4 Ministers.. 95
15.5 Executive privilege.. 96
15.6 Collective responsibility................................. 97
15.7 Cabinet confidentiality 97

16. **Emergency Powers (Article 28.3)**............................ 99
16.1 Declarations of war 99
16.2 Actual invasion... 99
16.3 Constitutional exemption 100

17. **The Attorney General (Article 30)**........................ 102
17.1 Appointment of the Attorney General........... 102
17.2 The role of the Attorney General 102

18. **The Courts (Articles 34-37)**.................................. 107
18.1 The court system 107
18.2 Appointment of judges 109
18.3 Judges' salaries... 110
18.4 Justice to be administered in public 111
18.5 Exclusive powers of the courts...................... 111
18.6 Exercise of a judicial function...................... 113
18.7 Article 37... 117

Part IV
Human Rights and the Constitution

19. **Human Rights and the Constitution**........................ 119
19.1 Human and constitutional rights.................... 123
19.2 No right is ever absolute................................. 126
19.3 Distributive justice 127

20. **Trial of Offences (Article 38)** 128
20.1 The principles of a fair trial............................ 128

21. **Trial by Jury**... 139
21.1 Jury trial matters... 139
21.2 Basic principles of jury trials........................ 141
21.3 Criminal trials where juries are not constitutionally
       required... 141

22. **Equality (Article 40.1)**... 146
22.1 Inequality established 146
22.2 Sex discrimination.. 147

22.3 Cases in which a breach was not established 149
22.4 Discrimination must be based on human
     characteristics 150
22.5 The failure to take into account relevant
     differences 151
22.6 Other legal provisions requiring equality of
     treatment 151

23. Personal Rights (Article 40.3) 152
23.1 The source of unenumerated rights 152
23.2 The content of unenumerated rights 154
23.3 Summary 165

24. The Right to Life 166
24.1 The right to life of the unborn child 167

25. Personal Liberty: Rights on Arrest and in Detention 171
25.1 The power to arrest 171
25.2 Detention for other reasons 176

26. Freedom of Expression (Article 40.6.1.i) 180
26.1 Restrictions on freedom of expression 181

27. Freedom of Association 189
27.1 Limits 189
27.2 Right to dissociate 191
27.3 Trade union recognition 192

28. The Family and Education (Articles 41-42) 193
28.1 The "Constitutional Family" is the family based
     on marriage 193
28.2 Individual rights and family rights 194
28.3 Family right to autonomy 194
28.4 The constitutional preference for marriage 196
28.5 The rights of unmarried parents and their children 197
28.6 The guardianship, custody and adoption of children 198
28.7 Divorce 200
28.8 Education 200

29. Property Rights (Article 43) 205
29.1 The scope of Article 43 205
29.2 Rent restrictions and property rights 207
29.3 Arbitrarily selective impositions on property rights 208
29.4 The right to compensation 209

30. Freedom of Religion (Article 44) 211
   30.1 Free conscience and profession of religion 212
   30.2 Supporting the practice of religion 212
   30.3 State aid for schools 215
   30.4 Autonomy of religious denominations 215

31. Amendments to the Constitution 216
   31.1 Requirements of a referendum 217
   31.2 Successful Amendments 217
   31.3 Defeated referenda 219
   31.4 Article 27 219

Appendix A 221
Appendix B 222
Index 223

TABLE OF CASES

Abbott and Whelan v. IT & GWU and Southern Health Board
(1982) 1 JISLL 56 .... 27.3
Abingdon School District v. Schempp 374 U.S. 203 (1963) 30.3
Article 26 and the Criminal Law (Jurisdiction) Bill, 1975,
In the Matter of [1977] I.R. 129 ....3.8, 7.1, 7.3
Article 26 and the Employment Equality Bill, 1996,
In the Matter of [1997] 2 I.R. 321 .... 29.3
Article 26 and the Equal Status Bill, 1997, In the Matter of
[1997] 2 I.R. 387 .... 29.3
Article 26 and the Housing (Private Rented Dwellings) Bill,
1981, In the Matter of [1984] I.L.R.M. 246 .... 29.2
Article 26 and the Matrimonial Home Bill, 1993,
In the Matter of [1994] 1 I.R. 305 .... 28.3
Article 26 and the Offence Against the State (Amendment)
Bill, 1940, In the Matter of [1940] I.R. 470 .... 6.1.5
Article 26 and the Part V of the Planning and Development
Bill, 2000, In the Matter of Supreme Court,
August 28, 2000 .... 29.3
Article 26 and the Regulation of Information Bill, 1995,
In the Matter of [1995] 1 I.R. 1 .... 3.7, 5.5, 8.3, 31.
Article 26 and the Section 4 of the School Attendance Bill,
1942, In the Matter of [1943] I.R. 334 .... 28.8.2
Association of General Practitioners v. Minister for Health
[1995] 1 I.R. 382 .... 27.3
Attorney General (S.P.U.C.) v. Open Door Counselling
[1988] I.R. 593 ....3.5, 24.1.3
Attorney General for England and Wales v. Brandon
Books [1987] I.L.R.M. 135 .... 19.1.3
Attorney General v Lee [2001] 1 I.L.R.M. 553............................ 17.2.3
Attorney General v. Cooke (1924) 58 I.L.T.R. 157 .... 26.1.4
Attorney General v. Cunningham [1932] I.R. 28 .... 20.1.1
Attorney General v. Hamilton (No. 1) [1993]
2 I.R. 250 .... 15.7, 17.2.3
Attorney General v. Hamilton (No. 2) [1993] 3 I.R. 227 .... 13.8
Attorney General v. Paperlink [1984] I.L.R.M. 373
.... 3.2, 3.3, 23.1, 23.2.9, 26.

Attorney General v. Southern Industrial Trust (1957)
    94 I.L.T.R. 161 .... 29.1.2
Attorney General v. X. [1992] 1 I.R. 1
    .... 3.5, 17.2.1, 17.2.3, 23.2.10, 24.1.1, 24.1.2, 31.3

B. v. D.P.P. [1997] 2 I.L.R.M. 118 .... 20.1.3
Baehr v. Lewin 852 P. 2d. 44 (Haw. 1993) 23.2.4
Baker v. Nelson 191 NW2d 185 (Minn., 1973) 23.2.4
Blake v. Attorney General [1982] I.R. 117 ....29.1, 29.2
Blascaod Mór, An v. Commissioner for Public Works
    [2000] 1 I.L.R.M. 401 .... 13.8, 22.1
Boland v. An Taoiseach [1974] I.R. 338 .... 7.3
Brady v. Donegal County Council [1989] I.L.R.M. 282 .... 23.2.11
Brennan v. Attorney General [1984] I.L.R.M. 355 ....3.6, 29.2
Buckley v. Attorney General [1950] I.R. 67 ....11.1, 18.5, 29.1.2
Byrne v. Ireland [1972] I.R. 241 .... 8.2, 8.3, 15.5, 23.2.11

C.M. v. T.M. [1988] I.L.R.M. 456 .... 22.2
Cahill v. Sutton [1980] I.R. 269 .... 4.4
Campaign to Separate Church and State v. Minister for
    Education [1998] 2 I.L.R.M. 81 .... 30.2.1, 30.3
Campus Oil v. Minister for Industry and Energy [1983]
    I.R. 88 .... 10.1
Cassidy v. Minister for Industry and Commerce [1978]
    I.R. 297 .... 22.5
Central Dublin Development Association v. Attorney
    General (1975) 109 I.L.T.R. 69 .... 18.7, 29.4
Charlton v. Ireland [1984] I.L.R.M. 39 .... 21.3.1
Christie v. Leachinsky [1947] A.C. 537 .... 25.1
Cityview Press v. AnCO [1980] I.R. 381 .... 13.4, 13.9
Clarke, In re Philip [1950] I.R. 253 .... 25.2.2
Comerford v. Minister for Education [1997] 2 I.L.R.M. 134 ...... 28.8.4
Comyn v. Attorney General [1950] I.R. 142 .... 8.2
Conroy v. Attorney General [1965] I.R. 411 .... 21.3.1
Cooke v. Walsh [1984] I.R. 710 .... 13.5
Corway v. Independent Newspapers [2000] 1 I.L.R.M. 426 .... 26.1.1
Costa v. E.N.E.L. [1964] E.C.R. 585 .... 10.1
Cotter v. Ahern [1975-1976] I.L.R.M. 248 .... 27.2
Coughlan v. RTÉ unreported, Supreme Court, January, 26, 2000 ... 31.
Cowan v. Attorney General [1961] I.R. 411 .... 18.7
Cox v. Ireland [1992] 2 I.R. 503 .... 20.1.12, 23.2.8, 29.1.2, 29.2

Crotty v. An Taoiseach [1987] I.R. 713
................................4.4, 4.6, 8.3, 9.1, 10.5, 11.1, 17.2.3
Crowley v. Ireland [1980] I.R. 102 .... 28.8.3
Curran v. Attorney General unreported, High Court,
     February 27, 1941 .... 20.1.8

D.G. v. Eastern Health Board [1998] 1 I.L.R.M. 241 .... 25.2.2
D.P.P. (Stratford) v. Fagan [1994] 3 I.R. 265 .... 25.2.4
D.P.P. v. Best [2000] 2 I.L.R.M. 1... 28.8.2
D.P.P. v. J.T. (1988) 3 Frewen 141 .... 28.2
De Burca v. Attorney General [1976] I.R. 38 ....4.5, 21.1.3, 22.2
Deaton v. Attorney General [1963] I.R. 170 ....11.1, 18.6.4, 18.6.6
Dennehy v. Minister for Social Welfare unreported, High Court,
     July 26, 1984 .... 22.3
Desmond v. Glackin (No. 1) [1993] 3 I.R.1 .... 9.4
Dillane v. Ireland [1980] I.L.R.M. 167 .... 3.4
Donnelly v. Ireland [1998] 1 I.R. 325 .... 20.1.8
Donovan v. Minister for Justice (1951) 85 I.L.T.R. 134 .... 23.2.4
Draper v. Attorney General [1984] I.R. 277 .... 22.3
Dublin Colleges Academic Staff Association v. CDVEC
     unreported, High Court, July 31, 1981 .... 27.3
Duggan v An Taoiseach [1989] I.L.R.M. 710 .... 13.5

East Donegal Co-op. v. Attorney General [1970] I.R. 317 .... 3.8, 3.9
Educational Company v. Fitzpatrick (No. 2) [1961]
     I.R. 345 ....19.1.3, 23.1, 27.2
ESB v. Gormley [1985] I.L.R.M. 494 .... 29.4

Finn v. Attorney General [1983] I.R. 514 ....4.6, 19.1.2, 31.
Flynn v. Power [1985] I.R. 648 .... 30.2.2

G. v. An Bord Úchtála [1980] I.R. 32 .... 28.5, 28.6.1
Gallagher, In re, [1991] 1 I.R. 31 .... 18.6.5
Garvey v. Ireland [1981] I.R. 75 .... 23.2.12
Gilligan v. Ireland [2001] 1 I.L.R.M. 473 .... 21.3.2
Goodman International v. Hamilton (No. 1) [1992]
     2 I.R. 542 .... 18.6.1
Greene v. Minister for Agriculture [1990] 2 I.R. 17 .... 10.2, 28.4

H. v. D.P.P. [1994] 2 I.L.R.M. 285 .... 17.2.2

Hand v. Dublin Corporation [1991] 1 I.R. 409 .... 23.2.8
Hardy v. Ireland [1994] 2 I.R. 550 .... 20.1.4
Haughey, In re [1971] I.R. 217 .... 3.9, 18.6.3, 20.1.8, 21.1.1, 21.3.1
Heaney and McGuinness v. Ireland [1994] 3 I.R. 593,
    (H.C.), [1996] 1 I.R. 580, (S.C.) .... 20.1.10, 26.
Hempenstall v. Minister for Environment [1994] 2 I.R. 20 .... 29.1.2
Holohan v. Donohue [1986] I.R. 45 .... 21.1.1
Howard v. Commissioners of Public Works [1994]
    1 I.R. 101 .... 8.3, 18.5.1

Íarnród Éireann v. Ireland [1996] 3 I.R. 321 .... 19.1.3
Ireland v. Mulvey *Irish Times*, November 11, 1989 .... 8.2
Irish Times v. Ireland [1998] 1 I.R. 359 .... 26.0.1

J.H.; K.C. and A.C., Re v. An Bord Uchtála [1985] I.R. 375 ...... 28.6.2

K. v. W. [1990] 2 I.R. 437 .... 28.5
Kane v. Governor of Mountjoy Prison [1988] I.R. 757 .... 25.2.5
Kavanagh v. Ireland [1996] 1 I.R. 321 .... 4.6, 21.3.2
Keady v. Garda Commissioner [1992] 2 I.R. 197 .... 18.6, 18.6.2
Kearney v. Minister for Justice [1986]
    I.R. 116 .... 19.2, 23.2.3, 23.2.9
Kennedy and McCann, Re [1976] I.R. 382 .... 26.1.4
Kennedy v. Hearne [1988] I.R. 481 .... 18.6
Kennedy v. Ireland [1987] I.R. 587 .... 3.7, 19.1.2, 23.1, 23.2.3
King v. Attorney General [1981] I.R. 233 .... 20.1.1, 20.1.4
Kostan v. Ireland [1978] I.L.R.M. 12 .... 21.3.1

Landers v. Attorney General (1973) 109 I.L.T.R. 1 .... 23.2.8, 28.8
Laurentiu v. Minister for Justice *Irish Times*, May 21, 1999 .... 13.6
Lennon v. Ganly [1981] I.L.R.M. 84 .... 23.2.10
Lotus case, The (1927) P.C.I.J. Ser. A No. 10 .... 9.5
Lovett v. Minister for Education [1997]
    1 I.L.R.M. 89 .... 29.1.2, 29.2
Lynham v. Butler (No. 2) [1933] I.R. 74 .... 18.6

M, an Infant, In re [1946] I.R.334 .... 28.5
M. v. An Bord Uchtála [1975] I.R. 81 .... 28.6.1, 30.2.2
M. v. An Bord Uchtála [1977] I.R. 287 .... 18.7.1
M.C. v. Legal Aid Board [1991] 2 I.R. 43 .... 23.2.11

M.M. v. P.M. [1986] I.L.R.M. 515 .... 13.3
Macauley v. Minister for Post and Telegraphs [1966]
    I.R. 345 .... 23.2.11
MacGairbhíth v. Attorney General [1991] 2 I.R. 412 .... 23.2.11
Madigan v. Attorney General [1986] I.L.R.M. 136 .... 4.4, 22.4
Magee v. O'Dea (1991) [1994] 1 I.R. 500 .... 20.1.7
Maher v. Attorney General [1973] I.R. 140 .... 11.1, 13.3, 13.9
Mallon v. Minister for Agriculture [1996] 1 I.R. 517 .... 21.3.1
Martin v. Dublin Corporation unreported, High Court, November
    14, 1978 .... 4.4
McDaid v. Sheehy [1991] I.L.R.M. 250 .... 13.6
McDonald v. Bord na gCon (No. 2) [1965] I.R. 217 .....3.9, 18.6, 18.7
McGee v. Attorney General [1974] I.R. 284 ...... 3.6, 3.7, 3.8, 4.2, 4.4,
    ....6.1.3, 6.1.4, 19.1.2, 23.1, 23.2.1, 23.2.3,
    ....23.2.4, 23.2.5, 24.1, 28.3, 30.1, 31.
McGimpsey v. Ireland [1990] 1 I.R. 110 .... 4.4, 4.6, 7.3, 7.4
McGrath and Ó Ruairc v. Maynooth College [1979]
    I.L.R.M. 166 .... 30.2.2
McGrath v. McDermott [1988] I.L.R.M. 647 .... 13.3
McKenna v. An Taoiseach (No. 2) [1995] 2 I.R. 10 ....4.6, 22.1, 31.
McKinley v. Minister for Defence [1992] 2 I.R. 333 .... 13.3, 22.2
McLoughlin v. Minister for Social Welfare [1958] I.R. 1 .... 17.2.1
McMahon v. Attorney General [1972] I.R. 69 .... 14.1.4
McMahon v. Leahy [1984] I.R. 525 .... 22.1
McMenamin v. Ireland [1996] 3 I.R. 100 .... 18.3
Meagher v. Minister for Agriculture [1994] 1 I.R. 329 .... 10.4, 13.5
Melling v. Ó Mathghamhna [1962] I.R. 1 ....3.3, 3.6, 21.3.1
Meskell v. CIÉ [1973] I.R. 121 .... 27.2
MhicMhathúna v. Ireland [1995] I.L.R.M. 69 .... 22., 28.4
Miller v. California 413 U.S. 15 (1973) 26.1.1
Muckley v. Ireland [1985] I.R. 472 .... 4.5
Mulloy v. Minister for Education [1975] I.R. 88 .... 30.2.2
Murphy v. Attorney General [1982] I.R. 241 .... 22.3, 28.4
Murphy v. Dublin Corporation [1972] I.R. 215 .... 4.5, 15.5
Murphy v. Independent Radio and Television Commission
    [1998] 2 I.L.R.M. 360 .... 26.
Murphy v. Stewart [1973] I.R. 97 .... 27.1.2
Murray v. Ireland [1985] I.R. 532, (H.C.) [1991] 1 I.L.R.M.
    465, (S.C.) 6.1.5, 19.2, 23.2.5, 28.1, 28.2, 28.3, 28.3.1
Murtagh Properties v. Cleary [1972] I.R. 330 .... 23.2.8, 27.2

National Irish Bank Ltd, Re [1999] 1 I.L.R.M. 321 .... 20.1.10
Norris v. Attorney General [1984] I.R. 36 .... 3.6, 3.7, 4.4, 6.1.1,
.... 13.3, 13.5, 13.9, 17.2.2, 19.2, 22.3, 23.2.3, 27.1.1, 30.
Northants. County Council v. A.B.F. [1982] I.L.R.M. 164 .... 19.1.2

Ó Beoláin v. Ireland unreported, Supreme Court, April 4, 2001 .. 8.5.1
Ó Domhnaill v. Merrick [1985] I.R. 151 .... 9.4
Ó Láighléis, In re [1960] I.R. 93 .... 9.3, 25.1
O'B. v. S. [1984] I.R. 316 .... 3.4, 9.3, 22., 22.3, 28.4
O'Byrne v. Minister for Finance [1959] I.R. 1 .... 3.3, 18.3
O'Callaghan v. Attorney General [1993] 2 I.R. 17 .... 21.2
O'Callaghan v. Ireland [1994] 1 I.R. 555 .... 25.2.4
O'Donovan v. Attorney General [1961] I.R. 114 .... 14.1.1
O'G., T.v. Attorney General [1985] I.L.R.M. 61 .... 22.2
O'Leary v. Attorney General [1993] 1 I.R. 102, [1993]
    2 I.R. 254 .... 20.1.4
O'Malley v. An Ceann Comhairle [1997] 1 I.R. 427 .... 13.8
O'Malley v. An Taoiseach [1990] I.L.R.M. 461 .... 12.5
O'R., W. v. E.H. [1996] 2 I.R. 248 .... 28.1, 28.5
O'Reilly v. Limerick Corporation [1989] I.L.R.M. 181.................. 19.3
O'Shaughnessy v. Attorney General unreported,
    High Court, February 16, 1971 .... 23.2.11
O'Shiel v. Minister for Education [1999] 2 I.L.R.M. 241 .... 28.8.3
O'Sullivan v. Hartnett [1983] I.L.R.M. 79 .... 21.3.1
O'T., I.v. B. [1998] 2 I.R. 321 .... 23.2.5
Osheku v. Ireland [1986] I.R 733 .... 6.1.5

People (A.G.) v. Dwyer [1972] I.R. 416 .... 24.
People (A.G.) v. Edge [1943] I.R. 115 .... 20.1.1
People (A.G.) v. O'Brien [1965] I.R. 142 .... 23.2.2
People (A.G.) v. O'Callaghan [1966] I.R. 501 .... 25.1.6, 25.2.1
People (A.G.) v. Singer [1975] I.R. 408 .... 20.1.7, 21.1.2
People (AG) v. Messitt [1972] I.R. 204 .... 20.1.5
People (AG) v. O'Brien [1965] I.R. 142 .... 20.1.11
People (D.P.P.) v. Farrell [1978] I.R. 336 .... 25.1.2
People (D.P.P.) v. Healy [1990] I.L.R.M. 313 .... 3.6, 25.1.2
People (D.P.P.) v. Higgins unreported, Supreme Court,
    November 22, 1985 .... 25.1.3
People (D.P.P.) v. Kelly [1982] I.L.R.M. 1 .... 20.1.5
People (D.P.P.) v. Lawless (1985) 3 Frewen 30 .... 20.1.11

People (D.P.P.) v. McNally (1981) 2 Frewen 43 .... 25.1.5
People (D.P.P.) v. O'Shea [1982] I.R. 384 .... 3.2, 20.1.13
People (D.P.P.) v. Pringle (1981) 2 Frewen 57 .... 25.1.2
People (D.P.P.) v. Quilligan (No. 1) [1987] I.L.R.M. 606 .... 25.1.4
People (D.P.P.) v. Shaw [1982] I.R. 1
.... 3.5, 19.2, 20.1.11, 24., 25.1.5
People (D.P.P.) v. Walsh [1980] I.R. 294 .... 25.1.2
Pigs Marketing Board v. Donnelly [1939] I.R. 413 .... 13.4
Pine Valley Ltd. v. Minister for the Environment [1987]
    I.R. 23 .... 18.5.1, 19.1.3
PMPS v. Attorney General [1983] I.R. 339 .... 19.1.3
Prince v. Massachusetts 321 U.S. 158 (1944) 30.1.1

Quinn's Supermarket v. Attorney General
    [1972] I.R. 1 .... 3.1, 6.1.1, 8.5, 19.1.3, 22.4, 30., 30.2.2

R. Ltd., In re [1989] I.R. 126 .... 18.4
R.C. v. C.C. [1997] 1 I.R. 334 .... 28.7
Reynolds v. United States 98 U.S. 145 (1878) 30.1.1
Riordan v. An Tánaiste [1997] 3 I.R. 502 .... 15.3
Riordan v. An Taoiseach (No. 2) Supreme Court,
    November 19, 1998 .... 4.6, 7.6, 31.
Rock v. Ireland [1997] 3 I.R. 484 .... 20.1.10
Russell v. Fanning [1988] I.R. 505 .... 6.1.2
Ryan v. Attorney General [1965] I.R. 294 .... 3.7, 23., 23.1, 23.2.1,
    .... 23.2.4, 23.3, 28.8
Ryan v. D.P.P. [1989] I.R. 399 .... 25.1.6

S.P.U.C. v. Coogan [1989] I.R. 734 .... 4.4, 17.2.3, 24.1.3
S.P.U.C. v. Grogan [1989] I.R. 753 .... 10.2, 24.1.3
Savage v. D.P.P. [1982] I.L.R.M. 385 .... 4.6, 21.3.2
Shanley v. Galway Corporation [1995] 1 I.R. 396 .... 23.2.8
Sinnott v. Minister for Education (2001) unreported,
    Supreme Court, July 12, 2001.. 28.8
Sinnott v. Minister for Education High Court, October 4,
    2000 .... 28.8.4
Skinner v. Oklahoma 316 U.S. 535 (1942) 23.2.4
Solicitors Act 1954, Re The [1960] I.R. 239 .... 18.6.2, 18.7
State (Buchan) v. Coyne (1936) 70 I.L.T.R. 185 .... 8.5.1, 20.1.6
State (Burke) v. Lennon [1940] I.R. 136 6
State (Byrne) v. Frawley [1978] I.R. 326 .... 4.5

State (C.) v. Frawley [1976] I.R. 365 ....23.2.1, 23.2.2
State (D.P.P.) v. Walsh (No. 3) High Court, October 21, 1981 ..26.1.4
State (D.P.P.) v. Walsh and Conneely [1981] I.R. 412 ....22.2
State (Gilliland) v. Governor of Mountjoy Prison [1987]
      I.L.R.M. 287 ....9.2, 14.3.4
State (Gilsenan) v. McMurrow [1978] I.R. 360 ....7.4
State (Harrington) v. Garvey unreported, High Court,
      December 14, 1976 ....25.1.2
State (Healy) v. Donoghue [1976] I.R. 325 .... 1., 3.6, 6.1.3, 20.1.9,
      ....23.2.11, 25.1.2
State (Keating) v. Ó hUadaigh unreported, High Court,
      May 11, 1984 ....20.1.12
State (Killian) v. Attorney General [1954] I.R. 207 ....4.6, 17.2.1
State (Lynch) v. Cooney [1983] I.L.R.M. 89 ....26.1.3
State (M.) v. Attorney General [1979] I.R. 73 ....23.2.10
State (MacFhearraigh) v. Gaffney (MacGhamhna) unreported,
      High Court, June 1, 1983 ....8.5.1
State (McCormack) v. Curran [1987] I.L.R.M. 225 ....4.6
State (McFadden) v. Governor of Mountjoy Prison [1981]
      I.L.R.M. 113 ....19.1.2
State (Murphy) v. Johnston [1983] I.R. 235 ....13.3, 13.9
State (Murray) v. McRann [1979] I.R. 133 ....18.6.2
State (Nicolaou) v. An Bord Úchtála [1966] I.R. 567 ....28.1, 28.5
State (O.) v. O'Brien [1973] I.R. 50 ....18.6.4, 20.1.12
State (O'Connell) v. Fawsitt [1986] I.L.R.M. 639 ....20.1.3
State (O'Rourke) v. Kelly [1983] I.R. 58.....................................18.6.6
State (Pheasantry) v. Donnelly [1982] I.L.R.M. 512 ....21.3.1
State (Richardson) v. Governor of Mounjoy Prison [1980]
      I.L.R.M. 82 ....23.2.1
State (Rollinson) v. Kelly [1984] I.L.R.M. 248 ....21.3.1
State (Sheehan) v. Government of Ireland [1987]
      I.R. 550 ....13.7, 18.6.4
State (Trimbole) v. Governor of Mountjoy Prison [1985]
      I.L.R.M. 465 ....19.1.2, 25.1.1
Street v. New York 394 U.S. 576 (1969) 8.4

Texas v. Johnston 491 U.S. 397 (1989) 8.4
Tierney v. Amalgamated Society of Woodworkers [1959]
      I.R. 254 ....27.1.2
Tilson, Re [1951] I.R. 1...28.6
Tuohy v. Courtney [1994] 3 I.R. 1 ....23.2.11

U.S. v. Eichman 496 U.S. 310 (1990) 8.4, 26

W. v. W. [1993] I.L.R.M. 294 .... 22.2
Ward of Court (Withdrawal of Medical Treatment), Re a,
    [1996] 2 I.R. 79 ....23.2.1, 23.2.3, 23.2.7
Webb v. Ireland [1988] I.R. 353 .... 8.3
Wise v. Dunning [1902] 1 K.B. 167 .... 26.1.2

Zablocki v. Redhail 434 U.S. 374 (1978) 23.2.4

TABLE OF STATUTES

Act of Union 1801 .... 1, 4.2
Adoption Act 1952 .... 23.2.10, 30.2.2
Adoption Act 1988 .... 28.6.1
Aliens Act 1935 .... 13.6
Broadcasting Act 1960
    s 31 .... 26.1.3
Censorship Act 1946
    s 6 .... 26.1.1
Censorship of Films Acts 1923-1992 .... 26.1.1
Censorship of Publication Act 1929
    s 16 .... 26.1.1
Censorship of Publications Acts 1929-1967 .... 26.1.1
Civil Liability Act 1961
    s 60 .... 13.7
Companies Act 1990
    s 10 .... 20.1.10
Courts Act 1988 .... 21.
Courts of Justice Act 1928
    s 5 .... 20.1.13
Criminal Evidence Act 1992 .... 20.1.8
Criminal Justice Act 1984
    s 25 .... 21.2
Criminal Justice (Drug Trafficking) Act 1996 .... 25.1.3
Criminal Justice (Public Order) Act 1994
    s 7 .... 26.1.2
Criminal Justice Act 1951
    s 23 .... 12.2
Criminal Justice Act 1957
    s 15(3) 25.1
Criminal Justice Act 1984 .... 21.2
    s 4 .... 25.1.3
    s 15 .... 20.1.10
    s 16 .... 20.1.10
    s 18 .... 20.1.10
    s 19 .... 20.1.10
    ss 18, 19 .... 20.1.10

Criminal Justice Act 1990 .... 12.2
Criminal Law (Amendment) Act 1935 .... 3.6, 3.8
    s 17 .... 23.2.1
Criminal Law Act 1976
    s 2 .... 27.1.1
Criminal Law Jurisdiction Act 1977 .... 9.5
Crown Proceedings Act 1947 .... 8.3
Customs Consolidation Act 1876 .... 18.6.4

Data Protection Act 1988 .... 26.1.5
Defamation Act 1961
    s 13 .... 26.1.1
Defence Act 1954 .... 21.3.3
Dentists Act 1985 .... 18.6.2
Drug Trafficking Act 1996 .... 25.1.3

Employment Equality Act 1998 .... 5.9, 22.6, 27.1.2, 28.4, 30.2.2
Equal Status Act 2000 .... 5.9, 22.6, 28.4, 30.2.2
European Communities Act 1972 .... 13.1
    s 2 .... 10.3
    s 3 .... 10.4, 13.5
        (1) 10.4
Extradition (Amendment) Act 1987 .... 17.2, 25.2.3

Family Law (Divorce) Act 1996 .... 28.7
Farm Tax Act 1985 .... 13.5
Foyle Fisheries Act 1952 .... 9.5
Freedom of Information Act 1997 .... 26.1.3, 26.1.5
    s 26 .... 26.1.5
    s 28 .... 26.1.5

Guardianship of Infants Act 1964
    s 6A 28.6

Health Act 1970
    s 72 .... 13.5

Imposition of Duties Act 1957 .... 13.6
Irish Nationality and Citizenship Acts 1956-2000 .... 8.6

Juries Act 1927 .... 4.5, 21.1.3

Medical Practitioners Act 1978 .... 18.6.2
Mental Treatment Act 1945
    s 260 .... 23.2.11
Mental Treatment Acts 1945-1961 .... 25.2.2
Ministers and Secretaries Act 1924
    s 6 .... 17.2, 17.2.3

Nurses Act 1985 .... 18.6.2

Offence Against the State (Amendment) Act 1940
    Pt II 9.3, 25.2.1
    s 9 .... 20.1.10
    ss 2, 5 .... 20.1.10
Offences Against the State Act 1939 .... 4.6, 23.2.8, 25.2.4
    Pt V 21.3.2
    s 10 .... 26.1.3
    ss 18, 19, 21 .... 27.1.1
    s 30 .... 25.1.3, 25.1.4
    s 39 .... 25.1.3
    s 46 .... 21.3.2
    s 52 .... 20.1.10
Offences Against the State (Amendment) Act 1998
Official Secrets Act 1963
    s 4 .... 26.1.3
    s 9 .... 26.1.3

Petty Sessions Act 1851 .... 10.4
Prohibition of Incitement to Hatred Act 1989 .... 13.8
Prohibition on Incitement to Hatred Act 1989 .... 26.1.2
Prosecution of Offences Act 1974 .... 17.2.2

Regulation of Information Act 1995 .... 24.1.3, 26.1.1
Rent Restriction Acts 1960 and 1967 .... 29.2
Republic of Ireland Act 1948 .... 8.

Sexual Offences (Jurisdiction) Act 1996 .... 9.5
Sexual Offences Act 9.3
Single European Act 10.5
Single European Act 1986 .... 9.1
Sinn Féin Funds Act 1947 .... 18.5
State Act 1939 .... 29.2

Status of Children Act 1987 ....28.4
Statute of Limitations 1957 .... 4.4, 23.2.11
Succession Act 1965 .... 9.3, 28.4

Video Recordings Act 1989 .... 26.1.1
    s 3(3)(a)(i) 26.1.2
        (iii) 26.1.1
        (b) 26.1.1

Constitution of Ireland

Constitution of Ireland 1922 1
    Art 2 .... 8.3
Constitution of Ireland 1937.............................. 1, 3.6, 8, 12
    Art 1 .... 7.1
    Art 2 ....4.4, 4.6, 6., 7.2, 7.3, 7.3.1, 7.4, 7.6, 7.6.1, 31.
    Art 3 ....4.4, 4.6, 6., 7.2, 7.3, 7.3.1, 7.4, 7.6, 7.6.1, 31.
    Art 3.1 ....9.5, 13.1
    Art 5 ....8.1, 8.3
    Art 6 .... 8.3
    Art 6.2 .... 2.4, 11
    Art 7 .... 8.4
    Art 9 ....8.6, 22.6
    Art 9.1 .... 8.6
    Art 9.2 .... 8.6
    Art 10.1 .... 8.3
    Art 12 ....12.1.1, 12.1.2
    Art 12.3 .... 18.1.1
    Art 12.4 .... 8.5
    Art 12.8 .... 12.1.3
    Art 13.1.1 ....12.2, 14.3.3
    Art 13.1.2 .... 12.2, 14.3.3, 15., 15.2.2
    Art 13.10 .... 12.2.1
    Art 13.2 .... 12.2
    Art 13.2.1 .... 12.2
    Art 13.2.2 .... 15.2.2
    Art 13.4 .... 12.2
    Art 13.6 ....12.2, 24., 31.2

Constitution of Ireland 1937— *contd.*

Art 13.7 .... 12.2
Art 13.8 .... 4.6, 12.5
Art 13.9 .... 12.2, 18.2
Art 14 .... 12.4
Art 15 .... 10.2
Arts 15-27 11
Art 15.5 .... 20.1.2
Art 15.10 .... 13.8
Art 15.12 .... 13.8
Art 15.13 .... 13.8
Art 15.14 .... 14.
Art 15.2 ....9.3, 10.2, 10.3, 10.4, 11.1, 13.1,
 .... 13.3, 13.5, 13.9, 17.2.2
Art 15.4 .... 4.1, 13.2
Art 15.4.1 .... 3.8
Art 15.5.1 .... 13.2
Art 15.5.2 .... 13.2, 24., 31.2
Art 16 .... 22.6
Art 16.1.2 .... 31.2
Art 16.2.6 .... 14.1.4
Art 18 .... 3.2, 15.2.2
Art 18.4.2 .... 31.2
Art 20 .... 14.3.1
Art 20.2 .... 14.3.1
Arts 21-22 .... 14.3.2
Art 21.1 .... 14.3.1, 14.3.2
Art 22 .... 12.2, 14.3.2
Art 23 .... 5.2, 12.2, 14.3.1, 31.4
Art 24 .... 5.2, 12.2
Art 25 .... 12.2, 14.3.1
Art 25.5.4 .... 3.1, 8.5
Art 26 .... 3.7, 3.8, 4.3, 5., 5.3, 5.7, 5.8.2, 5.10,
 ....6.1.5, 7.1, 8.3, 12.2, 14.1.3, 16.3.3,
 ....18.1.1, 25.2.1, 28.3, 28.8.2, 29.2, 29.3, 31
Art 26.2.2 .... 5.7
Art 26.3 .... 5.8
Art 27 .... 12.2, 31.4
Art 28 .... 11., 15.4
Art 28.10 .... 14.3.3, 15.2.3
Art 28.11 .... 15.2.3

Constitution of Ireland 1937— *contd.*
  Art 28.3 ....4.6, 14.3.4, 16., 16.3, 16.3.1,
  ....16.3.2, 16.3.3, 16.3.4, 24., 31.2
  Art 28.3.1 ....9.1
  Art 28.3.2 .... 16.2
  Art 28.4 .... 14.3.3
  Art 28.4.2 ....15.6, 15.7
  Art 28.4.3 ....31.2
  Art 28.5.2 ....15.2.2
  Art 28.6 .... 15.3
  Art 28.6.1 ....15.2.2
  Art 28.9.4-6 ....15.2.2
  Art 28A 31.2
  Art 29 ....8.1, 9.1, 16.1, 31.2
  Art 29.1 ....9.1
  Art 29.2 ....9.1
  Art 29.4 ....9.1
  Art 29.4.3 ....31.2
  Art 29.4.7 ....10.2, 10.3, 10.4, 13.1, 13.5, 13.9
  Art 29.5 ....9.2, 14.3.4
  Art 29.6 ....9.3
  Art 29.7 ....31.2
  Art 29.8 ....9.5, 13.1
  Art 30 ....17.2, 17.2.3
  Art 30.2 ....12.2, 15.2.2
  Art 30.3 .... 17.2.2
  Art 30.4 .... 17.1
  Arts 31-32 .... 12.3
  Art 31 ....15.2.2
  Art 32 .... 12.2
  Art 34 ....4.1, 4.1.1, 4.2, 11, 18.7
  Art 34.1 .... 18.4
  Art 34.3 .... 18.1.2
  Art 34.3.2 ....4.1
  Art 34.3.3 ....5.8.2, 10.1
  Art 34.4.3 ....3.2, 20.1.13
  Art 34.4.4 ....4.1, 18.1.3
  Art 34.4.5 .... 4.1.1
  Art 34.5 .... 18.2
  Art 35 11
  Art 35.1 .... 12.2

Constitution of Ireland 1937— *contd.*

Art 35.2 .... 11.1, 18.5
Art 35.5 .... 18.3
Art 36 11
Art 37 .... 11, 18.6, 18.7
Art 37.2 .... 18.7.1, 31.2
Art 38 .... 2.3, 21.2, 3.6
Art 38.1 .... 20.1.4, 20.1.13
Art 38.2-4 .... 21.1.1
Art 38.3 .... 4.6, 21.3
Art 38.4 .... 21.3, 21.3.3
Art 38.5 .... 21., 21.1.1, 21.1.3
Art 39 .... 22.6
Arts 40-43 .... 3.7
Arts 40-44 .... 2.3
Art 40.1 .... 3.4, 19.1.1, 19.1.3, 22., 22.1, 22.2, 22.3, 22.4, 31
Art 40.3 .... 19.1.1, 19.1.2, 19.1.3, 22., 22.4, 23,
.... 23.1, 23.2.5, 23.2.9, 23.2.12, 26., 28.2, 28.5, 29.1
Art 40.3.1 .... 3.3
Art 40.3.2 .... 3.3, 3.4, 23., 23.2.6, 23.2.8,
.... 23.3, 24.1, 26.1.5, 28.5
Art 40.3.3 .... 23.2.10, 24.1, 24.1.1, 24.1.2, 24.1.3, 31.2
Art 40.4 .... 19.1.1, 23, 25
Art 40.4.7 .... 25.1.6, 31.2
Art 40.5 .... 20.1.11, 23.1, 25
Art 40.6 .... 19.1.1
Art 40.6.1.i 23., 26., 26.0.1, 26.1.3, 26.1.5
Art 40.6.1.iii 27.1.2
Art 41 .... 3.4, 10.2, 19.1.2, 22.3, 23.1, 28,
.... 28.1, 28.2, 28.3.1, 28.4, 28.5
Art 41.2 .... 22.3
Art 41.3.1 .... 28.4
Art 41.3.2 .... 28.7, 31.2
Art 41.4.2 .... 28.
Art 42 .... 28., 28.1, 28.5, 28.6.1, 28.8, 28.8.1,
.... 28.8.2, 28.8.3, 30.2.1
Art 42.1 .... 28.8.1
Art 42.2 .... 28.8.1
Art 42.3 .... 28.8.1
Art 42.3.2 .... 28.8.2
Art 42.4 .... 28.8.3

Constitution of Ireland 1937— *contd.*
Art 43 ....19.1.3, 22.6, 23.1, 29., 29.1, 29.1.2
Art 43.1 .... 29.1
Art 43.1.2 .... 29.1
Art 43.2 .... 29.1.1
Art 44 ....3.1, 8.5, 19.1.3, 22.6, 23., 26.1.1,
.... 30, 30.1, 30.2.2, 30.4, 31.2
Art 44.1 ....30., 31.2
Art 44.2.3 6
Art 44.2.4 .... 28.8.1
Art 44.2.6 .... 29.4
Art 45 ....23.1, 23.2.8
Art 46 ....4.6, 5.2, 31
Art 46.2 .... 14.3.1
Art 47 31
Art 47.2 .... 31.4
Art 50 .... 4.2

Amendments
First Amendments 1939 .... 31.2
Second Amendment 1941 .... 31.2
Third Amendment 1972 .... 8.3, 10, 31.2
Fourth Amendment 1973 .... 31.2
Fifth Amendment 1973 .... 31.2
Sixth Amendment to the Constitution 1979 .... 31.2, 18.7.1
Seventh Amendment 1979 .... 31.2
Eighth Amendment 1983 .... 31.2
Ninth Amendment to the Constitution 1984 .... 14.1.3, 31.2
Tenth Amendment 1987 .... 8.3, 10, 31.2
Eleventh Amendment 1992 .... 31.2, 8.3, 10
Twelfth Amendment of the Constitution Bill 1992 ..... 24.1.1, 31.2
Thirteenth Amendment 1992 .... 24.1.2, 31.2
Fourteenth Amendment 1992 .... 24.1.3, 26.1.1, 31.2
Fifteenth Amendment 1995 .... 28.7, 31.2
Sixteenth Amendment 1996 .... 31.2
Seventeenth Amendment 1997 .... 15.7.1, 31.2
Eighteenth Amendment 1998 .... 8.3, 10, 31.2
Nineteenth Amendment 1998 .... 7.6, 7.6.1, 31.2
Twenty-first Amendment 2001 .... 13.2, 24, 31.2
Twenty-second Amendment 2001 .... 31.2

TREATIES

Amsterdam Treaty 10.5
Anglo-Irish Treaty of 1921 .... 1, 30

European Convention on Human Rights 9.3, 9.4
    Art 8 .... 9.3

Maastricht Treaty 10.5

Single European Act 10.5

Treaty of Nice 10, 10.5, 31.3
Treaty of the European Community 24.1.3

Part I

General Issues

1. A BRIEF HISTORY OF THE CONSTITUTION

The creation of the 1937 Constitution owes as much, if not more, to the political as to the legal pressures existing in the late 1930s. In fact, in many respects the inception of *Bunreacht na hÉireann* can only properly be explained by going back some 136 years, to the Act of Union 1801.

As a result of that Act, Ireland became part of the United Kingdom of Great Britain and Ireland. Parliamentary responsibility for the island was transferred to the Imperial Parliament in Westminster, London. Throughout the nineteenth century, however, support for the restoration of "Home Rule" in Ireland gathered pace. Ireland, it was argued, would be better governed if it had its own native parliament, with a limited degree of autonomy from London. Yet, while two Liberal-led British Governments sponsored Home Rule Bills (in 1886 and 1893) proposing such a Parliament, both were defeated. A third such Bill was finally passed in 1914 but was sternly opposed by Northern Unionists. Its commencement was ultimately suspended due to the outbreak of the First World War.

Faced with the relative lack of progress from the parliamentary route, others decided to take more direct action. In Easter, 1916, a small group of Republicans staged a failed rebellion in Dublin, demanding the immediate establishment of an Irish Republic, fully independent from the U.K. Initially, a majority of the Irish public opposed the Rising. The ensuing execution of 16 of the rebellion's leaders, however, prompted widespread sympathy and growing political support for the more hard-line perspective put forward by these revolutionaries. In the election of 1918, Sinn Féin, the party representing the Republican perspective, won a majority of the Irish allocation of seats in the U.K. Parliament. In pursuance of its policy of "abstention", however, it refused to take its seats in Westminster. Instead, on January 21, 1919, the Sinn Féin MPs first sat as part of Dáil Éireann, electing a separate "provisional government" for the island. A bitter War of Independence followed.

The Anglo-Irish Treaty of 1921 finally gave Ireland its independence, but with certain limitations. The first, and perhaps the most contentious, was that of partition. The "Ireland" that was granted independence (known as the Irish Free State or Saorstát Éireann) was a 26-county rather than a 32-county Ireland. In 1920, under the Government of Ireland Act, Northern Ireland had been created as a jurisdiction separate from the south, with its own parliament and government. Though it was given the option to join the newly independent Irish Free State, it declined.

The other contentious issue related to the quality of independence granted. Ireland was to be a "Dominion" like Canada or New Zealand and not a republic as many people had hoped. Thus, under the Treaty, the monarch of England would also be the head of state in Ireland and the head of the government of the new State. All members of the *Oireachtas* had, furthermore, to take an oath of allegiance to the King of England before they could take their seats. The Treaty further outlined that several key Irish ports were to be kept in British hands and that the new Irish government would pay the pensions of retired judges, civil servants and policemen who had worked for the British government in Ireland.

In 1922, a new Constitution, based on this Treaty, came into force in the Free State. The key feature of this Constitution, for our purposes, is that no term in it could be altered if such alteration conflicted with the Treaty.

The terms of the Treaty became the subject of a particularly vicious civil war lasting from 1922 to 1923, leaving in its wake a legacy of bitter divisions. On one side, stood the Pro-Treaty supporters, mainly Cumann na nGaedhal (now Fine Gael). Whilst acknowledging the limitations of the Treaty, they believed that the Treaty was a good start and that with a little bit of work it could be improved upon. On the other side stood the Anti-Treaty supporters, and in particular, what in 1926 became Fianna Fáil, led by Éamon de Valéra. This group opposed the Treaty: they wanted to see a United Irish Republic and felt that the partitioned dominion offered by the Treaty was a "sell-out".

From 1922 to 1932 the Cumann na nGaedhal party held the reins of government. In 1932, however, Fianna Fáil, with the support of the Labour Party, won a majority of seats in the Dáil. Éamon de Valéra was elected President of the Executive Council (head of government under the 1922 Constitution). He immediately set about doing away with the Treaty, and the Constitution on which it was based. Piece by piece, the Treaty was dismantled. First, the oath of allegiance was removed. The power to appeal a case from the Irish Supreme Court to the Judicial Committee of the Privy Council (effectively the House of Lords) in London, was abolished soon afterwards. The new Government also refused to pay pensions and land annuities as agreed by the Treaty.

But it was the abdication of King Edward VIII, in 1936, that gave de Valéra the opportunity he had been looking for finally to remove the King from Irish politics. King Edward, facing stern opposition to his proposal to marry a divorced woman, gave up the throne. In the ensuing crisis, the Dáil passed the Executive Authority (External Relations) Act 1936 which removed the King from his position as Head of State and Head of the Executive in Ireland. The King would now represent Ireland only in its dealings with the outside world: insofar as the *internal* workings of the State were concerned, the King no longer held any position.

Even at that time, steps were already underway to create a new Constitution, one that would better reflect the type of state that Fianna Fáil wanted Ireland to be. Key among the concerns of those drafting the new Constitution was to reassert Ireland's full independence from the U.K. and rid the Constitution of all reference to the King of England.

A Committee of civil servants and lawyers was set up to consider drafts for a new Constitution. The draft finally agreed was debated in the Dáil in 1936. Rather than amend the 1922 Constitution by the means laid out in that document, however, (legislative vote), the Government decided that a referendum was desirable. To that end, the Constitution was put before the people on July 1, 1937. The result was a healthy, though not resounding, 62 per cent in favour — even then there were mixed views about the Constitution.

The Irish Constitution came into operation on the December 29, 1937. It has remained in force since then but has been amended on 21 occasions. Despite its age, however, several eminent judges have noted that the Constitution is not frozen in time. It is a dynamic document capable of changing with the times and catering to new situations. In *State (Healy) v. Donoghue* (1976), for instance, O'Higgins C.J. observed that the values underlying the Constitution

> "...may gradually change or develop as society changes and develops and...fall to be interpreted from time to time in accordance with prevailing ideas.".

The Constitution did not, he added, impose for all time the ideas and values current in 1937.

Nonetheless, the complaint is regularly made, that in reality, the Constitution largely reflects the values and priorities of another time and is out of keeping with the Ireland of today. The Constitution of 1937 was written in respect of a state that was still dominated by the fallout from the Civil War and the effects of partition. It was written to assert an autonomy from outside interference that jars with Ireland's present-day membership of the European Union. Others point to the unmistakeable religious overtones of the Constitution and complain that it unfairly privileges a Christian (and maybe even a Roman Catholic) viewpoint over more secular perspectives.

It is easy to forget, however, that the Irish Constitution was, in Professor Farrell's words, "...devised...at a dangerous time for democracies.". (Farrell (ed.) *De Valera's Constitution and Ours,* (1988) at page 198). Germany, Austria, Spain, Italy, Russia were, by 1937, all under the thumb of authoritarian regimes with little respect for the rule of law. Despite its many difficulties, Ireland, which itself survived a bitter civil war, has largely managed to remain free of such malign influences. This in itself, perhaps, is a testimony to the many strengths of the 1937 Constitution, and to the many people — judges, lawyers, politicians and members of the public alike — who have sought to ensure that it is at all times respected and observed.

Further Reading: Fanning, "Mr de Valéra Drafts a Constitution", Chap. 3 in Farrell (ed.) *De Valera's Constitution and Ours* (1988)

2. THE PURPOSE OF A CONSTITUTION

A constitution is, in short, a basic legal framework setting out the rules by which a state is to be governed. Almost every state in the world has a constitution. It is not, however, a necessary feature of a constitution that it be written or indeed that it all be written down in the same place. The United Kingdom, for instance, has what is sometimes called an "unwritten constitution", a constitution that consists of a variety of well-settled customs and conventions by which that state is governed.

Ireland, however, follows the general international trend in setting out its constitution in one basic document, *Bunreacht na hÉireann*. While constitutions vary considerably in their length and detail, most are comparatively brief and are rarely as specific as a statute. Ireland's constitution is admittedly more detailed than most of its counterparts but remains remarkably short when compared, say, to a Finance Act.

Most constitutions, broadly speaking, have three main purposes:

2.1 Defining the jurisdiction of the State

The primary function of a constitution is to define the State and to assert its jurisdiction (power) over a defined territory. Very often, a constitution acts as an assertion of sovereignty, that is, a statement of ultimate power in respect of a particular territory. Sometimes, of course, such claims are disputed. Indeed, before 1999, Ireland maintained that it had a legal claim over the entire island of Ireland, including Northern Ireland, and the surrounding seas. In December 1999, however, the State dropped its legal claim in respect of Northern Ireland. (See below in Chap. 7).

2.2 Establishing a framework for governing the State

Constitutions invariably create an institutional framework by which a state is to be governed. A constitution then typically sets up various institutions of state. Typically, the various responsibilities and powers of the state are divided between these institutions in a process termed "the Separation of Powers". Generally, there will be a legislature, invested with law-making powers, an executive, charged with the day-to-day governing of a state, and a judiciary, responsible for resolving legal disputes. (See below in Chap. 11).

2.3 Regulating the relationship between the State and its inhabitants

A constitution typically contains provisions that regulate the relationship between the state and its inhabitants. The most common example of such measures are the fundamental rights provisions contained in most constitutions, that attempt to restrain the state from unduly interfering with the freedoms of its citizens. These fundamental rights provisions are contained in Articles 38 and 40-44 of the Irish Constitution. (See below in Chaps 19-30).

2.4 The "Rule of Law"

At the heart of modern constitutionalism is the principle of the rule of law. In short, this requires that a state be run in accordance with pre-ordained rules and regulations that are clear, precise, laid down in advance and made known to the public at large. The public, as a result, should be able to tell in advance whether particular conduct is or is not permitted, and act accordingly. A related aspect of this rule concerns the exercise of the powers divided between the various institutions of state. These powers cannot be exercised by an institution unless it is authorised to do so by the constitution (see Article 6.2). Even if it is self-evidently "good" for an institution of state to take certain steps, it should not do so unless the constitution (and the laws made under that constitution) permits the institution to take such steps.

3. CONSTITUTIONAL INTERPRETATION

As with all legal documents and legislation, judges are often called upon to interpret the Constitution, that is, to determine in a final manner its legal meaning and effect. In doing so, the judiciary is mindful of the fact that the Constitution is more than just a legal document. It also has significant political dimensions, for example as an assertion of the right of the nation to determine its own destiny, and as a statement of the political values and ideals that we hold true. As such, it is inevitable that at least some of the Constitution will contain clauses that owe more to political rhetoric than to careful legal parsing. In determining for legal purposes the meaning of the Constitution, it is thus generally necessary to avoid an over-literal approach.

3.1 In the case of conflict between texts, the Irish text prevails

The Constitution has not one, but two, official texts — one in Irish and one in English. Obvious difficulties may arise in the case of conflict between the different linguistic versions. In such cases, however, Article 25.5.4 asserts that the Irish language text shall prevail. This is despite the fact that in the Dáil debates preceding the adoption of the Constitution, the Irish text received comparatively little attention.

The reality, for good or ill, is that most cases proceed by reference to the English language text, with relatively little attention being given to its Irish language counterpart. Nevertheless, the Irish text has proved useful in resolving a number of difficulties with the English text. In *Quinn's Supermarket v. Attorney General* (1972), for instance, the Supreme Court ruled that the religious "discrimination", prohibited by Article 44, included positive as well as negative discrimination. This conclusion was supported by the use of the term "idirdhealú" in the Irish text, a word bearing the more neutral meaning "to distinguish between".

3.2 Literal interpretation

A literal interpretation involves reading the text of the Constitution in a strictly literal or basic manner. The emphasis here, in short, is on giving plain words their plain meaning. This approach was adopted, for instance in *People (D.P.P.) v. O'Shea* (1982). In that case the Supreme Court had to consider whether the State could appeal a verdict of acquittal handed down by the High Court (acting as the "Central Criminal Court") in a criminal trial. The standard principles of the common law generally precluded such an appeal as being an infringement of the accused's rights (the rule against "double jeopardy"). Article 34.4.3 of the Constitution, however, extends a right of appeal to the Supreme Court from "all decisions" of the High Court. Read literally, the Court concluded, the State was entitled to appeal the acquittal, notwithstanding the fact that this was contrary to well-established principles of natural justice in criminal trials. Unless there was an ambiguity, O'Higgins C.J. observed, "the Constitution, as the fundamental law of the State, must be accepted, interpreted and construed according to the words which are used ...".

Doubtless, several provisions of the Constitution are so clear that they should only be read literally. The requirement in Article 18 that the Seanad consist of 60 members, for instance, could hardly be given anything other than its plain meaning. Not every provision, however, is quite so definitive. The Constitution, after all, is a relatively broad document. It neither has, nor was intended to have, the level of specificity or the detail of an Act of Parliament. As such, an over-literal interpretation may serve more to distort the intentions of its drafters than to clarify them. In this regard, the observations of Costello J. in *Attorney General v. Paperlink* (1984) are most instructive. Noting that the Constitution is a political as well as a legal instrument, Costello J. warned that in interpreting the Constitution:

> "the courts should not place the same significance on differences of language used in two succeeding sub-paragraphs as would, for example, be placed on differently drafted sub-sections of a Finance Act. A purposive, rather than a strictly literal, approach to the interpretation of the sub-paragraphs is appropriate.".

3.3 Broad interpretation

Given the shortcomings of the literal approach in this context, it is suggested that a broad or "purposive" approach will generally be preferred. This perspective looks beyond the plain meaning of words used in the Constitution to the broader purpose and objectives — the "spirit" so to speak — behind those words. In this regard, it is crucial to remember that the Constitution, itself, is, according to Dixon J. in

O'Byrne v. Minister for Finance (1959), "a unique, fundamental document, concerned primarily with the statement of broad principles in general language.". As such, a literal approach may be out of place. In short, the court may prefer to look to the spirit rather than the letter of the law, the overriding sentiment behind an article rather than its strict, literal meaning. This is particularly the case where the protection of human rights is concerned. In *Melling v. Ó Mathghamhna* (1962), Ó Dálaigh J. observed, concerning the right to trial by jury, that "the Constitution is to be read not as dealing with words but rather with the substance of liberty.".

In *Attorney General v. Paperlink* (1984) an argument was made that certain semantic differences between Article 40.3.1 and Article 40.3.2 meant that the level of protection provided by each was different. Article 40.3.1 talks of "respecting", "defending" and "vindicating" personal rights whereas Article 40.3.2 refers only to their "protection" and "vindication". Costello J. ruled that while such differences might have been relevant in a Finance Act, they were of no significance in the context of personal rights protection. He considered that a "purposive rather than a strictly literal approach" was the more appropriate method of interpreting these Articles.

3.4 Harmonious interpretation

The harmonious method of interpretation entails interpreting Articles of the Constitution in the light of other provisions in the document. The various parts of the Constitution, in other words, are not to be read in isolation from each other. The Courts, in following this approach, seek to steer a middle route that achieves a "harmony" between different articles of the Constitution. A useful (if controversial) example of this is in *O'B. v. S.* (1981). The plaintiff in that case was a child born outside marriage whose father had died "intestate", that is, without making a will. At that time, a child born outside wedlock was not entitled to claim any property from the estate of her intestate parents. The Court agreed that, at first glance, this did constitute unequal treatment contrary to Article 40.1 of the Constitution, but ultimately concluded that such unequal treatment was justified by the constitutional preference for marriage expressed in Article 41. Article 40.1, therefore, had to be read in harmony with Article 41, the net result being that such treatment was not unconstitutional.

O'B. v. S. illustrates how one article of the Constitution may be used to cast light on the meaning of another article. A similar approach was

taken in *Dillane v. Ireland* (1980). In that case, the plaintiff had been
denied his legal costs arising from an unsuccessful prosecution taken
against him by a Garda (on behalf of the public). Had the prosecution
been pursued by any other member of the public, the plaintiff argued,
he would have been entitled to have his costs paid by that member of
the public. The Court agreed that this did amount to unequal treatment
but concluded that such treatment was permitted by the proviso to Article 40.1, which allows the State to have regard to "differences in social
function". The Garda's role in such prosecutions was, after all, distinctly different from that of an ordinary person. The Court went on to
conclude that such treatment, having been justified by Article 40.1,
could not then be construed as an "unjust attack" on the personal rights
of the plaintiff under Article 40.3.2. In short, what was deemed "just"
in the context of one article of the Constitution, could not simultane-
ously be deemed "unjust" under another article.

3.5 Hierarchical interpretation

Where harmony between conflicting rights cannot be achieved, however, the Courts have sometimes acknowledged that certain rights take
precedence over others. The starkest example is *People (D.P.P.) v.
Shaw* (1980). That case concerned a man accused of having kidnapped
two women. The Gardaí had detained him for longer than was permitted by law, thus infringing his right to personal liberty. This illegal
detention however, was justified, the Supreme Court found, by the
overriding intention of the Gardaí to save the life of one of the women
who had been kidnapped. The Gardaí honestly believed that the life of
this woman was in imminent danger and that if they detained the
defendant for longer than permitted that they might obtain evidence of
her whereabouts from him. The right to life being superior to the right
to liberty, the right to life was held to prevail.

A somewhat more controversial example is provided by various
cases concerning the right to life of the unborn child. In *Attorney General (S.P.U.C.) v. Open Door Counselling* (1988), the Supreme Court
held that that right took precedence over any right to disseminate information on abortion that the defendants might have had. But where the
right to life of one human being conflicts with that of another, more
difficult questions arise. In *Attorney General v. X* (1992), a young girl,
pregnant as a result of an alleged rape and considerably traumatised by
this fact, had threatened to kill herself if she were not permitted to have
an abortion. The Courts, thus, were faced with a dilemma: should they

permit the taking of the life of the child in order to save the mother from likely death? Costello J. in the High Court believed that the abortion should not be permitted and accordingly placed an injunction on the girl, preventing her from travelling to the U.K. to obtain an abortion. He made a straightforward comparison of the risks, noting that the chances of the mother taking her own life if the pregnancy proceeded were much less likely than the absolute certainty that the abortion would result in the death of her child. The Supreme Court, by a majority, took a different perspective, one that seemed to lean marginally in favour of the mother's right to life. It reasoned that where there was a real and substantial risk to the life of the mother, an abortion would be permitted with a view to saving the life of the mother.

3.6 Historical approach

The historical approach to constitutional interpretation presupposes that the court will look at the meaning of constitutional provisions in the light of the conditions and attitudes prevailing at the time that they were enacted. The danger in such an approach is obvious, dooming the Constitution to an existence frozen in time, and becoming increasingly meaningless to new generations. In fact, several judges have noted that, on the contrary, the Constitution is a dynamic document that is capable of changing to cater for new times and fresh challenges.

Nonetheless, some judges, at least, have found it hard to resist the lure of this approach. For instance, in both *Melling v. Ó Mathghamhna* (1962) and *Conroy v. Attorney General* (1965), the courts, in considering the meaning of a "minor offence" in Article 38, looked in part to the "state of the law when the Constitution was enacted and public opinion at [that] time...". The offences having been treated as minor at the time the Constitution was enacted, it must be assumed that the Constitution (not having expressly stated otherwise) did not alter this state of affairs.

In *McGee v. Attorney General* (1974) O'Keefe P., President of the High Court, had to consider whether the Constitution permitted a ban on the importation of artificial contraception imposed by the Criminal Law (Amendment) Act 1935. He noted that the Act in question had been passed without substantive opposition, just two years before the creation of the Constitution. This, he felt, indicated that the people who adopted the Constitution in 1937 were overwhelmingly opposed to the importation of contraception. As such, it was highly unlikely, he argued, that the people of 1937 would have envisaged that the new Constitution would have created a right to import such items.

In the Supreme Court, however, Walsh J. expressly rejected this historical approach. For him, the Constitution was a dynamic document, not to be frozen in history but designed to change and develop in line with social and moral developments in society at large. As such, an approach that looked to the state of public opinion at the time of the adoption of the Constitution could not be conclusive as regards the existence of rights.

This scepticism regarding the historical approach is reflected in certain comments of O'Higgins C.J. in *State (Healy) v. Donoghue* (1976). In that case, the learned Chief Justice rejected the proposition that the Constitution could only be read from the perspective of those who had first passed the Constitution in 1937. The Constitution was, he asserted, a dynamic document that "...may gradually change or develop as society changes and develops ...". It had, thus, to be "interpreted from time to time in accordance with prevailing ideas.".

The pitfalls involved in taking a historical approach to the Constitution were underlined by certain comments made by McCarthy J. in *Norris v. Attorney General* (1984). The majority in that case had ruled that a ban on male homosexual sexual conduct was not unconstitutional. The majority seemed partly to have been influenced by what they perceived to be the view of the people who had enacted the Constitution in 1937. O'Higgins C.J. (apparently ignoring the comments he had made earlier in *Healy!*) refused to envisage that the people who enacted the Constitution had thereby "rendered inoperative laws which had existed for hundreds of years prohibiting unnatural sexual conduct which Christian teaching held to be gravely sinful.". In his minority judgment, however, McCarthy J. noted the great dangers involved in trying to discern with any accuracy the views of the people in 1937. In his view,

> "...it passes from the realm of legal fiction into the world of unreality if the test sought to be applied is one based on some such question as: Did the people of Saorstát Éireann in 1937 consider that the offence created by some Victorian Statute should no longer be in force?".

The best view, in short, may be that of Barrington J. in *Brennan v. Attorney General* (1983): while looking to the historical context of the Constitution may be influential or "persuasive", it will rarely be decisive in determining the existence or otherwise of various constitutional rights.

3.7 Natural law approach

One of the most interesting — and perhaps controversial — ideas
about the Constitution is that it acknowledges the existence of a higher
law. This higher or "natural law", as it is called is to be distinguished
from "positive" or man-made law. Every person is said to have natural
rights, a set of universally applicable rights that exist not by virtue of
man-made laws but as a consequence of our human personality. It is
said that each person can determine the content of those rights by using
his or her reason or common sense.

The Constitution quite clearly acknowledges the existence of such
rights. In *McGee v. Attorney General* (1974), Walsh J. noted the references in Articles 40-43 to various rights (some expressly described as
"natural") that were "antecedent and superior to positive law". This
confirmed the view that the Constitution protected rights other than
those created by law. Although these "natural rights, or human rights,
are not created by law…the Constitution confirms their existence and
gives them protection". In short, the Constitution places "justice …
above the law".

The difficulty here lies in identifying these rights. One person's reasoned view of what is natural, after all, may be another person's heresy.
In *Ryan v. Attorney General* (1965), Kenny J. said that these rights
could be identified as flowing from "the Christian and Democratic
Nature of the State", a test used, for example, to pinpoint the right of
individual privacy in *Kennedy v. Ireland* (1987). Henchy J., in *McGee
v. Attorney General* (1974), speaks of rights that "inhere in the citizen
in question by virtue of his human personality" and that are "fundamental to the personal standing of the individual" viewed in the context
of the overall best interests of society. Whatever the merits of these for-
mulae, they share a tendency for vagueness and uncertainty that is
hardly helpful in determining the specific content of various rights. If
evidence is needed of this uncertainty, one need go no further than
Norris v. Attorney General (1984), where the majority and minority
alike in the Supreme Court used natural law arguments to justify
entirely *opposite* conclusions.

It is important to note, however, that while natural law is described
as a "higher law" (and even as a derivative of "divine law") it cannot
prevent the people from enacting a constitutional amendment that is
contrary to natural law. In the Article 26 reference of the *Regulation of
Information Bill 1995* (1995), the Supreme Court ruled that the people,
being the Sovereign power, could change the Constitution in whatever

way they wished. The Court was obliged to enforce the express terms of the Constitution, as dictated by the People, whether or not it infringed some higher law. The net result then, may be, that the natural rights perspective is simply a method of interpreting the Constitution, to be used where the Constitution does not provide express guidance on a particular issue.

3.8 The presumption of constitutionality

One must assume that the *Oireachtas*, in creating legislation, normally strains to ensure that it is in keeping with the terms of the Constitution. Article 15.4.1 specifically prohibits Parliament from enacting "any law which is in any respect repugnant to this Constitution or to any provision thereof". There is, therefore, a presumption that legislation that is enacted by the *Oireachtas* is not unconstitutional. This does not mean that such legislation can *never* be found to be in breach of the provisions of the Constitution. The presumption simply casts the onus or burden of proving the unconstitutionality of a piece of legislation onto the person alleging such unconstitutionality. In other words, if you allege a breach you must be both willing and able to prove it. In cases of doubt as to the constitutionality of a piece of legislation, the benefit of that doubt will be given to the *Oireachtas*. An Act, in short, is presumed to be constitutional until proven otherwise. One further consequence is that it is assumed that where a body is given statutory power, that the *Oireachtas* intends that it be exercised in compliance with the Constitution (*East Donegal Co-op v. Attorney General* (1970)).

The presumption, however, only applies to legislation passed after the enactment of the Constitution. The reason for this is simple: it could hardly be assumed that the Parliament that enacted such legislation intended to do so in compliance with a Constitution that had not yet been written. Thus in *McGee v. Attorney General* (1974) the Supreme Court noted that the presumption could not be applied in considering the constitutionality of a 1935 Act (the Criminal Law (Amendment) Act 1935).

The presumption, however, does apply in the case of Bills sent to the Supreme Court under the procedure outlined in Article 26. This is despite the fact that a Bill is not yet technically speaking a "law" for the purposes of Article 15.4.1. This technical point was overlooked, however, in favour of a more purposive approach in the Article 26 reference of the *Criminal Law (Jurisdiction) Bill 1975* (1977). Essentially, a Bill referred under Article 26 has been passed by both Houses of the *Oireachtas*. One must assume that they did so, mindful of the terms of the Constitution.

3.9 The double construction rule

The "double construction" rule is a rule of interpretation that flows from the presumption of constitutionality. The rule was first laid down in *McDonald v. Bord na gCon* (1965) and applied in *East Donegal Co-op v. Attorney General* (1970). The basic premise of this rule is that where there are two or more possible interpretations available to the court, one or more of which would mean that the legislation was unconstitutional and one of which would render it constitutional, the interpretation that is constitutional must, *if possible,* be chosen. A good example of this is to be found in *Re Haughey* (1971), where the Supreme Court had to consider legislation concerning the operation of a Dáil committee. The legislation allowed the Committee to "certify" that a person had committed a particular offence.

There were two possible views as to the interpretation of this clause:

- One, that the Committee was given the power to find the person guilty of the offence (something only a Court can do)

- Two, that the Committee could refer the matter to the Court, which would then determine the guilt or innocence of the person.

Both interpretations being open to the Court, and the first involving an unconstitutional act, the second interpretation was to be preferred.

4. JUDICIAL REVIEW: CHALLENGING THE CONSTITUTIONALITY OF STATE CONDUCT

The Constitution consists of the fundamental law of this State. Where the conduct of the State, or any of its institutions, conflicts with the Constitution, the consequences can be quite dramatic. A provision of law or a government measure that conflicts with the Constitution cannot have legal effect. It is null and void, and legally unenforceable. A court of law, thus, cannot generally enforce a law that contravenes the Constitution.

The Constitution gives judges of the High Court and Supreme Court various powers to declare that certain measures are illegal because they are contrary to the Constitution or any provision thereof. This is called the power of "judicial review".

4.1 Acts of the Oireachtas enacted after 1937

Article 15.4 of the Constitution prohibits the Oireachtas from enacting a law that infringes the Constitution or any part thereof. While there is a presumption that the Oireachtas did not act in contravention of the Constitution, this presumption can be displaced by evidence establishing the unconstitutionality of the legislation. Where a part of an Act is found to be unconstitutional under Article 34, however, only that part will be regarded as unlawful. The act in question will have no force in law *only to the extent that it is unconstitutional*. The remaining (constitutionally sound) provisions, thus, continue to enjoy the force of law.

While all State courts are obliged to act in accordance with the Constitution, only the High Court and Supreme Court are empowered to make a declaration to the effect that a measure is unconstitutional. Article 34.3.2 allows the High Court to determine whether or not a law enacted after 1937 is in keeping with the Constitution. A decision of the High Court can be appealed to the Supreme Court (Article 34.4.4). Such an appeal is usually heard by several judges sitting together, usually five, although three judges may also consider such an appeal.

4.1.1 The "one judgment" rule

Where a matter is being dealt with by the Supreme Court under Article 34, an important limitation applies. Where the constitutionality of a post-1937 statute is being considered, the Supreme Court may issue only one judgment. No other decision or opinion may be pronounced in court. In fact, Article 34.4.5 precludes the judges or any of them from revealing the very existence of such alternative opinions. This is not to say that judges cannot *hold* differing opinions, simply that they cannot express them in open court. The decision of the Court in cases where there is dissent, presumably represents the view of the majority, although again the Court is precluded from revealing whether the judgment is a unanimous or majority verdict, and who, if anyone, disagreed with the decision.

4.2 Article 50 — laws created prior to 1937

Article 34 only relates to measures passed by the institutions of this State. Yet many of the laws presently applicable in Ireland were created long before this State was created. Certain laws of the Irish Free State (1922-1937), the United Kingdom (1801-1922) or Ireland before the Act of Union (pre-1801) still have the force of law in this State. These measures are dealt with under Article 50.

Article 50 states that all laws applicable in the Irish Free State immediately before the enactment of the Constitution are carried over into the law of the new State subject to two conditions. Those conditions are that the old laws have not been repealed and that they are not inconsistent with the Constitution. To the extent that such laws are inconsistent with the Constitution, such provisions shall not be "carried over" into the law of this State.

Again, if only part of a law is contrary to the Constitution, only that part will fail to be carried over. In *McGee v. Attorney General* (1973), one section of a 1935 Act was found to be inconsistent with the Constitution. Only that section was not carried over — the rest of the Act remained enforceable in this State (subject to the possibility of its being repealed, of course).

There are two important differences between measures found to be unconstitutional under Article 34, and under Article 50. The first is that, because measures passed before 1937 were passed without reference to the 1937 Constitution, they do not enjoy any presumption of constitutionality. The second is that the Supreme Court is not restricted in such cases to handing down only one judgment. In *McGee,* for instance, all five judges gave their opinions on the section of the 1935 Act. Indeed, one dissenting judgment was delivered in favour of the section's constitutionality, that of the then Chief Justice, Fitzgerald C.J.

4.3 Article 26 — reference of Bills to the Supreme Court

Article 26 is dealt with further below in Chap. 5. The main aspects of Article 26 is that it allows the Supreme Court to consider the constitutionality of Bills (proposed legislation) before they become Acts of the Oireachtas. Only the President can refer such a Bill, and only to the Supreme Court. If the Bill, or any part thereof, is found to be unconstitutional, no part of the bill may become law.

4.4 Who may take a case — "locus standi"

The law generally requires that a person who takes a constitutional case in Court must have the standing — *"locus standi"* — to do so. As a general rule, a person will not have *locus standi* to challenge a measure unless they can show that they have been personally affected by its existence. A person for instance can only seek to have a statute invalidated on the grounds that it infringes their personal constitutional rights and not that of another person.

In *Cahill v. Sutton* (1980), the Supreme Court laid down the test that a person would not ordinarily have standing to take a constitutional case unless his or her interests "have been adversely affected, or stand in real imminent danger of being adversely affected" by the measure being challenged. The plaintiff in that case had sought to sue her doctor for medical negligence. Owing to a delay of four years after the personal injuries arose, however, she was prevented from doing so. This was because the Statute of Limitations 1957 required that actions for personal injuries be taken within three years of their occurrence. The plaintiff, however, alleged that this statute was unconstitutional as it failed to account for those who only discovered their injuries after the limitation period had run. But the plaintiff herself did not fall into this category — she was aware of her injuries from the time she had first sustained them. The plaintiff, in essence, was trying to invoke the rights of third parties (a *"jus tertii"*) as a defence to the Statute of Limitations, something which, the Supreme Court concluded, she could not do.

Another example is provided by one of the arguments in *Norris v. Attorney General* (1984). In that case the plaintiff was challenging statutes that criminalised male homosexual sexual conduct. The plaintiff alleged that one of the statutes that made "buggery" (anal intercourse) illegal contravened the right to privacy of married persons, as established in the earlier *McGee* case. The Supreme Court, however, refused to entertain this ground on the basis that the plaintiff was not himself a married person and could not thus plead the rights of third parties in his own defence. Likewise, in *Madigan v. Attorney General* (1986), the plaintiffs, who were residents of Ireland, were prevented from raising the possible impact of Residential Property Tax legislation on non-resident persons.

Even in *Cahill* itself, however, the Court admitted that there might be exceptional cases in which the rule of *locus standi* might be relaxed. Such a case arose in *S.P.U.C. v. Coogan* (1989). In that case the plaintiffs, a voluntary organisation which sought to protect the interests of unborn children generally, sought an injunction against several student unions which had been distributing information on abortion. This, they argued, indirectly threatened the right to life of the unborn child. The case clearly involved pleading the rights of a third party. Logically speaking, the plaintiff was not itself (nor could it ever be) a "victim" of abortion. Under the circumstances, however, the Court was willing to entertain the arguments of the plaintiff, it being a body with a genuine (*"bona fide"*) interest in the protection of the unborn child.

In the course of his judgment, Walsh J. noted that "every member of the public has an interest in seeing that the fundamental law of the State is not defeated". This is illustrated by the earlier decision of the Supreme Court in *Crotty v. An Taoiseach* (1987), a case in which the plaintiff challenged the right of the State to ratify an international agreement on European integration. It was argued that Mr. Crotty had no greater interest than any other member of the public in the ratification — he could not point to a personal grievance distinct from that of every other citizen in the State. Nevertheless, both the High Court and Supreme Court on appeal ruled that the plaintiff had *locus standi* to take the case. In *McGimpsey v. Ireland* (1990), the Courts followed *Crotty*, ruling that a citizen need not present evidence of "special or individual grievance" in order to plead a breach of Articles 2 and 3 of the Constitution by the State.

This gives rise to the possibility that an individual citizen may take an *"actio popularis"*, a case alleging the illegality of activity that is allegedly prejudicial to no one particular person but rather to the public at large. In *Martin v. Dublin Corporation* (1990), for instance, the late historian, Fr. F.X. Martin, took a case against the defendant for the alleged desecration of Wood Quay. The case, (though ultimately unsuccessful) was allowed to proceed even though Fr. Martin was not airing a personal grievance but rather one that, he believed, affected the people of Dublin generally.

4.5 Retrospectivity of a finding of unconstitutionality

A finding of unconstitutionality means not only that the measure is illegal but that it was always illegal. A verdict of unconstitutionality, in other words, does not "make" a law illegal but declares that it was never legally enforceable in the first place. Any action that has already been taken on the basis of an unconstitutional law is itself also rendered invalid. In this respect a finding of unconstitutionality is said to be "retrospective" in effect. The judge is not simply saying that the provision will no longer be legally enforceable ("future" or "prospective" effect) but that it *never* had the force of law in this State. With respect to laws passed before 1937, to the extent that such laws were unconstitutional, they did not become part of the law of the State. They were not "carried over" in 1937.

This means, in theory, that anything done under such a law after 1937 is invalid. For instance, a person imprisoned under an unconstitutional measure could claim not only that they no longer should remain in prison, but that they should never have been imprisoned in the first place. A person who has paid an unconstitutional tax could theoretically claim for the return of all payments made on foot of the unconstitutional measure.

This latter scenario arose in *Murphy v. Attorney General* (1982). In that case the plaintiffs complained that the way in which married persons were being taxed was unconstitutional. Having succeeded in establishing the unconstitutionality of the legislation, the Murphys attempted to recover the surplus of tax that they should not have been forced to pay from the time they had married. In strict theory, this money, having been secured illegally, should have been returned. However, there was a strong chance that if the State had been liable to every married couple who had paid too much tax, the State might have gone bankrupt.

The Supreme Court therefore limited the relief available.

- No married couple could be asked to pay more than was constitutionally permitted after the judgment in *Murphy* was handed down. However, only those who had commenced legal proceedings on this issue before the judgment was delivered could recover monies that had been paid in taxes *before* the judgment.

- Furthermore, that money could only be claimed from the date on which the relevant parties first submitted their claim. With regard to monies paid before that date, the State was entitled to assume, there having been no complaints about its payment, that it could be spent.

Such money, having been collected and used in good faith, could not now be recovered.

Of course, at the date of the judgment some people were in arrears of tax. After the judgment, the State attempted to collect these taxes. Because most of the people who had paid their taxes on time did so on the basis of the old (unconstitutional) provisions, the State tried to apply the same rules to those who had not. In *Muckley v. Attorney General* (1985), the Courts held that the old laws being unconstitutional, the State could no longer collect taxes on this basis. This gave rise to a rather perverse situation: those couples who had duly paid their taxes before 1982 could not recover the surplus unless they had put in a claim before the judgment. Those who were in arrears at the time, by contrast, could not be forced to pay the surplus. The result, to say the least, was most unsatisfactory.

Similar issues arose in *State (Byrne) v. Frawley* (1978). In a previous case, *de Búrca v. Attorney-General,* the Supreme Court ruled that the system of selecting juries set out in the Juries Act 1927 was unconstitutional. The system in question effectively excluded most women and all persons not owning property from jury service. This meant effectively that every jury selected since 1937 was a jury not selected in a constitutional manner, a point that put in doubt the legality of the convictions made by such juries.

The complainant in the later case had been convicted (after the decision in *de Búrca*) by a jury selected under the Juries Act. He had not, however, raised the issue as to the jury's unconstitutionality at his trial. Both the High Court and Supreme Court ruled that as the complainant had not, at the time of his trial, made any objection to the method of jury selection, he had effectively waived his right to do so. This conclusion seems to suggest an "estoppel" type reasoning — as the complainant knew of his right but did not act upon it, he could not subsequently object to the jury that he had accepted. Whether the same could be said of those convicted *before* the *de Búrca* decision is an open question. Arguably, it should have been obvious to any observant person that the jury system was seriously flawed: the fact that they failed to raise this issue at trial arguably disentitled them from raising the complaint after their conviction.

4.6 Are certain matters beyond judicial review?

The question arises whether there exists a certain class of issues into which the courts cannot inquire. In other words, are certain matters beyond judicial review? There are certainly some specific clauses preventing such review in specified cases. The Constitution, in Article 13.8, for example, expressly precludes the courts from reviewing the exercise and performance of the President's powers. The President, in other words, cannot be made accountable to a court for acts done in her official capacity as President. Nor can the courts review the validity of emergency legislation duly passed under Article 28.3 of the Constitution.

It seems, however, that there is a residue of sensitive issues into which the court cannot inquire. In *State (Killian) v. Attorney General* (1958), the Supreme Court ruled that it could not interfere with the discretion of the Attorney General in deciding whether or not to prosecute a person. The responsibility for such prosecutions was, in 1974, transferred to the Director of Public Prosecutions, but despite this change, the same principle applies. In *State (McCormack) v. Curran* (1987), the Supreme Court again reaffirmed that it could not force the D.P.P. to prosecute a person. Indeed, according to Finlay C.J., the Courts could not review a decision of the D.P.P. not to prosecute a person unless if could be shown that the D.P.P. had acted in bad faith or was acting with improper motives. The reasons for this reticence lie in the nature of the D.P.P.'s functions. The D.P.P. may decide not to prosecute someone for all sorts of reasons — lack of evidence or the prospect that the accused might not get a fair trial. If the D.P.P. were forced in open court to reveal certain facts in his possession, these facts might cast a shadow of guilt over an accused person and thus offend the right to be presumed innocent until proven guilty.

It seems also that the Courts cannot review the functions of the Legislature and Government in relation to the Special Criminal Court. Article 38.3 allows such a court to be set up where it is felt that the ordinary courts are inadequate to secure the effective administration of justice and the preservation of public peace and order. The Offences Against the State Act 1939 gave the Government the right to determine if such a court is needed at any particular time. In *Kavanagh v. Ireland* (1996), the Supreme Court ruled that the decision to establish and maintain such a court in existence is a matter for the Government alone. The Supreme Court could not consider whether the Government was justified in so doing. Nor can the Courts review the decision of the D.P.P. to refer an accused person for trial before the Special Criminal Court. (See *Savage v. D.P.P.* (1984)).

The substantive content of constitutional referenda also seems to be beyond judicial review. In *Finn v. Attorney General* (1983), the High

Court ruled that it could not review the content of a proposed constitutional amendment on the right to life. The reasoning of the Court seems to have been that the People, under Article 46, are entitled to amend, vary or repeal the Constitution in whatever way they wish. The Courts could not then question the content of a referendum proposal. In *Riordan v. An Taoiseach (No. 1)* (1998), for instance, the plaintiff complained that a proposal to change the Constitution to allow the Government at some time in the future to alter Articles 2 and 3 thereof was illegal. The Supreme Court, however, rejected this proposition, again affirming that the People are entitled to alter the Constitution in whatever way they wish.

These cases, then, do seem to suggest that there is a category of "politically sensitive" matters into which the courts cannot inquire. It is important, however, not to overemphasise the scope of this category. The courts have, over the years, reviewed Government actions in a series of very sensitive political matters. In *McGimpsey v. An Taoiseach* (1990), for instance, the Supreme Court reviewed, with little apparent reluctance, the legality of the Anglo-Irish Agreement of 1985. Another delicate international treaty was the subject of *Crotty v. An Taoiseach* (1987) in which the Supreme Court actually struck down the Irish legislation ratifying the Single European Act, a major treaty on further European integration. And while the courts will not inquire into the substantive content of referendum proposals, they did strike down a system of State funding for constitutional referenda on the grounds that it was used to support only one side of the argument (*McKenna v. An Taoiseach* (No. 2) (1995)). This willingness to step into what is largely a political arena of decision-making would seem to suggest that the category of cases in which judicial review is not possible is rather limited. It is suggested, that considering the importance of judicial review in protecting the rights of citizens, the Courts should not unduly extend this category beyond its present limits.

Table: Summary of Judicial Review

	Article 34	Article 50	Article 26
What type of legislation does this Article concern?	Measures adopted by the State *after* December 29, 1937	Measures adopted by the State *before* December 29, 1937 (and not repealed before that date)	Bills passed (or deemed to have been passed) by both Houses of the Oireachtas but not yet signed into law by the President
Who can make a challenge to such a measure?	Any person adversely affected by the measure	Any person adversely affected by the measure	The President of Ireland
Who decides such cases?	The High Court, or on appeal, the Supreme Court	The High Court, or on appeal, the Supreme Court	The Supreme Court
Does the presumption of constitutionality apply?	Yes	No	Yes
What is the effect of a ruling of unconstitutionality?	The parts of the measure that are unconstitutional are void and thus have no legal effect	The parts of the measure that are unconstitutional are deemed not to have been "carried forward" in 1937 into the law of this State	The entire Bill can never become law

5. ARTICLE 26 — REFERENCE OF BILLS BY THE PRESIDENT

One rather unique method of judicial review is outlined in Article 26 of the Constitution. Article 26 lays down a special method by which the constitutionality of Bills can be tested before they become law. The word "Bill" generally describes a provision that, although proposed before either House of Parliament, has not yet become an Act of Parliament. In this context, however, the term "Bill" refers specifically to a measure passed by both Houses of the Oireachtas but not yet signed by the President.

5.1 Who may make a reference?

Only the President may make a reference. He or she may do so only after having consulted the Council of State. The role of the Council, however, is purely advisory, and while the President is obliged to seek its opinion, she can ignore it once made. In other words, the President has an unqualified discretion: only he or she may ultimately decide whether or not the reference should be made.

5.2 What measures may be referred?

Only a bill and not an Act of Parliament can be referred. A Bill can be referred under this procedure only after it has been passed by both Houses of the Oireachtas. It is possible also to refer a Bill that has been deemed to have been passed by both Houses under the procedure laid out in Article 23. Certain Bills, however, can not be the subject of a reference. These are:

- A Money Bill, that is a Bill dealing exclusively with the raising of revenue or the payment of expenditure: (An annual Finance Bill, or Social Welfare Bill, would be good examples).
- A Bill "containing a proposal to amend the Constitution" under Article 46; and
- A Bill the time for consideration of which has been shortened under Article 24. (Article 24 allows for the time period during which the Seanad can consider a Bill to be reduced in times of public emergency.)

5.3 Can a part of a Bill be referred?

It is possible to refer a part or section of a Bill on its own for the consideration of the Supreme Court. Article 26 allows for the reference of "any specified provision or provisions" of a Bill. This was first used in 1942 when President de hÍde (Hyde) referred section 4 of the School Attendance Bill to the Supreme Court. In 1999, moreover, President McAleese referred Part V of the Planning and Development Act under Article 26.

5.4 To whom is the reference sent?

The President, if she so decides, makes the reference directly to the Supreme Court. This is one of only two situations in which the Supreme Court hears a case that has not first been heard by the High Court, in other words, where it has "original" (as opposed to "appellate") jurisdiction. The Supreme Court hearing such a case must comprise at least five judges.

5.5 What happens when a reference is made?

Once the President makes a reference, the Supreme Court has sixty days to determine whether the Bill or any part thereof is repugnant to the Constitution. The Court, consisting of not less than five judges, hears arguments put forward by Counsel appointed to represent various strands of the argument. It is possible in this context to have more than two sets of Counsel (barristers) in a case. In *The Matter of Article 26 and the Regulation of Information Bill 1995* (1995), the Supreme Court assigned three sets of counsel. One group of barristers was assigned to the defence of the Bill and two groups to argue against the Bill, one of the latter examining how it might infringe the rights of the mother, and the remaining group considering the rights of the unborn child.

5.6 Presumption of Constitutionality

From the very start, there is a presumption that the Bill does not infringe the Constitution. In all such cases the onus of proving the case lies on the lawyers alleging its unconstitutionality. This does not mean that a Bill can never be found to be unconstitutional, simply that its unconstitutionality must be proved on the balance of probabilities.

Where the Court is not convinced either way, the benefit of the doubt is given to those arguing that the bill is constitutional.

5.7 The "One Judgment" Rule

Once it has heard and considered the arguments, the Court makes its decision. Although the judges may have several different opinions on the issue, Article 26 allows only one judgment, that of the Court, to be handed down. This, effectively is, the decision of the majority of the judges. No other decision or opinion may be pronounced in court. In fact, Article 26.2.2 precludes the judges or any of them from revealing the very existence of such alternative opinions.

5.8 The consequences of the decision

The consequences of the court's decision are laid out in Article 26.3:

5.8.1 If any part of the Bill is found to be unconstitutional

The President cannot sign the Bill, or any part thereof, into law. This is an "all-or-nothing" situation: if even one section in a Bill is found to be repugnant to the provisions of the Constitution, the whole Bill cannot become law. This is different from cases involving the constitutionality of Acts of Parliament, where the Act is deemed invalid only to the extent that it infringes the Constitution (*i.e.* only those parts that are invalid are struck down).

One misconception that often arises is that the Bill, if found to be unconstitutional, is referred back to the Oireachtas for alteration. This is not the case. If any part of the Bill is found to be unconstitutional, the bill can never be enacted as an Act. The Oireachtas may choose to create a new bill along the same lines as the old one with the offending provisions omitted. It cannot, however, simply alter the old Bill to cure it of its unconstitutionality.

5.8.2 If no part of the provisions referred is found to be unconstitutional

The President must sign the Bill and put it forward as a law. She does not have any discretion to refuse to sign such a Bill. In such a case the bill becomes part of Irish law, an Act of Parliament.

The Act that results from a referred Bill enjoys a special status under Irish law. Once it has been found not to contain any unconstitutional provision under the Article 26 procedure, the constitutionality of its provisions can never be challenged again. [Article 34.3.3] Even if it is subsequently discovered that the act does offend certain provisions of the Constitution, the Act cannot be declared invalid by a court of law.

Where only part of a Bill was referred under Article 26, only that provision shall enjoy this constitutional immunity.

It is always possible, however, for the Parliament to repeal or amend the relevant Act, that is, change its provisions by means of an amending Act. There is nothing, in other words, preventing the Oireachtas from subsequently changing an act, the Bill for which was subjected to Article 26.

5.9 Bills and parts of Bills referred

To date, 14 references have been made. All but two of them have related to the entirety of a Bill, the two exceptions being section 4 of the School Attendance Bill 1942 and Part V of the Planning and Development Bill 1999.

Year	President	Bill	Result
1940	Hyde	Offences Against the State (Amendment) Bill	Not unconstitutional
1942	Hyde	Section 4, Schools Attendance Bill	Unconstitutional
1961	de Valéra	Electoral (Amendment) Bill	Not unconstitutional
1975	Ó Dálaigh	Criminal Law (Jurisdiction) Bill	Not unconstitutional
1975	Ó Dálaigh	Emergency Powers Bill	Not unconstitutional
1982	Hillery	Housing (Private Rented Dwellings) Bill	Unconstitutional
1983	Hillery	Electoral (Amendment) Bill	Unconstitutional
1987	Hillery	Adoption (No. 2) Bill	Not unconstitutional
1993	Robinson	Matrimonial Home Bill	Unconstitutional

Year	President	Bill	Result
1995	Robinson	Regulation of Information (Services outside the State for the Termination of Pregnancies)	Not unconstitutional
1996	Robinson	Employment Equality Bill	Unconstitutional
1997	Robinson	Equal Status Bill	Unconstitutional
1999	McAleese	Immigrants Trafficking Bill	Not unconstitutional
1999	McAleese	Part V, Planning and Development Bill	Not unconstitutional

In all, six Bills have been found to have contained provisions that were repugnant to the Constitution. In some of these cases the Oireachtas has created new Bills on the same issue absent the offending provisions (*e.g.* Employment Equality Act 1998, Equal Status Act 2000). In other cases (*e.g.* the Electoral Bill 1983), a constitutional amendment was enacted to allow the offending provisions to become part of law. There is, however, no obligation on the Oireachtas to reconsider the issue in question. The policy behind the Matrimonial Home Bill (the joint ownership by spouses of the Family Home) was effectively abandoned after the unfavourable decision of the Supreme Court. Nor is there any guarantee that new legislation following upon the rejection of a bill will itself be constitutional.

5.10 Is Article 26 a good idea?

There are advantages and disadvantages attaching to the Article 26 procedure:

- The key advantage is that the Bill's constitutionality can be scrutinised before the Bill affects the rights of any person. Problems can be anticipated before they arise and hence resolved, giving the Article a preventative role in the protection of rights. Article 26 is particularly useful in the defence of rights and principles that might otherwise not come before the court, because the affected parties would perhaps be insufficiently well-resourced to take such a case.

- The main disadvantage of Article 26 is the hypothetical nature of the debate before it. The arguments put forward depend solely on the creativity and imagination of the lawyers involved. The Bill may be found to "be" constitutional, despite the existence of unforeseen problems, not in the contemplation of the Court at the time of the reference. There is a distinct possibility that problems may arise that were not envisaged during the Article 26 hearing, at a point when the constitutionality of the provisions can no longer be challenged.

Part II

The Nation, the State and the Outside World

6. THE PREAMBLE TO THE CONSTITUTION

Most pieces of legislation have a "long title" or "preamble", a note at the start of the legislation explaining the reasons for its adoption. The Constitution also contains an introductory Preamble. Although it is quite controversial, it is clearly too general to be relied on without recourse to more specific articles. Thus, while it occasionally arises for consideration in the Courts, the Preamble has never been invoked as the *sole* source of a personal right.

The Preamble is largely a political statement unique to the time when it was written. It harkens back to the struggle for Irish independence, the "centuries of trial" during which Ireland was ruled by the British. The language of the Preamble is unapologetically defiant, and in particular unequivocally republican, an attribute that has been the source of some controversy. Indeed, some might say that it is not in keeping with the current spirit of reconciliation between the various cultures on this island and on the island of Britain. The Preamble refers to the "heroic and unremitting struggle" for independence, and suggests that this continues — indeed, one of the aspirations outlined is that "unity of our country be restored". In light of recent efforts to reconcile the two traditions on these islands, (not to mention the changes in Articles 2 and 3) it may be said that this strident language is somewhat redundant, if not even unhelpful.

The religious tone of the Preamble is also noteworthy. As Professor Beytagh observes "[t]he Preamble...indicates in unmistakable terms that the document is intended to be distinctly Christian (perhaps Catholic is more accurate) in its basic orientation". (Beytagh, *Constitutionalism in Contemporary Ireland,* (1997)). Indeed, in a State that supposedly opposes religious discrimination (see Article 44.2.3), it is strange to see reference to concepts that are not even accepted by all *Christian* traditions, let alone all Irish citizens. The reference to the "Most Holy Trinity" is clearly religiously exclusive — not every Christian accepts that there are three persons in one God. And what is an Irish citizen of the Jewish or Muslim faith, for instance, to think of the reference to "our Divine Lord, Jesus Christ"? Gavan Duffy J., in *State (Burke) v. Lennon* (1940), refers to this "most impressive Preamble", but who nowadays can be impressed by so exclusive and divisive an opening statement?

The Preamble, however, also outlines some less controversial goals. Its fourth paragraph introduces a constant theme of Irish constitutional jurisprudence, the need to balance the rights of the individual with the interests of society as a whole. The Preamble lists as an overall objective the promotion of the "common good", that is the best interests of society as a unit, but also mentions the importance of securing "the dignity and freedom of the individual". The Preamble thus sets, from the start, a tone of compromise and balance — protecting the freedom of the individual while working towards and maintaining "true social order".

6.1 Judicial comment on the Preamble

The Preamble is a broadly rhetorical introduction, containing only vague aspirations and the most general of aims. As such, it is difficult to discern any definitive rules or consequences from its terms. Yet the Preamble can be, (and on occasion has been) used in conjunction with other more concrete Articles to support certain conclusions on constitutional issues.

6.1.1 The religious values of the State

For instance, in *Norris v. Attorney General* (1984), (a case challenging the criminal prohibition on primarily homosexual sexual conduct) a majority of the Supreme Court invoked the Preamble to support their assertion that the Constitution broadly reflected Christian principles of right and wrong. In a similar vein, Walsh J., in *Quinn's Supermarket v. Attorney General* (1972), referred to the Preamble in support of his proposition that the Irish "are a Christian People".

6.1.2 The reunification of the Nation

In *Russell v. Fanning* (1987), moreover, Hederman J. referred to the Preamble for support in asserting that the re-unification of Ireland, North and South, was a "constitutional imperative", that is, a result required by the Constitution.

6.1.3 Prudence, justice and charity

The observance of "prudence, justice and charity" has been cited in several cases, including *McGee v. Attorney General* (1974). In that case, Walsh J. noted that the personal rights guaranteed by the Constitution should be interpreted in the light of these values. He did note that understandings of what is prudent, just and charitable may vary from time to time. "It is but natural", he observed, "that from time to time the prevailing idea of these virtues may be conditioned by the passage of time: no interpretation of the Constitution is intended to be final for all time". Similar remarks were made by O'Higgins C.J. in *State (Healy) v. Donoghue* (1976). The Chief Justice in that case noted that constitutional rights had to be "considered in accordance with concepts of prudence, justice and charity". He again observed, however, that the understanding of these values "may gradually change or develop as society changes and develops", in other words that the interpretation of these concepts is not frozen in time.

6.1.4 The dignity and freedom of the individual

Henchy J. also relied on the Preamble in *McGee*, noting that the conclusion in favour of the plaintiff in that case accorded with the Preamble's overriding aim to secure the "dignity and freedom of the individual". The plaintiff in *McGee* risked serious health complications if she became pregnant. Henchy J. thus felt that the ban on the importation of contraceptives, which was challenged in that case, condemned the plaintiff and her husband to a life "fraught with worry, tension and uncertainty". This was not in keeping, he suggested, with the overriding aims of the Preamble.

6.1.5 True social order

The Supreme Court in the Article 26 reference of the *Offences Against the State (Amendment) Bill, 1940,* however, observed that the dignity and freedom of the individual cannot be achieved without the maintenance of social order. The "true social order" spoken of in the Preamble has thus been invoked to justify the deportation of a dangerous foreign national in *Osheku v. Ireland* (1986) and was also pleaded by O'Higgins C.J. in *Murphy v. Attorney General* (1982). In the latter case, the Supreme Court had ruled that the method used to tax married couples since at least 1918 had been unconstitutional. This gave rise to the possibility of the State having to reimburse married couples to the tune, perhaps, of hundreds of millions of pounds. In deciding that the right to reimbursement should be strictly limited, the Chief Justice invoked in part the objective of achieving "true social order" cited in the Preamble. This, he suggested, justified his view that the State should not be subjected to such a steep compensation bill.

Generally, then, the Preamble is a statement of the broad aims of the Constitution. While the Preamble is too general to be used in isolation as a source of principles and rules, it has been invoked to support certain conclusions made on the basis of more specific Constitutional provisions.

7. THE NATION AND THE POSITION OF NORTHERN IRELAND (ARTICLES 1-3)

7.1 The concept of a nation

A nation (as distinct from a state) is a political rather than a legal concept. In short, a nation consists of a people who purport to share certain features in common and who assert (perhaps more importantly) that these common features set them apart from other peoples. The territory of a nation need not be the same as that of the state — indeed a people may assert "nationhood" without their having an independent state to speak of at all (*e.g.* the Tibetan "nation"). In the past, nationhood was defined in terms that today seem inappropriate, by reference for instance to a shared religion, language, genealogy, or race. There are, however, certainly many nations that cannot be defined in these terms, nations with considerable religious, racial and linguistic diversity. Take Belgium, for instance, with its three official languages, or Britain with its significant Muslim, Sikh and Hindu minority communities. Nationhood is a "spirit of affinity", thus, that can no longer be based simply on race, religion or language but on more complex factors.

It is obvious of course that there can, in respect of the same territory, be competing claims to nationhood. The classic European example of this is the dispute over the Basque territory. Closer to home, of course, one has the fraught situation of Northern Ireland. Some of the people in that jurisdiction claim to be part of the Irish Nation, others part of the British Nation. Indeed, the existence of that dispute largely explains the distinction in the Constitution between the "nation" and the "state". The Supreme Court, in the Article 26 reference of the *Criminal Law (Jurisdiction) Bill 1975* (1976), noted the theory, popular in 1937, "that a nation, as distinct from a state, had rights". One of those rights, it was felt, was "the right to unity of territory in some form", a right which, it was felt, had been infringed by the partition of Ireland. The right to "self-determination" was another of those rights. Article 1 of the Constitution asserts the Irish Nation's right to choose its own form of government, in other words to choose how and by whom it is governed. Ireland, Article 1 affirms, is entitled to chart its own course in the international realm, in particular "to determine its relations with other nations". Article 1 also asserts that Ireland as a nation was entitled to make decisions relating to its political life, its economy and its cultural development "in accordance with its own genius and traditions". In short, it says, Ireland's destiny should be determined by the Irish people.

7.2 Articles 2 and 3 — The position of Northern Ireland

One of the issues that especially concerned the drafters of the Constitution was that of partition in Ireland. The nation envisaged by the drafters of the 1937 Constitution comprised the whole island of Ireland, not just the Irish Free State. Since the enactment of the Government of Ireland Act 1920, however, Northern Ireland has been a jurisdiction separate from the South of Ireland. Thus, amongst the aims laid out in the Preamble of the Constitution is the reunification of the two jurisdictions on the island — "so that…the unity of our country [is] restored". To this end, Articles 2 and 3, prior to 1999, asserted a legal claim over Northern Ireland. This was obviously a serious point of contention between those who sought the end of partition and those who consider that Northern Ireland should remain within the United Kingdom. Subsequent to the Good Friday Agreements, Articles 2 and 3 were altered, one of the results of which was the dropping of that legal claim in favour of a broadly aspirational clause.

7.3 The old Articles 2 and 3

Before they were altered, Articles 2 and 3 read as follows:

> Article 2: "The national territory consists of the whole island of Ireland, its islands and the territorial seas".

> Article 3: "Pending the re-integration of the national territory, and without prejudice to the right of the Parliament and Government established by this Constitution to exercise jurisdiction over the whole of that territory, the laws enacted by that Parliament shall have the like area and extent of application as the laws of Saorstát Éireann [the Irish Free State] and the like extra-territorial effect".

The effect of these articles was considered in a number of prominent cases. For some time it was thought that the articles were merely political in nature and did not affect the legal standing of Northern Ireland (see *In the Matter of Article 26 and the Criminal Law (Jurisdiction) Bill, 1975* (1976)). In *Boland v. Taoiseach* (1974), however, the Supreme Court agreed that Articles 2 and 3 were not merely political aspirations but amounted to a legally binding claim over Northern Ireland. In other words, Ireland was laying out a claim in law to the six counties, a claim that was clearly in direct opposition to the assertion that Northern Ireland is part of the United Kingdom. In *McGimpsey v. Ireland* (1990), the Supreme Court repeated the fact that this was a legal and not merely a political claim.

One of the problems this posed was that it potentially restricted those in this state who wanted to make peace in Northern Ireland from conceding that Northern Ireland was part of the U.K. In both the Sunningdale Agreement (1973) and the Hillsborough Agreement (1985), Taoisigh Liam Cosgrave and Garret FitzGerald, respectively, conceded that the status of Northern Ireland as part of the U.K. would not be changed until the consent of the people of Northern Ireland was obtained. In other words, this state would not press for re-unification unless the majority in Northern Ireland wanted a united Ireland. Some people argued however, that this concession infringed Articles 2 and 3. It was alleged that these provisions undermined Ireland's legal claim over the six counties.

In both *Boland v. An Taoiseach* (1974) and *McGimpsey v. Ireland* (1990), these claims were tested and rejected by the Supreme Court. Each of these Agreements, the Court held, simply recognised a fact of political reality, that is that Northern Ireland is *de facto* a part of the U.K.. This was simply a recognition of the real situation on the ground in that jurisdiction. It did not compromise Ireland's *legal* claim, which remained intact.

7.3.1 McGimpsey v. Ireland (1989): Finlay C.J. explains the old Articles 2 and 3

In *McGimpsey v. Ireland,* Finlay C.J. took the opportunity to explain the legal effects of Articles 2 and 3 as they stood before the recent changes.

> 1. The learned judge first reiterated the fact that the old Articles 2 and 3 created a legal claim over Northern Irish territory. Re-unification was not an option but, rather, a constitutional imperative, something that the State was required actively to work towards.

> 2. This claim was not merely political but legal in nature, a "claim as of legal right".

> 3. Article 3 required that until there is actual re-integration the laws made by the Parliament and Government of the South would apply

only to the 26 counties. In other words, in the normal course, the laws of the Republic were not applicable in Northern Ireland. This did not, however, prevent the laws of the South from having normal extra-territorial jurisdiction.

4. Notwithstanding the inapplicability of Ireland's laws in the North, this "in no way derogate[d]" from the claim of jurisdiction over Northern Ireland as a claim of legal right. In other words, even though the State's laws did not apply to the whole "territory", Ireland still maintained its legal claim over the North.

7.4 Recognising Northern Ireland

The existence of the legal claim notwithstanding, the old Articles 2 and 3 did not prevent the courts in this jurisdiction from recognising the existence of Northern Ireland. In *State (Gilsenan) v. McMurrow* (1978) and *McGlinchey v. Ireland (No. 2)* (1990), the Courts acknowledged that, despite Articles 2 and 3, they would recognise the use of the term "Northern Ireland". Nor was there anything preventing the Courts from recognising the laws of Northern Ireland. In *McGlinchey v. Ireland (No. 2)* (1990), the plaintiff objected to being extradited to Northern Ireland on the grounds that the State could not recognise the laws of that jurisdiction. The Court rejected this claim.

7.5 The Good Friday Agreements, 1998

As a result of the Good Friday Agreements the Constitutional structures of Northern Ireland have been altered. A new Assembly has been created for the jurisdiction. From this Assembly a power-sharing Government (the "Executive") is elected, representing a cross-section of the political parties in the Assembly. Certain powers, once held by the U.K. Government in London, have been "devolved" to the Northern Ireland Assembly and its Government. This means that Northern Ireland is now largely run by Northern Irish people for Northern Irish people. New cross-border bodies have been established, the most prominent of which is the North-South Ministerial Council. This body consists of Ministers from the South and from the North meeting to discuss matters of common interest to both jurisdictions. In this capacity they can make executive decisions that affect the whole island of Ireland.

7.5.1 Summary of institutional changes:

Strand One	Strand Two	Strand Three
Northern Ireland	North-South Co-operation	British-Irish Co-operation
New Assembly New Executive	North-South Ministerial Council	Council of the Isles, representing England, Scotland, Wales, Northern Ireland and Ireland.

7.6 The new Articles 2 and 3

The new Articles 2 and 3 were introduced by the Nineteenth Amendment to the Constitution. The method of adopting these new articles was, however, unusual. While the Amendment was passed by an overwhelming majority in June 1998, the new Articles did not come into force until December 1999. The changes that were anticipated were contingent upon certain developments in the peace process, namely the creation of the North-South Ministerial Council. In other words, until such time as the Council was established, the old Articles 2 and 3 would remain in place. When the Council was established, in December, 1999, the Government passed a resolution replacing the old articles with the new ones. The new articles are now in place. While their insertion was contingent on the establishment of the North-South Council, it is important to note that they are no longer conditional upon the survival of that body. Indeed, even if the whole Good Friday agreement collapsed, the new Articles could only be removed by further referendum.

This conditional method of amending the Constitution was indeed very unusual. The people had allowed the Government to give effect to the changes on the happening of a particular event. In *Riordan v. An Taoiseach (No. 2)* (1998), however, the Supreme Court ruled that the people of Ireland, being sovereign, were entitled to alter the Constitution in whatever way they wished.

7.6.1 So what do the new Articles say?

* The old Article 2 defined the nation in terms of its geographical territory, *i.e.* the island of Ireland and its territorial seas. The new Article 2 defines the nation by reference to its people.

* Anyone who was born on the island of Ireland has a birthright and entitlement to be part of the Irish nation. The language of the article is noteworthy — those who were born on this island but do not want to be part of the Irish nation are merely given the opportunity (and not forced) to be part of the nation.

* Those who were not born on the island but who have otherwise acquired citizenship (through a parent, spouse or by naturalisation) are also part of the Irish nation.

* It is important to note that these articles do not in any way change the normal rules regarding citizenship. The citizenship of a person is still determined in accordance with Statute law.

* The Irish nation expresses an affinity with those of Irish origin living abroad. This does not automatically make such persons part of the Irish nation, however. Membership of the nation is reserved to those either born on the island or otherwise entitled to citizenship.

* The legal claim over Northern Ireland has been dropped.

* In its place is a broad aspiration to unity — the nation expresses a "firm will" for re-unification, but this falls far short of a legal claim.

* This unity can only be achieved by peaceful and democratic means.

* In particular, Article 3 implicitly recognises the status of Northern Ireland as part of the United Kingdom. This cannot be changed without the consent of a majority of people in the North, and a majority of people in the South.

* This consent is to be determined by peaceful and democratic means. In other words a referendum would be required both North and South before the status of Northern Ireland could change. While Article 3 is somewhat unclear on the point, the better view is that separate majorities would be required in the North and South respectively.

* The changes allow for the establishment of cross-border bodies having jurisdiction over the whole island of Ireland. Notwithstand-

ing the exclusive powers of the Parliament and Government of this state over the territory of Ireland, these bodies are allowed to exercise such power in respect of this jurisdiction.

In summary, the changes that followed the Nineteenth Amendment to the Constitution have resulted in the State dropping its legal claim over Northern Ireland. In its place is an aspiration for unity through peaceful means. In the meantime, however, any person born on the island of Ireland (as well as any citizen of Ireland) is entitled to claim membership of the Irish Nation.

Further reading: Clarke, "Constitutional Bootstrapping: The Irish Nation" (2000) 18 *I.L.T.* 74.

8. THE IRISH STATE (ARTICLES 4-11)

The Constitution of 1937 created a new legal entity, a new state with exclusive jurisdiction over all but six counties of the island of Ireland. According to Article 4 of the Constitution this state is quite simply called "Ireland", or in Irish, "Éire". While the state is in law *described* as a Republic (see the Republic of Ireland Act 1948), the name of the state remains as outlined in Article 4.

When discussing the Irish State, it is essential to distinguish between the concept of a nation (discussed above) and the concept of a state. Though these terms are often used interchangeably, they concern what are technically distinct concepts. A "nation" is effectively an abstract political idea rather than a strictly legal concept. Basically the concept of a nation is a political one, a moral assertion of the affinity of a people, based on characteristics that they claim to share. The exact boundaries of the "nation" are thus uncertain and depend largely on the extent to which one accepts certain political claims. For instance, in Northern Ireland some people claim to be part of the Irish nation, whilst others maintain that they are British.

The concept of "statehood", on the other hand, is strictly legal in nature. A state is a legal framework charged with the governance of a defined geographical territory. The State, then, is a legal mechanism, created by the people, to govern a particular territory.

8.1 The independence of the State

Article 5 describes the State as "a sovereign, independent and democratic state". The purpose of this Article is largely to assert the fact that the new "Ireland" established by the Constitution did not recognise the authority of any other state in respect of the island of Ireland. In particular, it sought to underline the end of British authority in Ireland. Nowadays, however, it is more difficult to maintain that Ireland is fully independent, in particular in light of the very significant impact of European Union (E.U.) law in the Irish legal order. Certain laws made by the institutions of the E.U. can have "direct effect", that is, acquire the force of law in the State even where they have not been approved by the Oireachtas. As such, the assertion of independence in Article 5 must be viewed as having been qualified by the provisions in Article 29 allowing Ireland full membership of the E.U. and of its constituent communities.

8.2 The State as a legal person

The State is a separate legal entity with its own legal personality. Like an incorporated company it can sue (see *Ireland v. Mulvey* (1989)) and be sued (*Byrne v. Ireland* (1972)). It can buy, sell and own property (*Comyn v. Attorney General* (1950)) and enter into contracts as an entity in its own right. In other words it can conduct itself, for legal purposes, in much the same way as an ordinary person.

8.3 Is the State a "Sovereign" State?

The State is also described as "sovereign", though this assertion is accurate, if at all, only in a limited sense. To be "sovereign" involves freedom from any external control, to be independent from outside interference. A "sovereign" power is one that is supreme within a particular field or in respect of a particular territory.

In British Constitutional Theory, the sovereign power is the monarch of England, *i.e.* the king or queen, (although *in practice* it is the elected Parliament that exercises this sovereignty). The Queen, then, in strict constitutional theory, is the "supreme power" in the U.K. Prior to 1947, for instance, the Queen could not be sued in her own Courts. Indeed, as a consequence of her sovereignty, the Queen enjoyed, at the time of Ireland's independence, several "Royal Prerogatives". These included the following:

- The right not to be sued (this has now been abolished by the Crown Proceedings Act 1947);

- The right to "treasure trove" (to claim items of national heritage, the ownership of which cannot be determined);

- The right to be free from having to obey Acts of Parliament (unless otherwise stated);

- The right to issue passports;

- The "executive privilege" — the right to prevent government documents from being admitted in evidence in court.

For a long time the Irish State simply assumed that it was the successor to the Crown in Ireland. As such, it argued that it was entitled to exercise these prerogative rights. In *Byrne v. Ireland* (1972), however, the Supreme Court ruled that the State could not invoke these prerogatives. The plaintiff in that case alleged that due to the negligence of the State, she had sustained injuries on a public footpath. The State, in response, pleaded its "prerogative right" not to be sued. The Court, however, ruled that the State did not enjoy such a right. The State was not, it pointed out, the successor to the Crown. The true sovereign power in Ireland since 1937, if not 1922, was the people of Ireland, not the State. Indeed, the Constitution of 1922, despite its supposed shortcomings, had made the people of Ireland the sovereign power in the State (see Article 2 of the 1922 Constitution). According to Budd J., thus, "it is the people who are paramount, not the State". Those people had created the State and made it subject to the Constitution, which itself limited the power of the State. The State was not, he thus concluded, "internally sovereign". The ultimate power on the island is not the State but rather the people of Ireland who created the State by means of the Constitution. There was nothing in that Constitution, the Court concluded, that prevented the State from being sued.

The Court based its judgment partly on Article 6 of the Constitution. That Article makes it clear that all powers of Government derive from "the people". The ultimate power to determine national policy lies with the people. Their decision furthermore is final and cannot be challenged. The people of Ireland, for instance, cannot be sued, (although the State *can* be sued). In the Article 26 reference of the *Regulation of Information Bill 1995,* (1995) the Supreme Court rejected the proposition that a constitutional amendment enacted by the people could be struck down on the grounds that it offended a higher "natural" law, said to have been ordained by God. The supreme power in the land, according to the Court, was the people. Their decision was final and conclusive and was not subject to review in the Courts.

The *Byrne* decision was followed in *Webb v. Ireland* (1988). That case concerned a claim that the ancient Derrynaflan chalice and paten, discovered by the Webbs, in fact belonged to the State as part of its "prerogative of treasure trove". The Supreme Court again ruled that the State did not succeed to the prerogatives of the Crown, although it could claim the right to items of national heritage on the basis of the Constitution itself, and in particular Article 10.1. That Article gave the State the right to all "royalties" in the State, subject to the estates and interests of other persons and thus created a foundation for a separate right to items of national heritage.

The royal prerogatives were finally put to bed in *Howard v. Commissioners for Public Works* (1993). In that case, the State claimed that it was not obliged by statute to seek planning permission for an interpretative centre built on a site of great natural beauty. The basis for this claim was that the State, as part of its supposed prerogative powers, was not obliged to obey its own statutes. Again the Supreme Court rejected this proposition. Denham J., indeed, noted that the whole idea of royal rights was repugnant to the "republican and democratic nature" of the Irish State, and could not thus have been carried over into Irish law after 1937.

The central point that these cases illustrate is that the State is not the supreme or sovereign power, at least from an internal perspective. So why then is the State described as sovereign in Article 5? In *Byrne v. Ireland*, Budd J. suggested that the sovereignty to which Article 5 refers is external sovereignty, that is, the exclusive power to rule Ireland as against any foreign power. Indeed, in *Crotty v. An Taoiseach* (1987), the Supreme Court ruled that the State, as part of its external sovereignty, had the exclusive right to determine Ireland's foreign policy. Any attempt to give away that right (without a prior constitutional mandate) would, furthermore, be unconstitutional. Yet even this external sovereignty has been eroded, in particular by Ireland's membership of the European Union. This has been permitted, however, by the Third, Tenth, Eleventh and Eighteenth Amendments allowing Ireland to ratify several E.U. Treaties which seek in part to promote greater co-operation on foreign policy and defence matters.

The result of this complex series of cases may be summarised as follows.

In Ireland, the people hold the sovereign power, not the State. The State, thus, is not internally sovereign although it can claim external sovereignty, that is the sole power to determine Ireland's relations with other states.

8.4 The national flag

Article 7 designates that the national flag is "the tricolour of green, white and orange". The colours are arranged in vertical rectangles of equal size, with the green portion nearest to the flagpole and the orange farthest therefrom. The idea for such a national emblem seems to have been inspired by the flag of the French Republic and was first used by adherents of the Young Ireland movement, in 1848. It is generally understood to symbolise the desire for peace and unity between the traditions of Roman Catholicism and Protestantism.

An interesting question (that has not yet arisen in this State but that has been litigated in the U.S.) involves the constitutionality of provisions penalising any defacement or desecration of the national flag. The U.S. Supreme Court has consistently upheld, as part of the right to free expression, the right of its citizens to burn in protest the "stars and stripes" (*Street v. New York* (1969), *Texas v. Johnson* (1989), *U.S. v. Eichman* (1990)). Whether such legislation would meet a similar fate in this State is open to question. It would seem, however, that the tighter restrictions on free speech under our Constitution might preclude such a result.

8.5 The languages of the State

Although the Irish language is designated the first official language of the State, Ireland, in fact, has two official languages, English also being an "official language". Indeed the Constitution itself was promulgated in two languages, Irish and English. Although both versions count as official texts, the text in Irish is the predominant text. Article 25.5.4 stipulates that in case of conflict between the two texts, the one in Irish shall prevail. Despite the apparent care taken in drawing up these texts, there are indeed some points where the meaning of each diverges, sometimes subtly, from the other. The English version of Article 12.4, for instance, stipulates that a candidate for the Presidency must have reached his thirty-fifth year of age. Read strictly this seems to indicate that the candidate may be thirty-four (*i.e.* a one-month old baby is in his first year of age, entering his second year of age on turning one). The Irish text however, designates that the person must have "survived" thirty-five years ("ag a bhfuil cúig blíana triochad slán") and seems then to reflect the better view that the President must be thirty-five or older.

The judiciary, however, is careful not to over emphasise such differences. More often than not, the courts have tended to read the two texts in a harmonious fashion, attempting to iron out any subtle differences that may emerge. In several cases the courts have used the Irish text to cast light on certain constitutional provisions in English. In *Quinn's Supermarket v. Attorney General* (1972), for instance, it was argued that the "discrimination" envisaged by Article 44 of the Constitution was confined to discrimination against (as opposed to discrimination in favour) of a religious denomination. Looking to the Irish text of Article 44, the Supreme Court refused to rule that the term "discrimination" should be viewed so restrictively. The corresponding term in Irish is "idirdhealú" — literally meaning "to divide" or "to distinguish between" — an interpretation that supported the view that "discrimination" for these purposes was not to be confined to situations where the discrimination was to the detriment of a religious denomination.

8.5.1 The right to use Irish in court

Notwithstanding the legal prominence given to the Irish language, it is a basic fact that in daily life the vast majority of Irish people use English as their primary language of communication. Correspondingly, most of the official business of the State is conducted through the medium of English. The work of the courts is no different.

That said, certain special requirements exist in relation to the linguistic competence of legal officers. Both barristers and solicitors are required, as a condition precedent to becoming qualified as such, to display a "competent knowledge" of Irish. A citizen, furthermore, has the right to put his or her side of a case before a court or tribunal through Irish, if so desired. In *State (MacFhearraigh) v. Gaffney and the Employment Appeals Tribunal* (1983), O'Hanlon J. ruled that a litigant has the right to argue his case through Irish. This extends to the cross-examination of witnesses, who may be questioned through Irish, subject to the right of those witnesses who are not proficient in Irish to have the proceedings interpreted. In a recent case, *Ó Beoláin v. Ireland* (2001), the Supreme Court held, furthermore, that for this purpose, the State had a constitutional duty to provide Irish language translations of the Acts of Parliament and other important statutory provisions.

The fact that the person asserting this right is proficient in English is irrelevant for these purposes. In *MacFhearraigh,* O'Hanlon J. ruled that the right to proceed through Irish can be invoked regardless of the fact that he might have put his case just as competently through English.

The right to proceed through Irish is, however, subject to an important principle of natural justice, that is that each party to a case must be able to understand the proceedings. Thus, it must follow that where one party asserts his right to present his arguments through Irish, the other party or parties will have a right to have the proceedings translated into English. To do otherwise would involve putting the Irish speaking litigant at an unfair advantage in the proceedings. In *State (Buchan) v.*

Coyne (1936), for instance, a Scotsman was tried and convicted of a road traffic offence before a Gaeltacht-based District Court, the court case having proceeded entirely through Irish. In a subsequent judicial review, the High Court quashed the verdict on the grounds that the accused did not understand, and had no means of understanding, the proceedings in the case.

8.6 Citizenship

A "citizen" of a state, is a person who, in respect of that state, enjoys certain rights and privileges and who is correspondingly subject to certain duties towards that state. The matter of who is or is not entitled to be a "citizen" of the state, is a matter generally determined by Act of Parliament. Nevertheless the Constitution provides some elementary guidance on the issue, most notably in Article 9 thereof.

Article 9.1 expressly states that any person who was a citizen of Saorstát Éireann immediately before the coming into operation of the 1937 Constitution is deemed to be a citizen of Ireland. Beyond that, a person's citizenship is to be determined by law, although the Constitution expressly ordains that a person cannot be denied citizenship on the grounds of their sex.

The Irish Nationality and Citizenship Acts 1956-2000 list the various ways in which Irish citizenship can be acquired:

- By birth — all persons born on the island of Ireland are entitled to claim citizenship.

- By descent — a son or daughter of an Irish citizen is generally entitled to claim citizenship. A grandchild of an Irish citizen will be entitled to citizenship only if his or her birth was registered with an Irish Embassy or with the Department of Foreign Affairs.

- By naturalisation — a person who has legally resided in the State for five of the previous nine years may become a citizen through a process called "naturalisation". To qualify, such a person must prove an intention to remain within the State for the foreseeable future.

- By marriage — the spouse of an Irish citizen (by birth or descent only) may apply for citizenship, but only after three years have passed since the marriage. (In the meantime, however, a spouse would ordinarily be entitled to a residence visa).

A citizen has obligations as well as rights. The main obligations of a citizen are outlined in Article 9.2 of the Constitution which states that a citizens has two "fundamental political duties", that of "fidelity to the nation" and loyalty to the State".

9. IRELAND IN THE INTERNATIONAL ORDER (ARTICLE 29)

Article 1 of the Constitution affirms the nation's aspiration to "self-determination", to be able to shape its own destiny "in accordance with its own genius and traditions". The reality, of course, is that Ireland is but a small part of an increasingly interdependent world. Since the early 1960s, Irish state policy has gradually shifted in line with a growing realisation that Ireland could not ever hope to thrive, either socially or economically, in isolation. This realisation culminated in our joining what was then the European Economic Community, the European Coal and Steel Community and the European Atomic Energy Community, in 1973. (Collectively, these Communities became part of the "European Union" in 1993). Ireland's relationship with the E.U. will be examined in the next chapter. For the moment, however, it is useful to examine the relationship between the State and the outside world and the effect of the Constitution upon this relationship.

9.1 International relations

In Article 29, Ireland commits itself to friendly relations with the outside world. Indeed, it is fair to say generally, that Ireland is a pacifist state. Article 29.1 affirms Ireland's "devotion to the ideal of peace and friendly co-operation". Disputes, where they arise, are to be resolved by peaceful means (Article 29.2), although it is worth noting that the Constitution does not entirely rule out the possibility of the State being involved in violent conflict. It is still possible, after all, for the Dáil to declare war. (Article 28.3.1).

The power to determine and exercise Ireland's foreign policy is vested in the Government alone. (Article 29.4). That power can be exercised only by or on behalf of the Government. Effectively, this precludes the State from giving away its power to determine Ireland's foreign policy, although our membership of the E.U. has qualified this restriction considerably. Yet before the E.U. had competence in the area of foreign affairs, the Supreme Court, in the important case of *Crotty v. An Taoiseach* (1987), ruled that the government could not give up its power to lay down Irish foreign policy to an international body. That case concerned a proposal in the Single European Act (1986) (an

E.U. treaty) to establish a forum called European Political Co-operation, a framework for co-operation between E.U. states on matters of foreign policy. The Supreme Court found that Ireland could not give up such powers to that body without a referendum on the Single European Act. (Although, see the arguments of Hogan, "The Supreme Court and the Single European Act", (1987) 22 *Irish Jurist* (n.s.) 55.)

9.2 How does Ireland become a party to international agreements?

While agreements are negotiated and signed by the Government, the Dáil also plays a limited role in their adoption. In particular, international agreements do not become effective as a matter of international law until the process outlined in Article 29.5 has been followed. This requires that all international agreements to which the State becomes a party must be "laid before" Dáil Éireann. This is probably best regarded as a formality, there generally being no requirement that the Dáil, in fact, approve the agreement, although certain international agreements do actually require Dáil approval. Where an international agreement proposes measures that would involve a charge on public funds, the agreement, to be binding in international law, must have been "approved" by Dáil Éireann. In other words, where the agreement requires that Ireland incur any financial costs, the Dáil must approve that agreement. In *State (Gilliland) v. Governor of Mountjoy Prison* (1987), the High Court thus ruled that an extradition agreement with the U.S., not having been approved by the Dáil, was not binding on Ireland. This was because the agreement presupposed a charge on public funds, namely in transporting persons being extradited to and from the United States.

9.3 Dualism v. monism

However, even where an agreement has received Dáil approval, this means only that Ireland is bound as a matter of international law *not* national law. Traditionally, Ireland is best described as a dualist (as opposed to a monist) state. This simply means that while Ireland recognises international law as binding upon the State, it does not regard international law as being part of domestic Irish law. In other words, until an international agreement is "incorporated" into national law by the Oireachtas, (Parliament, *i.e.* the Dáil and the Seanad) it cannot be

invoked in Ireland before an Irish Court. With the exception of E.U.
law, then, international law is not part of Irish law unless the Oireachtas decides otherwise. This is well illustrated by the decision in
O'B. v. S. (1984), where the Supreme Court ruled that the Succession
Act 1965 was to be applied notwithstanding the possibility that it
infringed the European Convention on Human Rights by discriminating against children born outside marriage.

Monist states, by contrast, take a different approach. In the Netherlands, for instance, international agreements signed by the Dutch Government are regarded as automatically part of Dutch law, whether the
Parliament has approved them or not. The Netherlands does not then
maintain the rigid distinction between national and international law.

Article 15.2 of the Irish Constitution is relevant here. It states that no
new law can be created in respect of the State other than by the Oireachtas. While this is now subject to a large exception with respect to
E.U. law, it means that until the Oireachtas passes legislation "incorpo-
rating" the international agreement it is not binding as a matter of Irish
law. This state of affairs is underlined by Article 29.6 of the Constitution, which prevents international law from becoming part of Irish law
except with the consent of the Oireachtas.

A good illustration of this is provided by the decision of the
Supreme Court in *Re Ó Láighléis* (1961). The plaintiff in that case had
been detained without trial under Part II of the Offences Against the
State (Amendment) Act 1940. As this Act had (while a Bill) been
found to be constitutional by the Supreme Court under the procedure in
Article 26, it could not be challenged as unconstitutional. Faced with
this barrier to his claim, the plaintiff asserted that the Act was contrary
to the European Convention on Human Rights. The Court however
refused to consider this matter, the Convention not being a part of Irish
law. Not having been incorporated into Irish law, the Convention could
not be invoked before a Court.

The aftermath to the decision of the European Court of Human
Rights in *Norris v. Ireland* (1989) is also instructive. There the Court
found that Irish law prohibiting most forms of male homosexual sexual
conduct, including acts between consenting adults, was in breach of
Article 8 of the European Convention on Human Rights (which protects the private life of the individual). Despite this ruling, however, the
offending Irish laws remained in force in Ireland until 1993. In that
year the Oireachtas enacted a Sexual Offences Act, creating an equal
age of consent. Until the Oireachtas did so, however, it was still possible, as a matter of Irish law, to penalise consenting adult male homo-

sexuals for private sexual conduct, despite the fact that this would have been in breach of International Law.

9.4 The impact of International Law in the Irish courts

Generally, this means that international agreements are not binding in a court of law. As such an Irish judge cannot require a person to comply with an international agreement unless it has been "incorporated" into Irish law by the Oireachtas. Some international agreements have been so incorporated, although many of the most important still await such endorsement. In the meantime, however, some judges have been willing to recognise that while not binding, such agreements can have a persuasive value. In other words they can be used to cast light upon Irish law, being used as an aid to the interpretation of national rules. (See *Ó Domhnaill v. Merrick* (1985), *Desmond v. Glackin* (No. 1) (1993).)

At present, there are proposals to incorporate the European Convention on Human Rights by means of an Irish statute. It is worth remembering, however, that being an Act of parliament, the provisions of such legislation will be subject to their compliance with the Constitution and could potentially be struck down on the basis of unconstitutionality.

9.5 Extra-territoriality

As a general rule, Irish law applies only within the confines of the State. There are however, some cases in which Irish Law can be applied to situations that arise outside Ireland. While International law generally requires that sovereign states respect each other's boundaries, it does recognise the principle of "extra-territoriality", that is the idea that one state can in limited cases impose its laws in respect of incidents that occur in another state. The best contemporary example of this involves what is sometimes called "sex tourism", where citizens of one state go to another state and commit a sexual offence in that other state, then returning to their state of origin. The Sexual Offences (Jurisdiction) Act 1996 allows Ireland to prosecute persons who have committed a sexual offence while abroad, notwithstanding the fact that, as the offence occurred outside Ireland, the State normally would not have the power to do so.

Article 3.1 and 29.8 of the Constitution clearly allow Irish legislation to have such "extra-territorial" effect. Being that the State shares a border with Northern Ireland, many of these laws involve relations between the two parts of this island. The Foyle Fisheries Act 1952, for instance, allows fishing offences allegedly committed on the River Foyle (which straddles the border between Derry and Donegal) to be prosecuted in either jurisdiction. While, technically, half of the width of the river lies in the Republic and half in the North, it would in practical terms be near impossible to pinpoint exactly where an offence was committed. In a similar manner (although for different reasons) the Criminal Law (Jurisdiction) Act 1977 allows certain crimes that have been committed in Northern Ireland to be prosecuted in this State, as if they had occurred here, and *vice versa.*

It is important to remember, however, that extra-territoriality tends to be the exception rather than the rule. According to the International Court of Justice's decision in the *Lotus Case* (1927), extra-territorial legislation should only be used where clearly necessary to promote "peace, order and good government" within the State that makes such laws.

10. IRELAND IN THE EUROPEAN UNION

Having examined the general relationship between the Constitution and International Law, it is now proposed that we turn to a very specific type of law that affects Ireland in a radical manner — the law of the European Union. In 1973, Ireland joined three communities, the European Economic Community (now the European Community), the European Coal and Steel Community and European Atomic Energy Community. In 1993, these three communities (along with agreements concerning issues of co-operation in the field of foreign policy and justice) were incorporated into what is called the "European Union", (E.U.) Ireland's membership of these entities has dramatically altered its power to determine its own destiny.

The Irish people have amended the Constitution four times to permit the ratification of the original treaties and subsequent amending treaties:

1973	Third Amendment	Ireland allowed to join EEC, ECSC and Euratom
1987	Tenth Amendment	Ireland could ratify Single European Act
1992	Eleventh Amendment	Ireland could ratify Maastricht Treaty (on European Union)
1998	Eighteenth Amendment	Ireland could ratify Amsterdam Treaty

An attempt to change the Constitution to allow for the ratification of the Nice Treaty was defeated in June 2001.

The European Union has its own framework for making and enforcing laws. These laws are generally created by the joint efforts of the European Parliament and the Council of Ministers of the European Union. While these laws can take many forms, the most common legally binding instruments are Regulations, Directives and Decisions. Regulations are of general application and, once created, are automatically applicable throughout the E.U. Decisions, though similar in their legal effects, differ from regulations in that they are of a more specific nature, being targeted at specifically identifiable persons and situations. Directives, by contrast with both regulations and decisions, are not automatically applicable in Member States. They require the Member States to which they are addressed to achieve a particular result but give the Member State the right to determine how best that result should be achieved.

10.1 The Supremacy of European Law

According to the case law of the European Court of Justice, E.U. law is supreme. (See, *e.g. Costa v. ENEL* (1962)). In other words, where there is a conflict between European and national law, European law will always prevail. The Irish Courts have accepted that this is the case. Indeed, the Supreme Court has gone so far as to acknowledge that E.U. Law is superior even to the terms of the Constitution. In *Campus Oil v. Minister for Industry and Energy (No. 2)* (1983), the Supreme Court held that where there was a conflict between E.U. Law and a term of the Constitution, E.U. Law would be applied, even in the face of a constitutional term. Thus the Supreme Court held that it could not hear an appeal from a decision of the High Court to refer a point of Community Law to the European Court of Justice. This was despite the terms of Article 34.3.3 of the Constitution, which gives a right to appeal all decisions of the High Court to the Supreme Court (except where legislation has provided otherwise).

In instances of conflict between E.U. Law and Irish Law, E.U. Law will always prevail. This is the case even where the Irish law concerned is part of the Irish Constitution.

10.2 Article 29.4.7

This preference for E.U. Law, even over the terms of the Constitution, is copper-fastened in the Constitution itself by Article 29.4.7. That provision effectively gives E.U. law an exemption from having to comply with the Constitution, with the result that an E.U. provision can become law in Ireland, even where it offends the terms of the Constitution. Article 29.4.7 basically covers two types of law:

1. The first type of law is that created by the Institutions of the E.U. itself. This means that regulations, directives and other types of legislation made by the E.U. can become part of Irish Law even where not in compliance with the Constitution. It also allows the measures

in question to become part of Irish Law, notwithstanding the fact that the Oireachtas played no part in their creation. Thus the legislative powers given to the Oireachtas by Article 15.2 have to be shared with the E.U. institutions, despite the fact that Article 15 says that only the Oireachtas can make laws for this State.

2. The second type of law exempted by Article 29.4.7 are laws created by the State itself in order to comply with the requirements of E.U. law. In other words, where the State enacts a measure that is "necessitated by the obligations of membership" of the E.U. or the European Communities, that law (and the manner in which it is enacted) need not be in compliance with the Constitution. This exemption, however, only applies to the extent that the State is doing what it is obliged to do by E.U. law. The State cannot claim exemption where it is exercising its own discretion.

In *Greene v. Minister for Agriculture*, (1990), for instance, the State was obliged by E.U. Law to make certain payments to farmers in disadvantaged areas. The State decided that for this purpose, persons would be means-tested, in other words farmers would only receive payment if their income was below a certain amount. However, the Minister designated that in calculating farmers' income, the income of their spouses would also be included. The scheme failed to place similar restrictions on unmarried farmers, and thus was found to have been contrary to Article 41 which requires the State to protect marriage against attack. Because the relevant E.U. directive did not require the State to discriminate against married farmers, the State could not claim an exemption under Article 29.4.7. The discrimination in question had not been necessitated by E.U. membership.

The consensus in the Irish Courts on the supremacy of E.U. Law is tempered by the judgment of Walsh J. in *S.P.U.C. v. Grogan* (1989). In that case, the learned judge suggested that because the amendment affirming the right to life of the unborn child was inserted after the amendment allowing Ireland to joining the European Community("E.C."), E.C. law did not prevail over that right to life. Even if this is correct, however, the subsequent amendments to allow the ratification of amending treaties presumably negate this argument.

10.3 The direct effect of E.U. Law

European Union Law can become part of Irish Law without ever having been approved by the Oireachtas. This is an exception to the general rule, laid out in Article 15.2, that only the Oireachtas can legislate for this State. By contrast with the provisions of most international agreements, E.U. Law is automatically incorporated into national law. In other words, it has "direct applicability". It can, furthermore, have direct effects, allowing ordinary individuals to rely on its terms as giving them rights in Irish Courts, notwithstanding the fact that the Oireachtas may not have approved the creation of such legislation. The net effect is that laws can be created that are applicable in Ireland by a process that effectively "by-passes" the Oireachtas.

This is permitted by Article 29.4.7 but is further facilitated by the European Communities Act 1972. Section 2 of that Act states that with effect from January 1, 1973, the law of the European Communities:

> "Shall be binding on the State and shall be part of the domestic law thereof under the conditions laid down in [the Treaties founding those Communities]".

Section 2 then automatically makes Community Law part of Irish law. This allows an individual to rely on European law in an Irish Court to give them legal rights, powers or immunities that they otherwise would not have.

10.4 Implementing Directives

Directives are a rather unique type of E.U. law. A directive is a measure that requires the states to which it is addressed to achieve a particular result as laid out in the text of the Directive. The Member States, however, retain a choice as to how that purpose is to be achieved. Thus Directives, unlike Regulations and Decisions, are not directly applicable — they must be implemented into national law in whatever manner the Member State chooses.

Ireland has chosen to allow the State to implement Directives by means of Ministerial Order or Statutory Instrument. Section 3 of the European Communities Act 1972 allows a Minister to implement a Directive by means of what are (rather confusingly) called regulations, in other words by means of a form of delegated legislation. In doing so the Minister is permitted to "vary, alter or repeal" any inconsistent piece of legislation, as he or she sees fit. This means that measures of E.U. law can be transposed into national law without having been approved by Parliament. In particular it allows legislation passed by Parliament to be amended by a Minister of Government, an approach which, as we shall see, offends the doctrine of the separation of powers. Only the Oireachtas can make law (Article 15.2) and therefore any attempt by a Minister to vary laws made by Parliament would normally be regarded as unconstitutional.

The Supreme Court had to consider this issue in *Meagher v. Minister for Agriculture* (1994). In that case, the Minister, in implementing an E.U. Directive under section 3(1) of the Act of 1972, purported to vary part of the Petty Sessions Act 1851. The plaintiff argued that this was unconstitutional, as only the Oireachtas could vary legislation. The High Court agreed and proceeded to consider whether this breach of the Constitution was necessitated by the obligations of membership of the European Union. If it was, the measure would have remained enforceable, as laws so necessitated enjoy an exemption from the terms of the Constitution. Johnston J., however, found that as Member States had a choice as to how they implemented Directives, it could not be said that Ireland was required to implement Directives in this manner.

The Supreme Court, however, decided otherwise. While Ireland may not have been legally obliged to adopt this particular method of implementing Directives, the *practical* reality was that it was effectively the only feasible way of so doing. There are so many Directives that have to be implemented every year, they reasoned, that the prospect of implementing them all by act of parliament would be unthinkable. The *Oireachtas* would not feasibly be able to keep up with the pace and Ireland would quickly default in its obligation to implement Directives. Thus the Supreme Court recognised that the term "necessitated" in Article 29.4.7 includes measures that are practically as well as legally necessary.

10.5 Is a referendum required *every* time there is a new E.U. Treaty?

In the course of its history the E.U. has developed considerably. Its competence has expanded into areas that at one point would never have been considered as matters relevant to the Common Market. These changes have been effected by a series of new Treaties, the most important of which are the Single European Act, the Maastricht Treaty and the Amsterdam Treaty.

Once signed by the State, these "amending" treaties do not come into effect until every state that has signed it ratifies the treaty in accordance with its own constitutional requirements. In theory, any state (including Ireland) may reject the treaty even after it has been signed (as Ireland has done with the Nice Treaty). In other words, Ireland is never obliged to ratify an amending treaty: it may choose to do otherwise. As a result it cannot be said that ratifying these treaties is "necessitated by the obligations of membership of the European Union".

Do we thus need a new referendum for every change in the Treaties of the European Communities and Union? This question was considered in *Crotty v. An Taoiseach* (1987) in which the Supreme Court had to rule on the legality of Ireland's ratifying the Single European Act without a referendum. In the course of his judgment, Finlay C.J. noted that Communities are dynamic in nature and must be expected to change and develop over time. When the Irish people passed the Third Amendment, allowing the State to join the Communities, such change must have been anticipated. To the extent, thus, that the proposed reforms to those Communities remained within the broad "purpose and objectives" of the original Treaties, the changes would be protected by the Constitution. If however, the changes in question altered the essential scope of the original objectives and aims of the Communities, they would not be afforded an exemption from the terms of the Constitution. In other words a referendum would be required.

In short if the proposed amendment to the E.U. is merely a development within the original aims and objectives of the Communities and Union, no referendum will be required. If, however, the changes proposed significantly alter the purpose of the Communities and Union, a new referendum will be required.

Applied to the various treaties passed since 1987, it might be said that the Maastricht Treaty, having made very significant alterations to the Communities, did require a referendum to give it constitutional immunity. The impact of the Amsterdam and Nice Treaties, however, is generally acknowledged as less dramatic and as such, these Treaties may not have required referenda. That said, both were subjected to a popular vote in referendum — the State has tended to "play it safe" when it comes to the constitutional validity of changes to the E.U. structures.

Part III

The Institutions of State

11. THE SEPARATION OF POWERS

Before dealing with the institutions and functionaries of state it is worth making some general introductory remarks about the concept of the "Separation of Powers". A broad appreciation of this concept is essential to an understanding of Irish Constitutional Law. The exact workings of each of the institutions and functionaries of state are outlined in greater detail in the following chapters. In each case, however, one should be mindful of the overall impact of the doctrine of the Separation of Powers. In sum, the principle requires that each institution exercise only the powers allocated to it. No other body may perform a role exclusively reserved to another institution of state. Article 6.2 makes it abundantly clear that the powers given to each institution by the Constitution are only to be exercised by (or on the authority of) those institutions.

In former times, the powers of state were vested exclusively in the monarch, the king or queen of a jurisdiction. For instance, in the United Kingdom all powers of state, in theory, belong to the Queen of England (although almost all of those powers are in practice delegated to other functionaries, the parliament, the government and the courts). It occurred to some Republican commentators that it was dangerous in the extreme to repose all power in only one person, no matter how well-meaning. As Lord Acton noted "power tends to corrupt, absolute power tends to corrupt absolutely". These republicans suggested that in a modern democracy the power to govern should be divided between different functionaries. Broadly, it was said that there were three types of power — legislative, executive and judicial.

Legislative power	This is the power to "make law" for the state. In a modern democracy this function is usually reserved to a legislature (parliament).
Executive power	This is the power to enforce and implement the law and policy of the state on a day-to-day basis. This power is usually reserved to an executive or "government".
Judicial power	This is the power to deliberate upon and resolve disputes about the meaning and application of law. This power is generally the preserve of judges in courts of law (the "Judiciary").

In Ireland these powers are distributed as follows:

Legislative power	The Oireachtas	Articles 15-27
Executive power	The Government	Article 28
Judicial power	The Courts	Articles 34-37

11.1 The exclusivity of roles

A key aspect of the separation of powers is that once powers are divided, a body can perform only those powers that are given to it. Each institution of state usually enjoys exclusive powers. No body or person can exercise the powers vested exclusively in another body or person.

In Ireland for instance, the Oireachtas makes the law of the State. Article 15.2 of the Constitution asserts that this role is exclusively reserved to the Oireachtas: "no other legislative authority has power to make laws for the State". This clause was designed mainly to exclude the prospect of the British Parliament in Westminster purporting to make laws for Ireland but its effects are clearly more extensive. In *Maher v. Attorney General* (1973), the Supreme Court refused to remove words from a piece of legislation in order to render the legislation constitutional. This, they said, would involve "law-making" on their part, a role that could only be performed by the Parliament.

The Executive too enjoys certain exclusive powers, for instance, the power to determine the foreign policy of the State. In *Crotty v. An Taoiseach* (1987) the Supreme Court struck down a piece of legislation that, amongst other things, allowed Ireland to participate in what was called "European Political Co-operation". The Supreme Court believed that this would undermine the Executive's exclusive right to determine Ireland's foreign policy and that it was therefore unconstitutional.

Article 35.2 states that judges are independent in the performance of their functions. In *Buckley v. Attorney General* (1950), the Supreme Court struck down an attempt by the Oireachtas to dictate the resolution of a case then being considered by the High Court. Legislation purporting to give away the courts' exclusive power to determine the appropriate punishment for a particular offender has met a similar fate. In *Deaton v. Attorney General* (1963), a law allowing the Revenue Commissioners to choose what penalty tax offenders would face was declared unconstitutional on the ground that only judges may make such a decision.

11.2 Some blurring of the lines of separation

While each of the institutions of state is technically independent of the others, the separation of powers in Ireland is not as rigid as it might otherwise be. For instance, there is an inevitably close relationship between the government and the Parliament. After all, the Taoiseach (who must be a member of the Dáil) and the Government (all of whom must be members of the Oireachtas) are essentially elected by the Dáil. It is sometimes said that the Government "controls" parliament, although technically the reverse is also true. The Government depends for its continuation in office on the support of the Dáil, to whom the Government is at all times answerable.

It is worth contrasting the Irish situation with that in the United States. There, the President (the head of the Executive) is elected not by Congress (Parliament) but by an electoral college of voters selected to represent each state. This means that a President could quite feasibly be elected without the support of a majority in Congress. An Irish Taoiseach, by contrast, could never be elected without Dáil support. While the U.S. President can veto certain measures of Congress, and Congress in turn can "impeach" a President that is considered no longer to be fit for office, the separation of the Executive and Parliament in the U.S. jurisdiction is relatively rigid in comparison with Ireland.

The strict separation of powers in Ireland is also undermined by the fact that the Taoiseach and Government have the power to appoint certain persons to Parliament and the Judiciary. The Taoiseach, for instance, appoints 11 of the 60 members of the Seanad, a power that usually secures for the Government the support of a majority in that House. The Government also effectively can tell the President whom to appoint as a judge. (Although, in practice, the Government now takes advice from the Judicial Appointments Advisory Board in relation to all but the highest judicial posts.)

Yet the courts in turn regularly supervise the activities of the parliament and government, in particular in constitutional challenges to their activities. The courts' powers of judicial review then, again illustrate the fact that while the various institutions of state are in strict theory independent of each other, there is a system of "checks and balances" that ensures that the Constitution is at all times observed.

11.3 Summary

In summary then, each institution of state is given certain powers b,
the Constitution. These must be exercised in compliance with the Con
stitution. In particular, no institution may take over a role allocated t
another institution unless permitted to do so by the Constitution.

12. THE PRESIDENT (ARTICLES 12-14)

The President is the Head of State in Ireland. The position of President was an innovation in the 1937 Constitution: the head of State in Saorstát Éireann was effectively the King of England. The extremely limited nature of the President's role reflects a very real fear in the 1930s that the position of President would be a stepping-stone to autocratic dictatorship, as had occurred in Nazi Germany for instance. Despite these fears, each incumbent without exception has served the State with distinction and within the bounds set by the Constitution.

Since 1938, there have been eight Presidents:

1938-1945:	Dubhghlas de hÍde (Douglas Hyde)
1945-1959:	Seán T. Ó Ceallaigh
1959-1973:	Éamon de Valéra
1973-1974:	Erskine Childers (Jnr.) (Died while in office)
1974-1976:	Cearbhall Ó Dálaigh (Resigned)
1976-1990:	Patrick Hillery
1990-1997:	Mary Robinson
1997-	Mary McAleese

12.1 Electing the President

12.1.1 Eligibility requirements

Any citizen of Ireland may run for the Presidency provided that he or she is aged 35 or over. The English text of the Constitution would seem to suggest that the candidate may be 34, one's "thirty-fifth year" being the year in which one reaches the age of 34. The (prevailing) Irish text would appear to conclude, however, that the candidate must be 35 or over. Despite the use of the male gender in the text of Article 12, it is indisputable that a candidate for the Presidency may be female, "every citizen" of the State being eligible for the post. A sitting President may not also be a member of the Oireachtas and if elected must vacate his or her seat therein.

12.1.2 Nominations

In order to run for the Presidency, a candidate must be nominated in the manner laid out in Article 12. There are three methods of nomination:

- An outgoing President may nominate himself or herself

- A candidate may be nominated by not less than 20 members of the Oireachtas (*i.e.* the Dáil and the Seanad).

- A candidate may be nominated by the councils of not less than four administrative counties or boroughs. (For example, Fingal County Council, Donegal County Council, Cork Corporation.) This method of nomination was first used by Dana Rosemary Scallan in the 1997 Presidential election, a ground-breaking move that tapped the potential for the nomination of persons other than the representatives of the larger Oireachtas political parties.

12.1.3 Election

Only citizens of Ireland otherwise qualified to vote in a Dáil election may vote for the President. The President is elected by direct vote at a secret ballot using the single transferable vote system of proportional representation. If there is only one candidate no election need be held. The President enters office upon taking the oath set out in Article 12.8.

12.1.4 Term of office

A President ordinarily remains in office, once elected, for seven years. A person may be elected President for two terms but no more (*i.e.* a total of 14 years), a privilege enjoyed by three Presidents, Ó Ceallaigh, de Valéra and Hillery.

12.2 The powers of the President

The President, in fact, has very few real powers, a situation that reflects the concern prevalent in the late 1930s that the role of President should not become a stepping-stone to dictatorship. As a general rule the functions that the President does enjoy must (*per* Article 13.9) be exercised "on the advice of the Government", a phrase that, despite its wording, effectively requires the incumbent to obey the will of the Government. Article 13.9 operates in respect of all of the President's constitutional powers, except where the contrary is clearly stated. The powers of the President are thus very limited.

The following functions or powers must be performed on the advice of the Government. In other words, while the President technically holds these powers, she must exercise them in line with instructions from the Executive:

- The President is (in name only) the Supreme Commander of the Defence Forces. All commissioned officers hold their positions on the authority of the President. (Article 13.4)

- The President appoints all judges, again on the direction of the Government. (Article 35.1)

- The President may pardon any person convicted of an offence on the direction of the Government. (Article 13.6) A pardon absolves a person from criminal responsibility for such offence. When the death sentence was available as a penalty, the President was allowed to commute or remit such a sentence. In fact the death penalty was abolished by the Criminal Justice Act 1990. The Twenty-First Amendment to the Constitution, passed in 2001, prevents the Oireachtas from passing a new law re-introducing the death penalty. As a result the President's right to commute a death sentence has also (logically enough) been removed.

The President was formerly entitled, though again under direction from the Government, to commute (shorten) or remit (change for a lesser penalty) any judicially imposed punishment. The Constitution, however, allowed this function to be delegated to another appropriate person. In fact, this function has now been transferred, by section 23 of the Criminal Justice Act 1951, to the Minister for Justice.

There are some situations where the President acts not on the advice of the Government but on that of other parties:

- The President appoints each new Taoiseach on the nomination of the Dáil. (Article 13.1.1)

- The President appoints the other members of each government on the nomination of the Taoiseach, with the prior approval of the Dáil. (Article 13.1.2)

- The President must dissolve the Dáil if the incumbent Taoiseach so requests, unless the latter no longer enjoys the support of the majority of Dáil members. (Article 13.2.1)

- The President (subject to Article 26) must sign every Bill passed or deemed to have been passed by the Oireachtas. (Article 25)

- The President appoints each new Attorney General on the nomination of the Taoiseach. (Article 30.2)

- The President appoints each new Comptroller and Auditor General on the advice of Dáil Éireann. (Article 32)

The President does, however, enjoy certain powers that can be exercised at his or her own discretion, regardless of the government's will (or anyone else's for that matter). These are as follows:

- Article 13.2: Where a Taoiseach requests that the President dissolve the Dáil, the latter may refuse, at his or her discretion, to do so if the Taoiseach no longer enjoys the support of a majority of T.D.s. In such a case, it is suggested, the President's role is confined to making the refusal. It is submitted, for instance, that it would not be advisable for her to arrange the formation of an alternative government.

- Article 13.7: Having consulted with the Council of State the President may convene a meeting of either or both Houses of the Oireachtas. The President may also, at her discretion and having consulted the Council of State, address either the Houses of the Oireachtas or the Nation as a whole on a matter of national or public importance. The content of such an address, however, is subject to the approval of the Government. To date four such addresses have been made, all to the Houses of the Oireachtas, one by President de Valéra, two by President Robinson and one by President McAleese.

- Article 22: Where the *Ceann Comhairle* of the Dáil determines that a Bill is a "Money Bill", this diminishes the role of the Seanad in its adoption. Article 22 allows the President, if requested by a majority of the Seanad and at least one-third of the membership of the Dáil, to refer a dispute concerning whether a bill is a "Money Bill" to a special Committee of Privileges.

- Article 24: The President may, at his or her discretion, accede to a request from the Taoiseach to shorten the time for consideration of a Bill by the Seanad, in times of "public emergency" as defined by Article 24.

- Article 26: The President may refer a Bill to the Supreme Court for its opinion as to whether the Bill or any part thereof is repugnant to the Constitution. (See Chap. 5 below.)

- Article 27: Where the Seanad has rejected a Bill that is subsequently deemed by the Dáil under Article 23 to have been passed by both Houses, the Seanad (together with at least one-third of the membership of the Dáil) may request that the President refer the matter to the People in referendum.

Each of the last six presidential powers gives real discretion to the President. While she is usually required to consult with the Council of State before making a decision, the President is otherwise fully entitled to act as she sees fit in these limited cases. It is worth noting that the President is not required to consult with the Council of State in respect of her powers under Article 13.2.

12.2.1 Other powers

While Article 13.10 empowers the Legislature to confer other powers upon the President, such powers may be exercised only on the advice of the Government.

12.3 The Council of State (Articles 31-32)

In some cases, the Constitution requires that the President consult with the Council of State before he or she makes a particular decision. The Council of State is required to "aid and counsel" the President in such matters, although its opinions are never binding. In every such case where required to do so, the President must seek the opinion thereof, although she may, in any case, choose to conduct herself contrary to such opinion. The members of the Council of State are listed below in the following table:

The persons presently holding the following positions	Any person still living who has ever held the following positions:
The Taoiseach	President

The Tánaiste	Taoiseach
The Chief Justice	Chief Justice
The President of the High Court	President of the Executive Council of *Saorstát Éireann*
The Chairpersons of both Houses of the Oireachtas	
The Attorney General	

In addition, the President herself, in his or her absolute discretion, may appoint up to seven members of the Council. Such members ordinarily remain in office until a new President is put in place.

12.4 Article 14 and the Presidential Commission

Where the President is not able or willing to perform his or her powers, Article 14 allows a Commission to be established to perform all or any of those functions in his or her place. The circumstances in which the Commission may be set up are comparatively wide. These include, where the President is absent from the State, temporarily or permanently incapacitated, where the incumbent President has died, resigned or has been removed from office and where the President has simply failed to perform certain required tasks.

The Commission consists of the Chief Justice of the Supreme Court, the *Ceann Comhairle* (Chairperson or Speaker) of the Dáil and the *Cathaoirleach* (Chairperson or Speaker) of the Seanad. Where one or more of these persons is unable to act as such, the following substitutions may be made:

- The President of the High Court may take the place of the Chief Justice.

- The Deputy Chair of each House may take the place of the Chairperson of the same House.

Any two members of the Commission may act, even in the absence of the third member, although in order for any decision to be taken it must be approved by at least two members. The Commission is subject to all the powers and privileges, requirements and restrictions that are vested in or placed on the President herself.

12.5 Dismissing the President

The President may not be subjected to legal proceedings or scrutiny before either House of the Oireachtas in respect of acts done in the exercise of his or her powers and functions. (Article 13.8). In other words the President enjoys an immunity from judicial or legislative scrutiny of her official actions (see the decision of Hamilton P. in *O'Malley v. An Taoiseach* (1989), refusing to interfere in the President's decision to dissolve the Dáil).

It is, however, possible to dismiss the President from office in two cases:

- Where he or she is found to have become permanently incapacitated. Such a step may only be effected by the Supreme Court, sitting with no less than five judges.

- The President may be impeached, but only for "stated misbehaviour". The steps leading to impeachment, (which are remarkably similar to those invoked in the United States against President Clinton in 1998) are as follows:

  (a) A proposal to lay a charge of impeachment must be made by notice of motion in either House of the Oireachtas. For this purpose at least thirty members of the relevant House must sign the motion in writing.

  (b) The proposal may only be adopted by that House with the support of at least two-thirds of the total members of that House, *i.e.* at least 40 senators or alternatively, at least 111 T.D.s.

  (c) If the charge is adopted by one House it must be investigated by the other House, *i.e.* the House that did not lay the charge. That House may impeach the President but only if at least two-thirds of its total membership determines that the charge is sustained and that the proven allegation would render the President unfit for office. In other words, the House may find that although the allegation of misconduct is true, it does not merit dismissal.

Only if all these conditions are met may the President be removed from office. It is worth noting that to date, the conduct of our Presidents appears to have been exemplary such that the impeachment process has never been invoked in this jurisdiction.

13. THE OIREACHTAS (ARTICLE 15)

The Oireachtas is Ireland's State Parliament. It consists of two Houses, a House of Representatives called *Dáil Éireann* and a Senate, called *Seanad Éireann*. It is important to note, however, that the President is also technically part of the Oireachtas. To become part of Irish law, all Bills passed (or deemed to have been passed) by the two Houses must be signed and promulgated by the President. At a later stage we will discuss the respective roles of these Houses but for now let us consider some important points about the Oireachtas as a whole.

13.1 Sole and exclusive right to legislate

Even when Ireland won its independence in 1922, it remained partly under the control of the U.K. Parliament in Westminster. Westminster retained certain rights to legislate in respect of Ireland. Article 15.2 of the new Constitution of 1937 was primarily designed to underline that Westminster was no longer entitled to make laws for Ireland. Only the Oireachtas, it asserted, could make laws for this State:

> "The sole and exclusive power of making laws for the State is hereby vested in the Oireachtas: no other legislative authority has power to make laws for the State".

Article 15.2, thus, fits perfectly into the scheme of the original drafters of the Constitution. Indeed it merely reflects the broad assertion in Article 1 that Ireland would determine its own destiny, free from external interference. Yet despite the rather absolute nature of the language, it is clear that Article 15.2 is now significantly qualified by other parts of the Constitution. It has to be read, in particular, in the light of Ireland's membership of the European Union (E.U.). In spite of Article 15.2, as we saw earlier, Article 29.4.7, in conjunction with the European Communities Act 1972, allows European Law automatically to become part of Irish Law, without ever having been approved by the Oireachtas. This was only made possible, of course, by Constitutional amendment. Without Article 29.4.7, E.U. Law could not (constitutionally) be enforced in Ireland without the approval of the Irish Parliament. (See Chap. 10.)

In a somewhat more limited manner, we also saw how laws created by parliaments can have "extra-territorial jurisdiction", that is can be found to apply to events and persons situated outside the State that has created the relevant law. Thus, just as Ireland can create laws that apply outside our jurisdiction, so too can laws be created abroad that concern persons and events in this State. (See Articles 3.1 and 29.8.)

13.2 The Oireachtas cannot pass certain laws

Generally, the Oireachtas has the sole discretion to decide on the content of laws. A Court cannot interfere with this discretion simply because it may disagree with the policy of the law. The Courts have regularly noted, for instance, that the primary responsibility for balancing the rights and interests of individuals and the State lies with the Oireachtas.

That said, the Oireachtas cannot pass certain laws. In general, it is precluded from passing "any law which is in any respect repugnant to th[e] Constitution or any provision thereof". (Article 15.4) To the extent that such a law infringes the Constitution it will have no legal effect. The Oireachtas is also specifically prevented from passing certain specific types of law. Article 15.5.1, for instance, precludes the Oireachtas from making something an offence with retrospective effect. The Oireachtas in other words, cannot declare that an act carried out in the past, and legal at the time, is now to be considered illegal. Parliament is also prohibited from enacting legislation that would provide for a death penalty (Article 15.5.2, inserted by the Twenty-First Amendment to the Constitution, 2001.).

13.3 The Oireachtas' exclusive powers within Ireland

Subject to the exceptions laid out above, a foreign body cannot make laws in respect of the State. Article 15.2 however, is not confined to preventing interference from outside the State. It also very clearly prevents any person or body within the State from taking over the exclusive role of the Oireachtas.

In fact, most cases concerning this issue involve the role of other State institutions. In *Maher v. Attorney General* (1972), for instance, the Supreme Court was called upon to alter a law so as to give it constitutional validity. That case concerned a motorist accused of a "drink-driving" offence. The law as enacted by the Oireachtas had purported to make a certificate, stating that the accused was driving under the influence of an excessive amount of alcohol, "conclusive" evidence of the guilt of the accused. This, in short, deprived the courts of their role in determining the truth or otherwise of the assertions made before it and was, therefore, unconstitutional.

Lawyers for the State had suggested that the legislation should be read without the word "conclusive". The Supreme Court, however, refused to alter the legislation so as to cure it of its unconstitutionality, noting that to do so would involve the Court in altering legislative policy. This was something that only the *Oireachtas* could do. In a similar manner, the courts have refused to rectify even the most obvious of mistakes in legislation. In *State (Murphy) v. Johnston* (1984), a provision of road traffic legislation wrongly referred to "Part III" when it should have referred to "Part V" of the legislation. The Court, nonetheless, declined to amend what was obviously an unintended error, again asserting that it would not engage in making legislation.

The role of the judiciary, it has frequently noted, is in interpreting and applying the law as it is, not as it thinks the law should be. Law reform, however desirable, "is not and can never be a function of [the courts]", as O'Higgins C.J. reminds us in *Norris v. Attorney General* (1984). Questions arise then as to the ability of the courts to extend the common (judge-made) law beyond its present confines. In *M.M. v. P.M.* (1986), McMahon J. rejected an attempt to extend the definition of a ground for the annulment of marriage. This was, he said, a task for Parliament and not the courts. Otherwise the courts would be *making* rather than following the law. Similarly, in *McGrath v. McDermott* (1988), the Supreme Court ruled that it had no general power to "add to or delete from express statutory provisions so as to achieve objectives which to the courts appear desirable". It could not, in particular, proceed to fill in loopholes in tax legislation so as to prevent the avoidance of tax.

Yet the courts have, on occasion altered common law rules in a manner that could quite feasibly be said to involve "making" law. In *McKinley v. Minister for Defence* (1993), the Supreme Court extended a common law cause of action to allow women as well as men to sue for loss of consortium (loss of sexual ability in one's spouse). It is arguable that this involved "mending" the law so as to prevent it from being struck down on the ground that it was discriminatory.

13.4 Delegated legislation

The process of making law, however, became progressively more complex over the last two centuries. Laws have become ever the more detailed and technical. In an increasing number of cases, the Oireachtas has delegated certain powers to other bodies, most notably the Government. These powers are generally exercised by means of the creation of "secondary legislation" statutory orders, or "Statutory Instruments" as they are sometimes called, whereby Ministers of Government create rules governing certain matters.

In practice, this is largely unobjectionable. The simple fact is that the Oireachtas has neither the time nor the resources to examine every technical detail of modern legislation. Nevertheless, this "delegation" of legislation is subject to the objection that it may involve a law-making role that infringes the Oireachtas' exclusive right to legislate.

The extent to which the Oireachtas can delegate its legislative functions is examined in a number of cases. The courts readily acknowledge the necessity of such delegation. As Hanna J. noted in *Pigs Marketing Board v. Donnelly* (1939), "[t]he functions of every government are now so numerous and complex that of necessity a wider sphere has been recognised for subordinate agencies ... ". In that case, which involved the price-fixing powers of a board established by statute, the Court noted that some matters are so complex and detailed that it is perfectly reasonable that they be delegated to experts. To do so does not involve the making of legislation, provided that the powers delegated involve no more than giving effect to policies already created by the Oireachtas. For instance, in *Pigs Marketing Board*, the Oireachtas had decided, in legislation, that prices for Pigs and Bacon should be controlled, in accordance with guidelines laid down in the legislation. The Board was merely charged with determining what those prices should be.

The general test to be applied in this context was laid down in *Cityview Press v. AnCO* (1980). This involved the Industrial Training Act 1967, which gave the defendant (a state body charged with training workers for employment) the power to set and collect levies from particular employers. This money was to be used to fund the training of workers for the industry in question from which the money was being collected. It was alleged that this was in breach of Article 15.2 in that it allowed the defendant to make legislation.

The Supreme Court laid down the test to be applied in this context:

> "The test ... is whether what is challenged as an unauthorised delegation of parliamentary power is more than a mere giving effect to principles and policies which are contained in the statute itself.".

If it is, the Court said, the delegation would be unconstitutional. If on the other hand, "the law is laid down in the statute and the details only filled in or completed by the designated Minister or subordinate body", the delegation will be legal. In other words, provided that the person to whom the power was delegated was following rather than making law, the delegation would be permissible.

13.5 Only the Oireachtas can change or repeal legislation

What is clear is that it is not possible to delegate the power to change ("amend, vary or repeal") existing Acts of Parliament. In *Cooke v. Walsh* (1984), the Supreme Court considered the Health Act 1970 which gave the plaintiff, amongst other people, the right to free medical care. Under section 72 of the Act, however, the Minister for Health was entitled to make Regulations providing that certain services available under the Act would be open "only to a particular class of the persons who have eligibility for that service". The Minister attempted, under section 72, to prevent persons who had been injured in road accidents from claiming free medical care unless they could show that they were not entitled to other compensation. The Ministerial order, in other words, attempted to deny the plaintiff rights given to him under legislation.

The Court ruled that the Minister did not have the authority to do so. The Minister had purported to change the legislation so as to deny persons of their statutory eligibility. In line with the presumption of constitutionality, the Court assumed that the legislature had not intended to give the Minister the power to change the legislation, and as a result ruled that the Minister had acted *ultra vires* (outside his powers).

Meagher v. Minister for Agriculture (1994) implicitly endorses the fact that, ordinarily, a Minister cannot be given the power to change legislation. That case concerned the validity of the European Communities Act 1972, section 3 of which allows a Minister implementing E.U. legislation in Ireland, to make such changes to Irish legislation as are deemed necessary. The Supreme Court decided that Article 29.4.7, exempting measures "necessitated by the obligations" of E.U. membership from constitutional scrutiny, did apply in this case and that thus the power in section 3 could not be challenged. It was clear, however, that absent Article 29.4.7 the power vested in the Minister would have been unconstitutional.

The Government cannot, by the same token, simply decide to refrain from enforcing or operating an Act of Parliament. In *Norris v. Attorney General* (1984), McCarthy J. noted (although it was not relevant to the decision of the Court) that a positive decision by the Government *never* to enforce a particular law would be unconstitutional. In *Duggan v. An Taoiseach* (1989), for instance, a Ministerial decision not to collect tax due under the Farm Tax Act 1985 was found to be in breach of Article 15.2. The Act was still in force, and as such the law required that the tax be collected. The Government could not by ministerial pronouncement "repeal" the legislation.

13.6 The Oireachtas cannot delegate the right to make policy

In *McDaid v. Sheehy* (1991), the courts had to consider the Imposition of Duties Act 1957, which allowed the Government to impose customs and excise duties as they saw fit. In the High Court, Blayney J. ruled this provision unconstitutional. Here, the details of State policy were not merely being "filled in". The legislation allowed for the creation of a tax, a "bare" power to make policy, with no guidance whatsoever from the Oireachtas. On appeal, the Supreme Court held that the consequent taxes were in fact valid but for reasons that in no way impeached the reasoning of Blayney J. The Supreme Court itself, indeed, used similar reasoning to strike down a section of the Aliens Act 1935 in *Laurentiu v. Minister for Justice* (1999). The legislation in question gave the Minister the power effectively to determine Ireland's policy on the deportation of non-E.U. nationals. This amounted to an unconstitutional delegation of legislative power.

13.7 The *Sheehan* principle

One strange aspect of the separation of powers flows from the decision in the *State (Sheehan) v. Government of Ireland* (1987). This concerned the age-old rule that a person can sue a local authority in respect of injuries sustained on the public highway only when those injuries are caused by the authority's action and not by their *in*action. In the Civil Liability Act 1961 (Section 60), the Oireachtas had purported to abolish this illogical distinction and allow the authorities to be sued for their omissions. It is quite common, however, for Acts of Parliament to allow the Government to decide when they should come into force, so that the Government could prepare for their operation. Section 60 thus gave the Government the discretion to decide when the provision would begin to operate. Forty years on, however, the Government have still not taken that decision!! Section 60 remains unenforceable. In

Sheehan, the plaintiff suggested that section 60 had to be brought into force within a reasonable timeframe. Although the High Court agreed, the Supreme Court on appeal disagreed, ruling that section 60 gave the Government an unfettered discretion to decide when the legislation should come into force. In doing so, the latter Court seems to have ignored the fact that this has allowed the effective repeal, by Government inaction, of legislative policy. Considering the judicial reaction to measures that purport to allow Ministers to change legislation, the decision in *Sheehan* seems oddly inconsistent.

13.8 Parliamentary privilege

Parliament generally enjoys a certain independence from outside control and supervision. Each House, for instance, is entitled by virtue of Article 15.10 to make and administer its own rules, and to impose penalties for the breach of those rules. The courts cannot review a decision of either House in respect of its internal operation. On this ground the High Court, in *O'Malley v. Ceann Comhairle (of the Dáil)* (1995), refused to entertain a challenge to the *Ceann Comhairle*'s (Speaker's) refusal to allow certain questions to be asked of a Minister in the Dáil.

Members of Parliament, in addition, have certain constitutional rights that are reserved only to them. Thus members of the two Houses, in certain limited circumstances, are exempt from the provisions of law that apply generally in the State.

- Articles 15.12 and 15.13 prevent T.D.s or Senators from being sued or prosecuted in court in respect of comments made in Parliament. For instance, a T.D. who makes defamatory remarks, or who makes comments calculated to incite to hatred (contrary to the Prohibition of Incitement to Hatred Act 1989) will not be amenable to a court of law for such conduct. A good hypothetical example would be that of a T.D. who makes inflammatory racist remarks in the Dáil. Neither he nor any person who re-publishes his remarks could be prosecuted for this. Indeed, not only are the comments themselves privileged: the privilege extends to any "publication" of the same comments, *e.g.* in a newspaper or on *Oireachtas Report.* In *An Blascaod Mór v. Commissioners for Public Works* (2001), Budd J. reaffirmed that the Courts could not act in respect of utterances in either House and that to do so would undermine the freedom of debate within the Oireachtas.

- In *Attorney General v. Hamilton (No. 2)* (1994), the Supreme Court ruled that members of Parliament could not be forced to reveal the identity of sources of information on which utterances in either House are based. That case concerned a number of T.D.s who had made statements in the Dáil based on information received outside the House. The Tribunal investigating irregularities in the Beef Industry failed in its attempt to force the deputies to reveal the sources of that information.

- Article 15.13 provides for a particular type of freedom of travel, reserved again only to T.D.s and Senators. No member of Parliament may be arrested going to, returning from or while "within the precincts of either House", except for certain alleged offences: these are treason, a felony (though the concept is now abolished) or a breach of the peace. This is designed to prevent the unlikely situation of a government arresting persons with the sole purpose of eliminating the votes of its opponents. One should note, however, that while it may not be possible to arrest a member of the Oireachtas, nothing in this subsection prevents the T.D. or senator from being charged and prosecuted in accordance with the law.

13.9 Summary

The Constitution originally envisaged that only the Oireachtas would be able to make legislation in respect of the State. The doctrine of the separation of powers precludes any other institution from performing the law-making powers of the Oireachtas. In particular, the courts have noted that they cannot "amend" legislation to prevent it from being unconstitutional (*Maher v. Attorney General* (1972)) or to repair even obvious mistakes in legislation (*State (Murphy) v. Johnston* (1984)). The Courts, moreover, leave the role of law reform largely to Parliament (see the comments in *Norris v. Attorney General* (1984)).

While the Oireachtas may delegate certain functions to Ministers, it can only do so in line with the "principles and policies" test outlined in *Cityview Press* (1980). A Minister cannot ordinarily act so as to amend or vary legislation as to do so would involve a breach of the separation of powers. Only the Oireachtas can make, amend or repeal a law.

Ireland's membership of the European Union, of course also qualifies Article 15.2. By virtue of Article 29.4.7 and the European Communities Act 1972 the Union can make laws that apply in Ireland even where they have not been passed by the Oireachtas. Article 29.4.7

exempts E.U. law from having to be validated by the Oireachtas and thus allows laws to be created and enforced in Ireland without parliamentary sanction.

14. THE DÁIL AND THE SEANAD (ARTICLES 16-24)

Most modern democracies have a bi-cameral legislature, that is, one with two houses, an upper chamber and a lower chamber. (Though some legislatures, like that of Nebraska, in the U.S., are uni-cameral, *i.e.* have only one single House). There are two Houses of the Oireachtas, a House of Representatives (the lower House), called *"Dáil Éireann"*, and a Senate (the upper House), named *"Seanad Éireann"*. A member of the Dáil is called a *"Teachta Dála"* (T.D.) or a "Deputy". A member of the Senate is a *"Seanadóir"* or Senator. Of the two houses, the Dáil is clearly the more powerful, in matters of legislation, finance, international affairs and in the supervision of the Government, alike. Indeed several commentators (President de Valéra amongst them) appear to have mooted the possibility of abolishing the Seanad altogether, a move that has, to date, been avoided.

Can one be a member of both Houses at the same time? No. Article 15.14 precludes this. If while a member of one House (A), a person is elected to the other (B), he or she will be deemed to have vacated his seat in House A.

14.1 The Dáil

14.1.1 Number of members: 166

There may be at most one T.D. for every 20,000 of the population, but at least one for every 30,000. (That is, with a population of 3.75 million there must be at least 125 and at most 185 T.D.s). Representation must be as equal as practicable throughout the State. For instance, measures that allowed for greater representation in rural areas were struck down as offending the guarantee of equality in *O'Donovan v. Attorney General* (1961).

14.1.2 Who may be elected?

Any citizen of Ireland, male or female, who has reached the age of 21 may be elected to the Dáil. Certain persons may, by law, be disqualified from election to the Dáil: these include a sitting President, judges, members of the Defence Forces or of the Garda Síochána, civil serv-

ants, lawfully imprisoned persons serving sentences exceeding six
months in duration and undischarged bankrupts.

14.1.3 Who is allowed to vote?

Any citizen of Ireland or of the United Kingdom who is, at the relevant
time, present in the State and registered to vote. Every such person
must have reached the age of eighteen and not be otherwise disqualified from voting. Originally, the Constitution only allowed "citizens"
to vote. Hence, in an Article 26 reference, the Electoral Amendment
Bill 1983 was struck down as unconstitutional on the grounds that it
purported to give U.K. citizens resident in the Republic of Ireland the
right to vote here. The Constitution was subsequently changed to allow
the Oireachtas to extend the right to vote to non-citizens. The Ninth
Amendment to the Constitution 1984 extended the franchise to "such
other persons in the State as may be determined by law, ...". So far
only U.K. citizens have been given such a right, on the basis of recipro-
cal rights for Irish citizens living in the U.K.

14.1.4 How does voting proceed?

Persons vote by means of a single transferable vote, a form of proportional representation. Constituencies are multi-seat, in other words
more than one seat (usually three, four or five), is assigned to each of
the 41 constituencies. In fact, according to Article 16.2.6, constituencies cannot legally consist of any less than three seats. Electors rank
the candidates in order of preference. When a candidate is eliminated,
his second or lower preferences are distributed amongst the remaining
candidates. Where a candidate reaches the "quota" required, he is
deemed elected, any surplus over the quota being distributed amongst
the remaining candidates until all seats in the constituency are filled.

Voting is by secret ballot. Any mechanism or procedure by which a
voter's vote may be identified is unconstitutional. In *McMahon v.
Attorney General* (1972), the courts struck down a system that allowed
votes to be traced back to the voter in cases of alleged electoral fraud.
This offended the secrecy of the ballot and was accordingly deemed
illegal.

14.2 The Seanad

The Seanad has 60 members, elected by a variety of means. Most, in
all 43, are elected by a vote of all present county and borough council-

lors, incoming T.D.s and outgoing senators. These 43 members are elected from five panels representing various strands of social and economic life (*e.g.* Agriculture and Fisheries, Workers, Industry and Commerce, etc.).

A further three members are elected by the graduates of the National University of Ireland (U.C.D./N.U.I.D., U.C.G./N.U.I.G., U.C.C./N.U.I.C., and N.U.I. Maynooth). The graduates and foundation scholars of the University of Dublin (Trinity College) also elect three members. Such graduates must also be citizens. It is arguable that this unfairly prejudices the graduates of other younger third-level institutions who are denied such a vote despite having similar qualifications to those of the graduates of the N.U.I. and Trinity College. It is worth noting that while the Seventh Amendment of the Constitution allowed the State to allocate some of these seats to the graduates of other universities and third-level institutions, this has not yet been done.

The remaining 11 members are appointed by the first Taoiseach to be elected immediately following a general election. It is worth noting however, that where the position of Taoiseach changes otherwise than after a general election, that new Taoiseach cannot replace the 11 members appointed by the previous Taoiseach.

The Seanad is elected after the Dáil, but not less than ninety days after the dissolution of the lower House.

14.3 The Dáil is the more powerful house

As a general rule, it must be said that the Dáil is the more powerful of the two Houses. Being the House that is directly elected by the people, it stands to reason that it is treated as the more important of the two. This is reflected in the different powers and duties that each House possesses:

14.3.1 Legislative powers

Most of the time, a Bill (a proposal for a law) may be introduced in either House (Article 20). It is possible, then, for the Seanad to initiate bills (Article 20.2). Certain Bills, however, can only be introduced in the Dáil: these are money Bills and Bills proposing an amendment to the Constitution (Article 21.1 and Article 46.2 respectively).

A Bill that is initiated in either House must be sent to the other House for its approval. If approved by both Houses without amendment the situation is straightforward: it is sent to the President who signs it and puts if forward as a law. (Article 25)

Different considerations apply, however, where either House wishes to amend or reject a Bill. Where the Dáil rejects a Bill it cannot become law. By contrast, where the Seanad rejects a Bill, introduces amendments to which the Dáil objects, or simply ignores the Bill, that Bill may still become law (Article 23). Effectively, the Seanad can only delay the Bill, for a period of ninety days. Once that ninety-day period has expired, it is open to the Dáil to pass a resolution deeming the Bill to have been passed by both Houses. This it must do within 180 days of the end of the delay period. Thus, even though the Seanad objects to the Bill, in part or in full, the Bill may become a law. This has only happened on very rare occasions. Because of the Taoiseach's power to appoint 11 members to the Seanad, it is almost invariably the case that the Government has a majority in that House. Article 23 has been invoked on only three occasions. The most notable was in 1959, when the Dáil attempted to pass a Bill for an Amendment to the Constitution purporting to abolish proportional representation. The Seanad having bravely refused this proposal, the Dáil used Article 23 to deem the Bill to have been passed by both Houses. Ironically, the Bill was subsequently rejected by the people in referendum.

14.3.2 The public finances

The Seanad's powers are even more limited in respect of what are called "Money Bills". (Articles 21-22). These are proposals concerning, in short, the collection or spending of public monies. A Finance or Tax Bill would be a good example. Bills concerning the creation or payment of a debt and anything to do with the supply of money would also be included in this category. Such a Bill may be introduced only in the Dáil (Article 21.1). The Seanad considers the Bill but may only make recommendations, which the Dáil may freely ignore. The Seanad indeed has only a short time to consider the Bill: if at the end of twenty one days the Bill is not returned, the Dáil may proceed to enact the bill as if it had been passed by both Houses.

It is the responsibility of the Chairman of the Dáil, under Article 22, to decide what is a Money Bill. If it disagrees, however, Seanad Éireann may ask the President to establish a Committee of Privileges to determine whether the Bill is indeed a Money Bill. The President may establish such a committee but she is not obliged to do so. The committee, if established, would consist of an equal number of Senators and

T.D.s, with a judge of the Supreme Court presiding as Chair. The decision of this committee is final and conclusive, and thus cannot be further challenged in a court of law.

14.3.3 The election and supervision of the Government

The Dáil alone has an exclusive supervisory role in respect of the Government. The Taoiseach, though technically appointed by the President, is selected by the Dáil (Article 13.1.1). It, in turn, must approve his selection of Ministers (Article 13.1.2). In fact, the Taoiseach and his Government ultimately depend on Dáil support alone for their continuation in office. If a Taoiseach loses the support of a majority of T.D.s, he or she must resign unless the President can be persuaded to dissolve the Dáil (Article 28.10). While in office, the Government is answerable to the Dáil alone in respect of its activities (Article 28.4).

14.3.4 The conduct of international affairs

Though it is the responsibility of the Government to sign international treaties, these may only bind the State if endorsed by the Dáil (Article 29.5). Unless the agreement requires that the State provide funding, the treaty need only be laid before the Dáil to satisfy this condition. Where a charge on public funds is anticipated, however, the Dáil must approve the terms of the agreement. Where it fails to do so (as in *State (Gilliland) v. Governor of Mountjoy Prison* (1987)), the agreement in question will not be binding on the State. An agreement that is merely of a technical or administrative nature, however, is entirely exempt from these requirements.

It is worth noting also that a declaration of war may be made only by the Dáil. The State may not participate in a war without the assent of the Dáil (Article 28.3).

14.4 Summary of voting rights

- European elections — any E.U. citizen resident in Ireland may vote.

- Presidential elections and referenda — only Irish citizens resident in Ireland may vote.

- Dáil elections — only Irish or British citizens resident in Ireland may vote.

- Seanad elections — only graduates of Trinity College Dublin and of the National University of Ireland, County Councillors, outgoing T.D.s and outgoing senators may vote.

- Local elections — all residents may vote.

15. GOVERNMENT (ARTICLE 28)

The Government, or "Executive" to give it its proper name, has overall responsibility for the day to day administration and running of the State. In the legal field in particular, it is charged with monitoring the implementation of laws and ensuring that the law of the land is being complied with.

In its widest sense, the term "Government" includes the civil and public service as a whole, including the Garda Síochána, that is, those generally responsible for ensuring the efficient and effective running of the State. The Constitution, however, uses the term in a narrower sense to describe what is sometimes known as the "Cabinet", the Taoiseach and his or her Ministers.

The Government presently consists of 15 members, including the Taoiseach. In fact, there may be as few as seven members of Government but no more than fifteen. The President officially appoints the members of Government, although they are effectively selected by the Taoiseach, subject to the approval of the Dáil (Article 13.1.2).

15.1 Membership of the Government

15.1.1 Eligibility

In order to be made a Minister, one must be a member for the time being of either Dáil or Seanad Éireann. A Taoiseach wishing to nominate a person who is not a member of Parliament has the option of first appointing that person as one of his or her 11 nominees to the Seanad. There are, however, certain restrictions on senators being members of the Government. At any one time, for instance, no more than two senators may be Ministers. In addition, only members of the Dáil are eligible to be appointed to the posts of Taoiseach, Tánaiste and Minister for Finance. In fact, it is quite rare for a senator to be appointed a Minister. In 1957, Senator Seán Moylan was appointed Minister for Agriculture. Professor James Dooge (Minister for Foreign Affairs, 1981-1982) is the only other sitting senator to have achieved ministerial status.

15.1.2 Resignation and removal

Contrary to perception, it is not possible for the Dáil to remove an individual Minister, although its members may, through political pressure, force such resignation or removal. An individual Minister may leave (or be forced to leave) office in several ways:

- **Voluntary resignation:** the Minister hands his resignation to the Taoiseach. This is then given to the President who, subject to the approval of the Taoiseach, will accept this resignation.

- **Requested resignation:** The Taoiseach may request a Minister to resign. The Taoiseach may do so for any reason which to him or her "seems sufficient". It would seem that the Taoiseach's decision in this regard is not subject to judicial review: the Taoiseach has an unfettered discretion to seek a resignation.

- **Termination:** if a Minister fails, once requested, to resign, the President, on the advice of the Taoiseach, may terminate his or her appointment. A well-known example of this was the removal from office in 1990 of the then Minister for Foreign Affairs, the late Brian Lenihan Senior, T.D. The amiable Foreign Minister, then a candidate for the Presidency, had refused to resign following allegations of improper conduct. Facing a Government revolt, the Taoiseach of the time advised the President to terminate his appointment.

15.2 An Taoiseach

15.2.1 Appointment of the Taoiseach

The head of the Executive is called the "Taoiseach", but is also described in the Constitution as "Prime Minister". The equivalent officer in *Saorstát Éireann* went by the rather grand title of "President of the Executive Council". Two persons held the latter post: William T. Cosgrave (1923-1932) and Éamon de Valéra (1932-1937). The Taoiseach is not directly elected but depends instead on the elected members of the Dáil for his appointment. Although it is the President who officially appoints the Taoiseach, he or she does so at the behest of the Dáil Deputies, who must choose a Taoiseach from among their ranks.

Éamon de Valéra:	1937-1948, 1951-1954, 1957-1959;
John A. Costello:	1948-1951, 1954-1957;
Seán Lemass:	1959-1966;
Jack Lynch:	1967-1974, 1977-1979;
Liam Cosgrave:	1974-1977;
Charles Haughey:	1979-1981, 1982, 1987-1992;
Garret Fitzgerald:	1981-1982, 1982-1987;
Albert Reynolds:	1992-1995;
John Bruton:	1995-1997;
Bertie Ahern:	1997-

15.2.2 Responsibilities of the Taoiseach

The Taoiseach has overall responsibility for the running of Government. Beyond this, however, his or her precise role tends to be a little vague. In addition to his or her overall brief, the Taoiseach has the following specific duties and powers:

- The nomination of Government Ministers. (Article 13.1.2)

- The power to ask the President to dissolve the Dáil: the latter may only refuse to do so when the Taoiseach has lost the support of a majority of Dáil members. (Article 13.2.2)

- The power to appoint 11 members of the Seanad: however, only a Taoiseach first appointed after a general election may do so. (Article 18)

- The responsibility to inform the President generally concerning matters of national and international policy. (Article 28.5.2)

- The power to nominate the Tánaiste. (Article 28.6.1)

- The power to ask a Minister to resign and, if the request is refused, to demand that resignation. (Article 28.9.4-6)

- The nomination of the Attorney General. (Article 30.2)

- The Taoiseach is automatically deemed a member of the Council of State as is each and every former holder of that office. (Article 31)

- The Taoiseach represents Ireland in the European Council, the body responsible for the overall policy direction of the European Union, and at Intergovernmental Conferences of the E.U. When the State holds the Presidency of the Council of Ministers (for six months out of every seven and a half years), the Taoiseach becomes the President of the Council of Ministers.

A Taoiseach may, in addition, assign himself or herself a specific ministerial responsibility, although this rarely happens. Charles Haughey was, for instance, Minister for the Gaeltacht from 1987-1991.

15.2.3 Resignation of the Taoiseach

Subject to certain conditions, a Taoiseach must resign if he or she loses the support of the majority in the Dáil (Article 28.10). The resignation of the Taoiseach has the knock-on effect of terminating the appointments of all the other Government Ministers (Article 28.11). In other words, every Minister depends for his or her continued appointment on the survival of the Taoiseach. That said, the members of the Government are entitled to continue their duties in a care-taking capacity until such time as a new Government is appointed. Similar provisions apply to Ministers in office immediately prior to the dissolution of the Dáil. They continue to hold office until their successors are appointed.

One rather strange option open to a Taoiseach is contained in Article 28.10. In circumstances where the Taoiseach has lost the support of a majority of Dáil Éireann, he or she normally must resign. The Taoiseach may, however, remain in office if the President, on the Taoiseach's advice, decides to dissolve Dáil Éireann. On such dissolution the Taoiseach and his or her ministers are entitled to remain in office until such time as the Dáil has reassembled. If at that point the Taoiseach can secure the support of a majority in the Dáil he or she need not resign at all. If however, he or she fails to secure such a majority when the Dáil first convenes after the election, the Taoiseach must resign. This occurred in 1989 when the outgoing Taoiseach, Charles Haughey, having failed to secure majority support after a general election, was prompted to resign his post.

15.3 The Tánaiste

The Tánaiste is a member of Government nominated by the Taoiseach from the ranks of the Government (Article 28.6). The Tánaiste must be a member of the Dáil: in practice he or she tends to be a senior Government Minister and in coalition governments the leader of the second largest coalition party invariably holds the position. Under normal circumstances the Tánaiste has no more power than any other Minister, although in cases where the Taoiseach cannot perform his functions the Tánaiste takes over the role as head of Government. This may occur when the Taoiseach has died, or where the Taoiseach is permanently incapacitated, in which case the Tánaiste acts as Taoiseach until such time as a new Taoiseach is appointed.

The Tánaiste may also deputise for the Taoiseach during the latter's temporary absence. A "temporary absence" is not defined but has been held to mean something more than mere physical absence from the State. Instead, it seems, the phrase is intended to cover the situation where a Taoiseach is unable to make executive decisions in respect of the State. Thus a Taoiseach may still be in charge of the Government of the State though he be in attendance at a European Council meeting — correspondingly, a Taoiseach who is lost in the Wicklow Mountains is effectively "absent" from his post, though he be physically within the territory of the State. It is not unconstitutional, according to the decision of the Supreme Court in *Riordan v. An Tánaiste* (1997), for both the Taoiseach and the Tánaiste to be physically absent from the State at the same time, provided that one or other of them is effectively in a position to make executive decisions in respect of the State.

15.4 Ministers

- There should be no less than seven and no more than 15 members of Government, including the Taoiseach.

- Ministers must be members of either the Dáil or the Seanad.

- The Taoiseach, Tánaiste and Minister for Finance must be members of the Dáil.

- No more than two senators at any one time may act as Ministers.

- The Taoiseach may assign Ministers "portfolios" making them responsible for certain tasks or issues, and for Departments of State. The allocation of responsibilities is determined by legislation. The exact confines of each Department and Ministerial position can change from time to time and it is not unusual for new Governments to alter the distribution of Ministerial responsibilities.

- A Minister may technically be appointed without any specific port-folio (this is extremely rare).

- Individual Ministers may represent Ireland at the E.U. Council of Ministers.

It is worth noting that while "junior Ministers" (or "Ministers of State") may be appointed, these persons are not technically members of the Cabinet Government of which Article 28 speaks. These members of the Oireachtas are appointed to assist cabinet Ministers with specific aspects of their brief. When the Constitution, however, refers to a "Minister", it means one of the 15 members of the Cabinet and no one else.

15.5 Executive privilege

Prior to 1972, it was widely believed that the Government enjoyed what was called an "executive privilege". The "executive privilege" afforded the Government the right to refuse to disclose the content of (or even sometimes the very *existence* of) documents relating to the operation of Government. This was a royal prerogative right enjoyed by the Queen and it was wrongly believed that the Executive in Ireland had inherited this right to refuse the courts access to its documents. (See also *Byrne v. Ireland* (1972), discussed below in Chap. 8.)

In *Murphy v. Dublin Corporation* (1972), the Supreme Court struck down the executive privilege as being inconsistent with the Constitution. The privilege, the Court held, infringed the Court's right and duty to consider all relevant evidence in a case before it. The lack of access to certain evidence potentially undermined its ability to achieve justice in a particular case. It was noted that certain documents could be with-held from evidence on the grounds that they, for instance, might under-mine the security interests of the State or that they attracted legal privilege. The decision as to whether such documents should be with-held, however, was a decision solely for the Court to make, not the Government. There was, furthermore, no class of documents that could generally be excluded from court scrutiny. The Court had to decide on a case by case basis whether certain documents could be withheld or not.

The key aspect of this case is that it restored to the courts the right to determine whether government documents should be admitted as evi-dence. As such, it is an important illustration of how the separation of powers operates between the Executive and the courts.

15.6 Collective responsibility

Article 28.4.2 underlines an important principle of cabinet government, that the Government is "collectively responsible" for its actions. This means that while the individual Ministers may disagree amongst themselves on policy issues, they are politically and legally responsible as a single unit for their various official actions. Each Minister, in other words, takes political responsibility for the official actions of his or her colleagues, even if the Minister disagrees with a colleague's stance. It also means that (in public at least) a Minister must be seen to support Government policy and to support his or her colleagues.

15.7 Cabinet confidentiality

Of late, one of the most prominent legal issues concerning the Government has undoubtedly been the issue of "cabinet confidentiality". This should not be confused with the now abolished royal prerogative of executive privilege. While executive privilege related to all documents held by the Government or its servants, cabinet confidentiality relates specifically to dealings amongst the 15 Ministers at official meetings of the Cabinet.

Cabinet confidentiality requires that the details of cabinet meetings, for instance the content of discussions, or the existence of memos or documents on which decisions were based, may not be revealed outside the confines of the cabinet room. It flows from the principle of collective responsibility, outlined in Article 28.4.2, that Government members are responsible as a unit for their decisions. This relates only to discussions of the Government ministers — it does not protect the civil service generally from disclosure of their deliberations.

This issue first arose in the *Attorney General v. Hamilton (No. 1)* (1993). A government minister, Ray Burke, was giving evidence before the Beef Tribunal regarding the content of a government meeting. The Tribunal wished to ascertain whether and why the Government, at a cabinet meeting, had allegedly decided to grant export credit insurance to only two beef companies in respect of their exports to the Middle East. The Attorney General claimed that Mr. Burke was precluded from answering that question as it would infringe the requirement of cabinet confidentiality. The Supreme Court ultimately agreed, ruling that the content of cabinet discussions could not be revealed to the tribunal.

The reasons given were three-fold.

- First, the Court argued that to allow public exposure would undermine the collective authority and responsibility of the Government. If the public knew for instance that some Ministers had disagreed with each other, it might undermine the sense that the Government "was thinking and acting as one".

- Second, in the absence of privacy, they argued, Ministers might not feel free to speak their minds. Confidentiality encouraged frank discussion of contentious issues.

- Third, (by far the weakest argument), if the deliberations of the courts and the Oireachtas could not be challenged, why should the Government not also enjoy such a privilege? (The simple answer to this is that the Constitution expressly extends such privileges to the other institutions but not to the Government.)

Ministers may not waive cabinet confidentiality. Thus, a retired minister wishing to write her memoirs may find herself legally precluded from discussing the content of cabinet discussions therein. Cabinet confidentiality, in other words, is not a right but a duty. It extends beyond the lifetime of the Government in respect of which it applies — in short a Minister may be precluded from revealing the details of discussions of a Government that has since left office.

15.7.1 Changes made by the Seventeenth Amendment

In response to concerns that the rule of cabinet confidentiality was too strict, the Constitution was, in 1997, amended to create some exceptions. Hence, since the enactment of the Seventeenth Amendment, it is possible to obtain a High Court order mandating the disclosure of information where required by either a court or a tribunal. Where a court seeks such information, it must be shown that disclosure is in the interests of the administration of justice. A tribunal, in a similar vein, may seek such an order where it can show that there is "an overriding public interest" in the disclosure. The Seventeenth Amendment is confined, it should be noted, to proceedings before either (1) a court of law or (2) a tribunal of inquiry established by the Government under legislative authority, to inquire into a matter deemed to be of public importance. In both cases, an order of the High Court *must* be obtained.

16. EMERGENCY POWERS (ARTICLE 28.3)

The Constitution was drawn up at a dark time in Europe's history and it is, thus, small wonder that the drafters made contingencies for times of war and emergency. Article 28.3 originally provided only for situations in which the State itself was a participant in a war or the subject of an armed rebellion. With the outbreak of the Second World War, however, the Oireachtas (as was then its right) amended the Constitution to allow Article 28.3 to apply in circumstances where the conflict takes place outside our borders. In fact, as a result of further amendment, a national emergency may continue to exist long after the armed conflict that caused it has ended.

16.1 Declarations of war

The State may not participate in a war without the approval of Dáil Éireann. This effectively precludes Ireland from being compelled into a war without democratic assent. An interesting question is whether this provision might preclude Ireland's participation in a military alliance, if that alliance purported to be able to commit its members as a whole to a war effort.

It is worth noting that Article 29 commits Ireland to "the ideal of peaceful and friendly co-operation amongst nations" and expresses a preference for the resolution of disputes by peaceful means. While this would not prevent the State from going to war, it does seem to suggest that a declaration of war should only be made as a last resort.

16.2 Actual invasion

Where the State is actually invaded, Article 28.3.2 allows the Government to take all reasonable steps considered necessary for the protection of the State. This may be practically important where circumstances are such that the Dáil is not in a position to meet to discuss the emergency. Where feasible, however, the Dáil is required to sit at the earliest possible date after such invasion.

16.3 Constitutional exemption

The main effect of Article 28.3 is to grant certain types of "emergency legislation" an exemption from the possibility of being struck down for unconstitutionality. If the procedure laid out in Article 28.3 is followed, any legislation passed using its provisions cannot be challenged on the basis of its being contrary to the Constitution.

16.3.1 Even emergency legislation cannot create a death penalty

There is one important exception to Article 28.3. The Twenty-First Amendment of the Constitution prevents the enactment of legislation providing for the death penalty *in all cases, even* where Article 28.3 has been invoked. In other words, legislation providing for the death penalty cannot be enacted as an emergency measure.

16.3.2 When can Article 28.3 be invoked?

In order for Article 28.3 to operate, it is not actually necessary that Ireland itself be at war. A "time of war", for these purposes, includes a situation where there is an armed conflict in which the State is not a participant. Each of the Houses of the Oireachtas must make a declaration to the effect that this armed conflict is such that "a national emergency exists affecting the vital interests of the State". A good example would be the security situation in Northern Ireland: as a result of mounting tension in that jurisdiction, the Dáil and Seanad passed declarations as to the existence of a national emergency in 1976. These declarations were only revoked in 1995. An earlier example is the outbreak of World War II. Though Ireland was not a participant, a state of emergency was declared in 1939. This State of Emergency remained in place, rather strangely, until 1976!

16.3.3 How does an emergency end?

The reason for this anomaly is that the resolutions allowing the passing of emergency legislation under Article 28.3 remain in force until both Houses have resolved that the emergency has ended. A state of emergency in fact may remain in place long after the situation that prompted its creation has ended. For example, as noted already, the resolutions passed in response to the Second World War were only revoked in

1976. At that point, however, a new set of resolutions was passed in response to the troubles in Northern Ireland. In the Article 26 reference of the subsequent *Emergency Powers Bill 1976* (1977) the Supreme Court made some interesting comments about the operation of Article 28.3. In short, while the Court cannot examine the content of legislation passed under it, it can check to see that the correct procedures have been followed in relation to its passing. In other words, the steps laid out in Article 28.3 must be followed in order for the constitutional exemption to apply. The Court also pointed out that while the legislation itself might contain provisions that offend the Constitution, the Court would not assume too readily that emergency legislation had been framed without any regard to the Constitution. Unless otherwise stated, for instance, it was to be assumed that the legislation left intact the rights of the accused not expressly mentioned by the legislation. For instance, while the Emergency Powers Bill allowed a person to be detained without charge for up to seven days, the Court observed that (in the absence of words to the contrary) the accused retained his right to legal advice, and medical treatment.

16.3.4 What would happen if the Houses of the Oireachtas invoked Article 28.3 in circumstances where there was clearly no threat to the State?

The Supreme Court expressly mentioned this possibility in their judgment but declined to comment definitively on the issue. While the Courts cannot generally review a parliamentary decision to use Article 28.3, it is arguable that they could be entitled to act when the Oireachtas has clearly conducted itself in bad faith.

17. THE ATTORNEY GENERAL (ARTICLE 30)

The Attorney General occupies two unusually conflicting roles. On the one hand, the holder of this post is the chief legal adviser to the Government. Although he is not strictly a member of the cabinet, the Attorney General is effectively hired and fired by the Taoiseach. Yet the Attorney General is also charged with protecting and vindicating the public interest, a role that might potentially bring him into conflict with the Government. At the heart of this role then lies a possible conflict of interest, one that has led some commentators to suggest that the work of the Attorney General should be divided between two officials rather than vested in only one.

17.1 Appointment of the Attorney General

The President, on the nomination of the Taoiseach, appoints the Attorney General, although it is effectively the Taoiseach who decides on the occupant of the post. While the Attorney General cannot be a member of the Government (Article 30.4), his or her continued occupancy of this role depends in essence on the continued approval of the Taoiseach. Just as the Taoiseach chooses the Attorney General, so too can the former demand the latter's resignation. If the Attorney General should refuse such request, the President shall terminate his appointment.

The Attorney General may be a member of the Oireachtas, although usually he is not. The Constitution does not lay down any qualifications that an Attorney General must possess, although the Attorney tends generally to be a high-ranking barrister with considerable legal experience.

17.2 The role of the Attorney General

Article 30 specifically refers only to the Attorney General's role as legal adviser to the Government. Section 6 of the Ministers and Secretaries Act 1924, however, refers in more extensive terms to the role of the Attorney General. It charges the Attorney with, amongst other things:

"...the representation of the Government of [Ireland] and of the public in all legal proceedings for the enforcement of law, the punishment of offenders and the assertion or protection of public rights and all powers, duties and functions connected with the same respectively, together with the duty of advising the [Government] and the several Ministers in matters of law and of legal opinion".

The Attorney, additionally, is allocated certain specific functions by legislation, one of which is to pre-approve certain extradition applications under the Extradition (Amendment) Act 1987.

17.2.1 Independence of the role

Despite depending on the Taoiseach for the continuation of his office, the courts have clearly asserted that the Attorney General is independent of the Government. In *McLoughlin v. Minister for Social Welfare* (1958), the Supreme Court had to decide whether an employee of the Chief State Solicitor's Office, which in turn answers to the Attorney General's Office, was a "government" employee for the purposes of social welfare law. Despite arguments to the effect that the Attorney General was an arm of Government, the Court ruled that the role of the Attorney General is technically "independent" of Government. As such, the plaintiff was not an employee of Government. In the course of his judgment, Kingsmill Moore J. observed that the Attorney General was not a servant of Government but rather an independent Constitutional Officer. That this was so, he said, was underlined by the fact that the Constitution provided for the forced or voluntary resignation of the Attorney, in recognition of the fact that the Attorney may be required, in certain circumstances, to pursue proceedings in the face of government opposition.

Indeed, the Attorney General is entitled, in his own right, to take steps to uphold the Constitution and the law, even where the Government opposes such action. In *Attorney General v. X.* (1992), the Attorney General took proceedings to restrain a fourteen and a half year old girl from going to the U.K. to obtain an abortion. There is little doubt that some members of the Government were actively opposed to such an action, or at least would not have proceeded in the manner chosen by the Attorney. Notwithstanding such disapproval, and the eventual failure of the Attorney's case, the Supreme Court expressly agreed that the Attorney was well within his rights to take such a case.

Prior to 1974, the Attorney General was charged with the prosecution of offences. In this role too, the Attorney was technically independent. In *State (Killian) v. Attorney General* (1950), the Supreme Court ruled that the Attorney General could not be forced by the courts to take a prosecution. In that case, a convicted prisoner alleged that another person had in fact committed the offence for which the prisoner had been incarcerated. The Attorney General, however, refused to reopen the case. The court refused to interfere with this decision, noting that the decision to prosecute was solely one for the Attorney to make.

17.2.2 Prosecution of offences

Article 30.3 states that all non-summary crimes and offences should be prosecuted in the name of the people. The Article applies to prosecutions other than those taken in a court of summary jurisdiction, meaning a court responsible for trying only minor offences (generally the District Court).

It was originally envisaged that the Attorney General would be primarily responsible for the taking of non-summary prosecutions. The Constitution, however, provides that "some other person authorised in accordance with law" may act instead of the Attorney. Due to the heavy workload of the Attorney General, the Prosecution of Offences Act 1974 created a new office of Director of Public Prosecutions (D.P.P.) with responsibility for taking prosecutions against alleged offenders. Nowadays, as a result, most non-summary prosecutions are taken by the D.P.P., although the Attorney General retains the sole power to instigate certain types of prosecution, for instance for genocide.

The D.P.P. retains the independence enjoyed by the Attorney General in respect of such offences. Thus, the courts cannot generally review a decision of the D.P.P. unless it can be shown that the D.P.P. acted in bad faith or in pursuance of an improper motive. In *H. v. D.P.P.* (1994), for instance, the High Court refused to hear a review of the D.P.P.'s decision not to prosecute a person in respect of the alleged sexual abuse of a minor. The D.P.P., in other words, has a largely unfettered discretion in deciding whether or not to pursue a specific prosecution.

In *Norris v. Attorney General* (1984), however, McCarthy J. warned that a policy decision *never* to prosecute a particular offence (in this case, the former crimes of buggery. and gross indecency between males) would be unconstitutional. The D.P.P. (and by implication the Attorney General) are obliged to obey and enforce the law. The D.P.P.

may, of course, decide that a prosecution is not appropriate in a *particular* case. The Constitution, however, precludes the D.P.P. (or anyone else for that matter) from making a positive decision *generally* to refrain from enforcing the law in all cases of a particular offence. To permit the D.P.P. to do so, McCarthy J. pointed out, would involve allowing the D.P.P. to change the law of the State, a task reserved by Article 15.2 to the Parliament.

17.2.3 The Attorney General as defender of public rights

In addition to his role advising the Government, the Attorney General is also charged with ensuring compliance with the Constitution. Section 6 of the Ministers and Secretaries Act 1924 makes the Attorney responsible for "the assertion or protection of public rights". To this end the Attorney General may take a case seeking to have the law (including, in particular, the Constitution) enforced. For instance, in the *Attorney General v. X.* (1992) the then Attorney General sought an injunction to prevent a fourteen and a half year old girl from travelling to Britain for an abortion. The Attorney General believed that this was necessary to defend the right to life of an unborn child. The Supreme Court ultimately ruled that, in the particular circumstances of that case, such an injunction should not be granted. It nevertheless expressly noted that the Attorney General had acted properly at all times to vindicate the rights of the unborn child, as was his right and duty under the Constitution. In *Attorney General v. Hamilton (No. 1)* (1993), the Attorney General again took an action seeking, this time successfully, to enforce the constitutional principle of cabinet confidentiality.

In taking such actions, the Attorney General may of course find that his actions bring him into conflict with the wishes of the Government. This is an aspect of the Attorney General's independence — his responsibility in upholding the public interest may bring him into conflict with his own Government. The worrying aspect of Article 30 is that the Taoiseach could theoretically demand the removal of an Attorney General for any reason, including the fact that the Attorney General has sought to pursue a course of legal action of which the Government disapproves.

The right to take a case asserting the public interest or attempting to enforce the law, however, is not reserved exclusively to the Attorney General. Any person who is personally affected by an alleged breach of the law or the Constitution (*i.e.* with *locus standi*) may take such a case. It is possible also for a concerned individual with a genuine, *bona fide* interest in the upholding of the law or the Constitution to take such a case. In *Crotty v. An Taoiseach* (1987), for instance, the courts accepted an attempt to assert the Constitution by a concerned citizen. In *SPUC v. Coogan* (1989), moreover, the Supreme Court allowed a case taken by the plaintiff, a voluntary body, asserting the constitutional rights of unborn children. According to Walsh J. in that case, every citizen has an interest in seeing that the Constitution is upheld. This right is all the more important considering that the Attorney General, being an adviser to the Government, is more likely to be predisposed to the view of the Government than the average person, not so closely linked to the Government.

In *Attorney General v. Lee* (2000) the Supreme Court has indicated that the role of the Attorney General in defending public rights is to be exercised only in "exceptional circumstances" where an alternative course of action is not readily available. This seems to suggest a narrowing of the Attorney General's role in this area, one that may ultimately lessen the conflict of interest discussed above.

18. THE COURTS (ARTICLES 34-37)

The Constitution provides for a system of courts in which justice shall be administered by judges, appointed in accordance with the law. While the precise operation of those courts is dealt with in legislation, the Constitution lays down several important guiding principles and rules for their running.

18.1 The court system

The Constitution divides the courts into two, the court of final appeal and the courts of first instance. A court of final appeal is ordinarily responsible for the rehearing of cases already heard in lower courts. A court of first instance, by contrast, is a court with "original jurisdiction", a court in which one may initiate a case for the first time, without having been to a lower court first.

18.1.1 The Supreme Court

The court of final appeal is called the "Supreme Court". This is the highest court in the land. Except in two specified cases, the Supreme Court can hear cases only on appeal, in other words after they have been heard in a lower court. An appeal basically involves a challenge to the correctness of the lower court's decision. Unless otherwise provided by law, any decision of the High Court can be appealed to Supreme Court. That is not to say, however, that a case can be reheard in its entirety in the appeal court. An appeal to the Supreme Court is usually limited to legal argument. The Supreme Court does not usually entertain challenges to decisions on the facts of a case, unless it is clearly established that the lower court made a decision that no reasonable person could have made.

The Supreme Court has eight judges in all, including the Chief Justice, the highest judicial position in the land. Ordinarily the Supreme Court sits in groups of three or five judges, but at least five judges must be present when considering the constitutionality of a Bill under Article 26. In addition, not less than five judges must be present when a question arises as to the President of Ireland's permanent incapacity (see Article 12.3). On at least one occasion, the Supreme Court has sat with no less than 7 judges, (*Sinnott v. Minister of Minister of Education* (2001)), although such an occurence would be quite rare.

Ordinarily, the Supreme Court can only hear a case after it has been heard in another court. There are, however, two situations in which the Supreme Court has original jurisdiction, that is where it can hear a case that has not been before another court.

- The first situation is where, under Article 12.3, it is alleged that the President has become permanently incapable of performing his or her job. The Supreme Court alone considers such a case.

- The second scenario arises under Article 26, where the President may refer a Bill directly to the Supreme Court in order to test its constitutional validity.

18.1.2 The High Court

The main court of first instance is the High Court. Article 34.3 gives the High Court the full power to determine all judicial matters and questions, whether of law or fact, civil or criminal. These powers include the right to determine the constitutional validity of any law. In fact, only the High Court or Supreme Court on appeal can consider such questions. The constitutional validity of a law cannot be questioned in any other court.

The High Court presently consists of 26 judges. Each judge usually sits alone, although it is possible to form a "Divisional High Court" consisting of an odd number of judges in certain rare circumstances. There is a President of the High Court who is responsible for the overall running of the court and the allocation of work amongst judges.

18.1.3 The lower courts

Article 34.4.4 also provides for the establishment of courts of local and limited jurisdiction. The main courts in this category are the District Court and the Circuit Court. The Circuit Court currently consists of 26 judges with responsibilities divided between eight "circuits". The Circuit Court is fast becoming one of the most important courts for Family hearings, with most divorce and judicial separation proceedings being held in this court. The Circuit Court can also hear contract and tort cases involving (unless otherwise agreed) sums of no more than £30,000 (€38,100). The court's criminal jurisdiction extends to most non-minor offences, with the result that criminal cases in the Circuit

Court are usually held in front of a jury. In addition to its original jurisdiction, the Circuit Court can hear appeals from the District Court.

The District Court is the lower of these two courts. It has jurisdiction to hear minor criminal offences (without a jury), contract and tort cases involving sums of not more than £5,000 (€6,350) and other miscellaneous matters, such as the renewal of liquor licences. There are presently 51 District Court judges, allocated to 23 districts throughout the State.

In addition to the four main courts noted above, there is a variety of other courts with specialised jurisdiction. The Small Claims Court hears cases involving relatively minor legal disputes, usually involving less than £1000 (€1,270) in damages. In the arena of criminal law, there are two additional courts, the Special Criminal Court, which hears cases that cannot, for security reasons, be heard in the ordinary courts, and the Court of Criminal Appeal, which hears appeals from the other criminal courts.

18.2 Appointment of Judges

Judges are formally appointed by the President, but in line with Article 13.9 the President only makes such appointments "on the advice of the Government". In fact nowadays, all but the very highest ranking judges (specifically the Chief Justice, and the Presidents of the High Court, Circuit Court and District Court) are effectively selected by an independent Judicial Appointments Advisory Board.

Supreme Court and High Court	Circuit Court	District Court
1. A practising barrister of at least 12 years standing.	1. A practising solicitor or barrister of at least 10 years standing.	A practising solicitor or barrister of at least 10 years standing.
2. A serving High Court judge or a judge or Advocate General of the European Court of Justice or European Court of first instance.	2. A District Court judge.	
3. A Circuit Court judge of at least 4 years standing.		

Only certain persons are eligible to become judges. One must generally be qualified either as a barrister or a solicitor to be eligible for consideration, as the table above illustrates.

Within 10 days of appointment, a judge is required to make the declaration laid out in Article 34.5. A failure to make such declaration will result in the judge being ineligible to continue in office. In the declaration, the judge promises to perform his duties as best he or she can, and in particular to act "without fear or favour, affection or ill-will" towards any person.

18.2.1 Retirement

Most judges must retire at the age of 70, except for the District Judge who retires at 65, although provision may be made for the year-by-year extension of a District judge's tenure until he or she reaches 70. Judges of the High Court and Supreme Court appointed before 1999 do not have to retire until they are 72.

18.3 Judges' salaries

Article 35.5 prevents the remuneration (salary) of a judge from being reduced during his tenure as a judge. The reason for this provision is based on the principle of the independence of the judiciary. Article 35.5 is designed to prevent a judge from being penalised for a decision unfavourable to the Government, or hounded out of office by a severe pay cut. According to the Supreme Court in *McMenamin v. Ireland* (1996) "remuneration" in Article 35.5 includes the pension of the judge after he or she retires. In that case, O'Flaherty J. also warned that judges' salaries must be increased broadly in line with inflation. A failure to account for significant increases in inflation would, thus, be in breach of this Article.

In *O'Byrne v. Minister for Finance* (1959) a judge's widow argued, rather ingeniously, that as a result of Article 35.5 a judge could not be taxed on his salary, as this amounted to a "reduction" in his take-home pay. The Supreme Court rejected this proposition (although only by a narrow 3-2). The Court took a purposive approach to the Article, ruling that the taxation of judges' salaries did not endanger the independence of the judicial role. There was nothing unconstitutional, thus, in requiring a judge to pay taxes like every other citizen of the State.

18.4 Justice to be administered in public

As a general rule, court proceedings must be held in public (Article 34.1). Part of the reasoning behind this provision is that an accused person is less likely to be treated unjustly when his trial is open to the public. A wider interest, however, is at stake. In *Re R. Ltd.* (1989), Walsh J. pointed out that justice is usually administered in public for the simple reason that the courts are administering justice "on behalf of all the inhabitants of the State". While it is not necessary, then, that any members of the public should be present at a court hearing, it is at least required that such court session should be open to the public.

Certain exceptions may be made, however, in "such special and limited cases as may be prescribed by law". Such private proceedings are termed *"in camera"* proceedings. This is done, for instance, to protect the identity of the victims of rape and sexual abuse. Additionally, all family law cases are heard *in camera* with the reported judgment referring to the litigants only by the initials of their names (*e.g. A.N. v. B.K.*). A case may also be held *in camera* because of a fear that matters seriously prejudicial to the interests of a company may be disclosed to the public at large.

18.5 Exclusive powers of the courts

Subject to certain exceptions, justice may only be administered in courts established by law and only by properly appointed judges. The "judicial function", in other words, is reserved to the judiciary. Article 35.2 moreover requires that the State respect the independence of the judiciary. Any attempt to take over this function, or alternatively to direct judges as to how they should perform this function, will be restrained as an unconstitutional breach of the separation of powers.

An important case in this area is *Buckley v. Attorney General* (1950), commonly known as the "Sinn Féin Funds" case. The High Court in this case had to consider who was entitled to the proceeds of money held in the name of "Sinn Féin". As that party had split several times since its foundation, several organisations claimed that the money was rightfully theirs. Yet, before the court could make its decision, the Oireachtas passed the Sinn Féin Funds Act 1947 requiring that the case be terminated and that the High Court order that the money be distributed amongst veterans and survivors of the War of Independence. The Supreme Court ruled that this was an unconstitutional breach of the separation of powers. Once a judge has started to hear a case, only he or she can determine its outcome. The Legislature, in passing this Act, had breached the independence of the judiciary by purporting to tell it how to do its job.

18.5.1 Can the Oireachtas reverse the effects of a court decision?

While the Oireachtas can change the law following a court case, it cannot do so in such a way as to deprive the winning parties of their victory. If a person, for example, were to win £1 million in a defamation case, and the Parliament thought this inappropriate, it might feasibly change the law to put a cap on winnings in subsequent cases. It could not, however, deprive the particular victor of his £1 million.

In *Pine Valley v. Minister for the Environment* (1987), the plaintiff had bought property in respect of which the Minister for Local Government (now Environment and Local Government) had granted outline planning permission. In a subsequent case, however, the local county council obtained an order quashing this planning permission, on the grounds that it infringed the County Development Plan. In the wake of this case, legislation was introduced to prevent a planning permission from being declared invalid by reason only of the fact that it infringed the local Development Plan. The legislation, however, contained a clause that effectively exempted from the Act any planning permission in respect of which a court judgment had previously been handed down. This meant that the Act did not validate the plaintiff's planning permission.

The Supreme Court agreed that this constituted discrimination but ultimately concluded that such discrimination was justified by the need to avoid interfering with the judgment of the Court in Pine Valley's case. If the legislation were to have overturned the verdict in the earlier case, this would have amounted to "an unconstitutional invasion of the judicial domain".

A good example of the care taken by the Oireachtas to prevent such invasions of the judicial realm can be seen in the aftermath of the *Howard v. Commissioners of Public Works* litigation (1993). There, the Supreme Court held that an interpretative centre at Luggala, Co. Wicklow required planning permission in order for it to be built. The judgment had implications for many other state-owned buildings, many of which had been constructed without planning permission. Within days of the judgment, the *Oireachtas* passed an Act retrospectively exempting such buildings from the need for planning permission. The Act, however, was worded such that it did not exempt the Luggala centre — to do otherwise would have amounted to an unconstitutional interference with the independence of the judiciary.

18.6 Exercise of a judicial function

Otherwise than in the exceptional cases outlined in Article 37, only judges may administer justice, and only in courts established by law. The question that thus inevitably arises concerns the meaning of this phrase "administration of justice". How does one define an "administration of justice"? In other words, what functions are reserved to the judiciary? This is a vexed question with no easy answer. One may generally say, however, that the role of the judiciary (the "judicial function") is to adjudicate in cases where there is a legal dispute as to the meaning or application of the law.

An "administration of justice" or "judicial function" basically involves the power to determine, in a final manner, the existence of legal rights and liabilities, or the imposition of legal penalties.

In the case of *Lynham v. Butler (No. 2)* (1933), Kennedy C.J. made some pertinent comments about the content of a "judicial function". As regards criminal proceedings, he noted, this embraced the determination of guilt or innocence, and the fixing of punishments. In civil cases the judicial function involved determining in a final manner the legal rights or liabilities of parties in dispute. In both cases, the decision of the court is binding upon the parties. The State, furthermore, is entitled (even obliged) to enforce that judgment. Subject to the possibility of appeal, such decision is usually final.

Some of the most extensive comments on this issue, however, derive from the judgment of Kenny J. in *McDonald v. Bord na gCon (No. 2)* (1965). Bord na gCon is a state body charged with the regulation of greyhound racing. Under powers granted to it by the Greyhound Industry Act 1956, the Board had issued an exclusion order against the owner of a greyhound. The owner claimed that this decision was, in essence, an administration of justice and that the Board, thus, had no authority to make such a decision.

In the course of his judgment, Kenny J. outlined five characteristic features of a judicial function:

- It involves a dispute or controversy as to the existence of legal rights or a violation of the law.

- It results in the determination or ascertainment of legal rights or obligations, the imposition of legal liability or the infliction of a legal penalty.

- The determination of the court is final (subject to appeal) as regards the existence of legal rights or liabilities or the imposition of penalties.

- The State must enforce those rights, liabilities or penalties when called on by the court to do so.

- The function is one which, as a matter of history, is an order characteristic of courts in this country.

Yet, even with the aid of these detailed criteria, deciding whether a function is judicial or not is still a complex and nuanced task. In fact, in *McDonald* itself, there was some disagreement on the correct result. Kenny J., in applying these principles, felt that the powers in question did involve the administration of justice. Yet, while the Supreme Court adopted the principles suggested by Kenny J., it rejected his conclusion on the facts. It considered that the decision had none of the characteristics of a judicial function noted above. That so many eminent judges could be in disagreement, thus, underlines how difficult it is to pinpoint exactly what an "administration of justice" entails.

Applying these criteria to specific cases, then, is no easy task. Some examples may, however, prove useful. In *Kennedy v. Hearne* (1988), for instance, the Supreme Court ruled that the Revenue Commissioners were not administering justice in assessing the tax liability of employers who fail to deduct tax from their employee's wages. In doing so the Revenue Commissioners were not determining a legal dispute between parties, nor were they performing a function traditionally reserved to judges. Similar reasoning was put forward in *Keady v. Garda Commissioner* (1992), where the defendant's right to dismiss members of the Garda was challenged. The Supreme Court dismissed the contention that this involved an administration of justice. Here there was no contest between the parties as regards the existence of legal rights, merely an inquiry into an alleged breach of discipline.

18.6.1 A Tribunal cannot perform judicial functions

Since the early 1990s many tribunals of inquiry have been established by the Oireachtas (*e.g.* the Beef Tribunal and the Flood Tribunal). These tribunals are charged with the determination of certain facts, usually concerning alleged irregularities in certain areas of public life. It is crucial to note that although many tribunals of inquiry are chaired by judges, tribunals are nonetheless *not* part of the court system. As such the chairpersons involved (even if they are judges) are not permitted to perform judicial functions.

This issue arose in litigation arising from the Beef Tribunal, *Goodman International v. Hamilton (No. 1)* (1992). The plaintiff had challenged the legality of the Tribunal on the ground that it was performing a judicial function. The Supreme Court rejected this proposition. A tribunal is set up merely as a fact-finding body: it investigates an issue or event and reports its findings of fact to the Oireachtas. It cannot and does not determine legal liability or punish individuals as a result of its findings. By contrast, it is not part of the function of the courts merely to find facts where such a finding of fact has no effect on the determination of a legal right or liability. A Tribunal is charged with finding facts as an end in itself; a court does so only to rule on the legal rights or liability of the person before it.

18.6.2 Matters of discipline

In *Re the Solicitors Act 1954* (1960), however, the Supreme Court ruled that a decision to strike practitioners from the roll of solicitors is a judicial function. The crucial factor in this decision, arguably, was that the function was traditionally one carried out by the Chief Justice, the solicitor being, historically, an officer of the Court. It involved also the "imposition of a penalty", which one judge (rather melodramatically) likened to a severe prison sentence.

The authority of the *Solicitors* case has since been doubted, with judges and lawyers alike tending to confine its influence to the specific facts of the case. Nonetheless, the fear that disciplinary procedures may be struck down as an invasion of judicial functions led the Oireachtas to require that certain decisions to dismiss a practitioner be endorsed by (or at least subject to cancellation by) a High Court judge. (See, *e.g.* Medical Practitioners Act 1978, Dentists Act 1985, Nurses Act 1985). That said, the better view nowadays (as *Keady* suggests) may be that employment-related disciplinary procedures are not part of the "judicial function" and that the *Solicitors* case was so decided only because of the historical role of solicitors in the work of the courts.

Matters of prison discipline, it seems, can quite feasibly be dealt with by the prison authorities without recourse to the courts. This is so even where the breach of discipline, if proved, would also amount to a crime. In *State (Murray) v. McRann* (1979), a prisoner was alleged to have assaulted a prison officer. The Governor of the prison, having investigated the matter, ruled that she should forfeit certain privileges normally extended to prisoners. The High Court rejected the prisoner's assertion that this amounted to the exercise of a judicial function. The Prison Governor was simply acting so as to maintain internal prison discipline and this was not a judicial matter. The fact that the alleged act might also have been prosecuted as a crime was irrelevant.

18.6.3 The determination of guilt or innocence is a judicial function.

A determination of guilt or innocence in a criminal matter is clearly a matter for the courts alone. In *Re Haughey* (1971), the Supreme Court ruled that a Dáil Committee had no power to "declare" that a person was guilty of an offence. Only a court (either a judge or a jury) could make such a determination.

18.6.4 The determination of punishment is a judicial function

Furthermore, only a judge may determine the nature and extent of punishment to be imposed upon convicted persons. In *Deaton v. Attorney General* (1963), legislation (the Customs Consolidation Act 1876) permitted the Revenue Commissioners to select the penalty to be paid by those convicted of customs offences. The Supreme Court ruled that such legislation was unconstitutional, as the choice of appropriate punishment for each particular offender was a function reserved to the judiciary.

A similar result was reached in the *State (Sheerin) v. Kennedy* (1966). In that case, the courts struck down legislation that allowed the Minister for Justice to impose hard labour on juvenile prisoners as an additional penalty for misbehaviour. Legislation that allows persons other than judges to choose the duration of imprisonment has met a similar fate. In the *State (O.) v. O'Brien* (1973), legislation purported to allow a person to be imprisoned indefinitely, to be released only when the Minister for Justice saw fit to do so. As this effectively allowed the Minister and not the court to determine the duration of a particular offender's punishment, the punishment was not allowed to stand.

18.6.5 What about persons found "guilty but insane"?

Where a person is found to have committed a crime while insane, he or she will be incarcerated at a mental asylum until such time as the Minister for Justice determines that he or she is no longer insane. In *Re Gallagher* (1991), the Supreme Court ruled that this was permissible. McCarthy J., for the court, noted that a verdict of "guilty but insane" technically amounts to a verdict of acquittal. As such, the incarceration is not a punishment and thus not a matter reserved to the courts to determine. The treatment of insane persons, he said, was a matter primarily for the Executive.

18.6.6 Can the Legislature set out a range of penalties for offences?

The Court in *Deaton* made it clear that while only judges may determine what sentence a particular offender should serve, it is well within the powers of the Oireachtas generally to prescribe minimum and maximum penalties for certain offences. Just as the Oireachtas is entitled to make something a crime, so too can it indicate what penalties should be available to the Court where such a crime has been committed. What happens, however, when the Oireachtas (as with murder), ordains that a particular offence should attract a *mandatory* sentence? No court has yet been asked to rule on this issue although in the *State (O'Rourke) v. Kelly* (1983), the Supreme Court suggested that the creation of mandatory sentences would be "within the competence of the Oireachtas".

18.7 Article 37

There are some functions of a judicial nature that may, notwithstanding Article 34, be performed by bodies other than the judiciary. Article 37 allows persons or bodies of persons that are not courts or judges to be given the power to perform "limited functions and powers of a judicial nature". In order to avail of this exception, however, certain conditions must be met:

- The functions performed must not relate to "criminal matters".

- The functions must be limited in terms of their impact.

By "limited" it is meant that the powers to be performed must not be far-reaching or serious in terms of their effects. The fact that only a small number of people may be affected is irrelevant: what is crucial here is the extent of the impact on the persons that the measure *does* affect. If the effects are serious then the power exercised is not a limited judicial function even if it only affects a small number of persons.

In *Re Solicitors Act 1954* (1960), two solicitors had been struck off the roll of solicitors by a disciplinary committee of the Law Society. The two solicitors claimed that this was a judicial function reserved only to the courts. The Supreme Court agreed that this was indeed a judicial function and proceeded to consider whether it fell within the exception in Article 37. As regards the meaning of the term "limited" it noted that:

> "If the exercise of assigned powers and functions is calculated ordinarily to affect in the most profound and far-reaching way the lives, liberties, fortunes and reputations of those against whom they are exercised, they cannot properly be described as 'limited'."

Thus, because of the severity of the sanction imposed (dismissal from one's profession), the Court considered that the powers of the committee could not be regarded as limited in nature.

Here are some other examples of the application of this test:

- In *McDonald v. Bord na gCon (No. 2)* (1965), Kenny J. ruled that an exclusion order restricting the racing of greyhounds was not limited as it had the potential to affect the livelihoods and reputations of the trainers in a serious manner. (On appeal, however, the Supreme Court ruled that the functions were not judicial: thus Article 37 did not apply.)

- In *Cowan v. Attorney General* (1961), Haugh J. determined that the functions of an Election Court were (a) judicial and (b) not limited as they were likely to affect the lives and reputations of the persons before it in a serious manner. The Election Court had the power to exclude candidates from an election and to punish individuals for electoral fraud. The latter being a criminal matter, Article 37 would not have applied, even if the functions had been found to be limited.

- By contrast, in *Central Dublin Development Association v. Attorney General* (1975), Kenny J. ruled that while a ministerial power to decide whether a building was exempted from planning permission was a "judicial function", it was only a limited one. The decision that development is not exempted, after all, simply means that planning permission must be obtained. It does not prevent development and therefore did not seriously affect the rights of developers.

It is important to remember that Article 37 concerns only situations where a body other than a court is found to be performing a judicial function. If it is not a judicial function, then *it need not be proved that the function is limited in nature.* Article 37 simply allows certain non-criminal judicial functions of a limited nature to be performed by bodies other than courts. By the same token, the fact that a function has far-reaching effects (*i.e.* is not "limited") does not make it a judicial function.

In summary one must ask

(a) Is this a judicial function?

- If not — it *can* be performed by a body other than a court, (subject, of course, to other provisions of the Constitution).
- If so — proceed to (b).

(b) If it is a judicial function, does it deal with a criminal matter?

- If so — it can *only* be performed by a court.
- If not — proceed to (c).

(c) Is this judicial function limited in nature?

- If so — it can be performed by a body other than a Court.
- If not — it can *only* be performed by a Court.

18.7.1 Adoption — The Sixth Amendment

Fears regarding the legality of procedures for the adoption of children led to the enactment of Article 37.2, introduced by Sixth Amendment to the Constitution 1979. Adoption orders are granted by a non-judicial body, *An Bord Uchtála* (the Adoption Board). In *M. v. An Bord Uchtála* (1977), a suggestion was made, though not pursued, that granting an adoption order was a judicial function. If this were so, then the validity of many thousands of adoption orders granted by the Board would be in question. An adoption, if it is a judicial matter, is hardly "limited" — it affects in a profound and lasting way the rights of all the parties to the adoption. Thus, the Sixth Amendment was enacted to prevent any adoption order from being challenged on the grounds that it was granted by a body other than a court. Thus, even if adoption is found to be a non-limited judicial function, the decisions of the Board, past and future, cannot be impeached.

Part IV

Human Rights and the Constitution

19. HUMAN RIGHTS AND THE CONSTITUTION

19.1 Human and constitutional rights

The Constitution recognises certain human rights and requires the State to guard and protect those rights as best it can. Some of these rights are listed in the Constitution itself, although it is important to note that the constitutional protection of human rights is not limited to those rights that are expressly mentioned in the text thereof. The Constitution protects certain "unenumerated" (unlisted) as well as "enumerated" rights. The reason for so doing will be examined further in Chap. 23, but for the moment it is worth noting that the fact that a right is not expressly mentioned in the Constitution does not mean that it is not protected thereby.

19.1.1 Can non-citizens enjoy constitutional rights?

Does one have to be a citizen to enjoy Constitutional rights? Despite the specific terms of several articles, it has been accepted that the various rights guaranteed by the Constitution are not confined to persons who are citizens of Ireland. In a number of prominent cases, non-citizens have succeeded in establishing that they may enjoy the protection of the various constitutional guarantees.

On a literal reading of the Constitution, it is hard to see how this is so. Various articles that guarantee the protection of constitutional rights are specific in their reference to "citizens". Article 40.3, for instance, guarantees the personal rights of "citizens". Articles 40.1 (equality) 40.4 (personal liberty) and 40.6 (the freedoms of expression, assembly and association) are similarly worded. Other terms, by contrast, though for no apparent reason, contain no such limitation.

19.1.2 The universal nature of rights

This strictly literal approach, however, may be rejected in favour of a broader perspective on the scope of these rights. In *McGee v. Attorney General* (1974), Walsh J. suggested that most of the rights guaranteed by the Constitution are natural rights that are "antecedent and superior" to positive (man-made) law. In other words, as human individuals we enjoy certain rights that pre-date the enactment of our Constitution. The latter document does not create these rights but simply recognises that they exist and pledges the State to guard these rights and in appropriate cases to defend and vindicate them.

The Constitution, then, does not create human rights. These rights already exist and inhere in every human individual regardless of nationality. It would be patently absurd, thus, to say that a person's right to life, for instance, derives from the fact that he or she is an Irish citizen. The personal rights guaranteed by the Constitution are basic human rights of universal application. They are enjoyed not by virtue of Irish citizenship but rather on account of our human personality. The decision of Hamilton J. in *Northants Co. Co. v. A.B.F. and M.B.F.* (1982) largely reflects these sentiments. That case involved the rights of the family as guaranteed by Article 41. In the course of his judgment, Hamilton J. rejected the argument that the (married) father, not being a citizen of Ireland, could not rely on the rights in that Article. The rights in Article 41, he observed were natural rights "antecedent and superior to all positive law". The natural law, from which these rights derived, he continued:

"... is of universal application and applies to all human persons, be they citizens of this State or not ..."

This view was, further, endorsed by the judgment of Barrington J. in *Finn v. Attorney General* (1983): the rights guaranteed by the Constitution, he noted:

"derive not from a man's citizenship but from his nature as a human being ... the Constitution accepts that these rights derive not from the law but from the nature of man and of society, and guarantees to protect them accordingly."

The fact that Article 40.3 refers explicitly to "citizens" was of no consequence, he continued. "The whole scheme of moral and political values which are clearly accepted by the Constitution" prevented the State from ignoring the personal rights of persons who are not citizens.

Several cases seem to endorse this view. In *Kennedy v. Ireland* (1987), Hamilton P. expressly noted that although one of the plaintiffs was not an Irish citizen, this was no bar to his prospects of establishing that the constitutional right to privacy had been breached. This, again, was in spite of the fact that Article 40.3 refers expressly to the personal rights of "citizens". Nevertheless, the High Court, in *State (McFadden) v. Governor of Mountjoy Prison* (1981) and the *State (Trimbole) v. Governor of Mountjoy Prison* (1985) alike, acknowledged that non-nationals were entitled to rely on Article 40.3, guaranteeing them the right to fair procedures.

19.1.3 Do legal persons enjoy constitutional rights?

Notwithstanding this decidedly broad approach, the Courts have proved somewhat less charitable when considering whether incorporated bodies and other non-natural legal persons enjoy constitutional rights. The term "legal person" is used to describe a body or organisation (as opposed to a "human" or "natural person") which has a legal personality independent of the persons who own or have created that body. As a general rule, certain rights guaranteed by the Constitution can be invoked only by human persons. In *PMPS v. Attorney General* (1983), Carroll J. ruled that the personal and property rights guaranteed by Articles 40.3 and 43 could not be invoked by the plaintiff, a body incorporated as an Industrial and Provident Society. In a similar manner the courts, in *Quinn's Supermarket v. Attorney General* (1972), refused to allow the plaintiff to rely on the guarantee of equality in Article 40.1, as it expressly refers to the rights of citizens as "human persons".

It appears from that case, however, that artificial persons may invoke certain other articles, the Supreme Court in *Quinn's Supermarket* having allowed the plaintiff to rely on Article 44 of the Constitution. Indeed, there is a spate of cases in which incorporated companies have been allowed, without any argument, to invoke constitutional rights, such as the *Educational Company v. Fitzpatrick (No. 2)* (1961) (the personal right to dissociate), and the *Attorney General of England and Wales v. Brandon Books* (1986) (freedom of expression). Indeed in *Iarnród Éireann v. Ireland* (1996), Keane J. expressly ruled that artificial legal bodies can avail even of the personal rights guaranteed in Article 40.3. To rule otherwise, he felt, would leave a serious gap in the Constitution's protection of property rights.

Of course, it is well established that individual (human) shareholders may take a case alleging that action in respect of a company infringes their personal rights. As such, a company wishing to avail of the personal rights provisions may be well advised either to put itself forward as agent for its shareholders (as in *Pine Valley v. Minister for Environment* (1987)) or otherwise to join a human shareholder as an additional plaintiff in its case. This seems, however, somewhat artificial and there is perhaps some merit in Keane J.'s approach to this problem. Behind the corporate veil, after all, are human individuals, investors and employees alike, all of whom rely on the success of the company for their continued well-being. To accord certain constitutional rights to these companies is simply to recognise that certain actions in respect of an artificial person can affect in a profound way the interests of those other persons.

19.2 No right is ever absolute

The exercise of every right, however crucial it may seem, is subject to limitations. No right is ever absolute. No right, in other words, can ever be said to be worthy of complete state protection *at any cost whatsoever.* The State may, for instance, curtail the exercise of a right with a view to vindicating the superior or more pressing right of another person. Here it is involved in the balancing of conflicting individual rights. A good example is the case of the *People (D.P.P.) v. Shaw* (1982). In that case the Supreme Court held that the right to liberty of the defendant could validly be abridged for the purpose of vindicating the superior right to life of other persons. The defendant had been detained for a longer time than permitted after his arrest. This was however justified, the Gardaí having genuinely believed that the defendant, if detained, might reveal the whereabouts of a kidnapped woman whose life was, they believed, in imminent danger.

Rights can also be restricted or curtailed where it is shown to be necessary to protect the common good, that is the good of society as a whole. In *Murray v. Ireland* (1985), for instance, the plaintiffs, a married couple both of whom were in prison, complained that the State was preventing them from engaging in sexual relations with a view to having children. Both the High and Supreme Courts acknowledged that the plaintiffs indeed did have a right to beget children. Under normal circumstances, then the State cannot prevent persons from procreating. The Courts ruled, however, that the requirements of security in prisons, designed as they were to safeguard the public in general, justified the restrictions in this specific case. A prisoner, while retaining most of his or her constitutional rights, may exercise those rights while imprisoned only insofar as they do not endanger prison security. A similar result was reached in another case involving a prisoner, *Kearney v. Minister for Justice* (1986). In that case, the High Court ruled that the prison authorities were justified in opening and inspecting prisoners' mail, this being necessary in order to maintain prison security, in particular in preventing the smuggling of contraband into prisons.

The broader common good was also invoked by the majority of the Supreme Court in *Norris v. Attorney General* (1984). In that case O'Higgins C.J. justified legislation that penalised male homosexual sexual activity on the grounds that such legislation was warranted by the common good. The legislation involved, he claimed, was necessary to protect "the health both of individuals and the public" and to safeguard the institution of marriage from unjust attack. It is arguable, however, that where the common good is invoked as justifying the curtailment of certain rights, the State must be able to prove the dangers to the common good posed by the exercise of such rights. In *Norris* itself, for instance, a minority of the Supreme Court felt that the State had not done enough to prove the supposed ill-effects of homosexuality. The implication is that the State cannot simply invoke the common good as a general catch-all justification for incursions on human rights. It must be able to prove that its action is justified.

19.3 Distributive justice

The Irish Courts have made it clear that their human rights brief does not include matters of "distributive justice". In other words, the judiciary will generally decline from making decisions regarding the appropriate allocation of financial resources by the State (see *O'Reilly v. Limerick Corporation* (1989)). This arguably undermines the courts' power to intervene on behalf of some of the most disadvantaged in our society — a significant flaw in the courts' human rights armoury.

20. TRIAL OF OFFENCES (ARTICLE 38)

Where a person has been accused of a crime, and there is a proposal that such person be punished for such crime, the Constitution demands that there be a trial "in due course of law". The meaning of the phrase "due course of law" is twofold:

The first and narrower aspect of this phrase is that a person has the right to be tried in accordance with pre-established and pre-publicised rules laid down by law.

The second and wider aspect is that the defendant is entitled, in particular in the course of his trial, to expect that he will be treated fairly, and in particular that the procedures to which he is subjected are fair and reasonable.

Broadly speaking, no person may be tried for an offence except by reference to clear and fair procedures as laid down by law. In this respect, one may have regard to several principles of a fair trial, some of which are long-established, all of which must be observed in the course of a trial of a criminal offence.

20.1 The principles of a fair trial

20.1.1 The allegation must concern a crime known to the law

A person cannot be tried except for a specified offence deemed criminal by law. In Latin, it is said that *"nullem crimen sine lege"* — if there's no specific law against it, it isn't a crime! In *Attorney General v. Cunningham* (1932), the Court of Criminal Appeal observed that it is a fundamental principle of law that

> "... the criminal law must be certain and specific, and that no person is to be punished unless and until he has been convicted of an offence recognised by law as a crime and punishable as such."

For instance, in the *People (A.G.) v. Edge* (1943), the Supreme Court held that the defendant could not be convicted of "kidnapping" a minor with the minor's consent but against the will of his parents. This was because the alleged offence (in the words of O'Byrne J.) was "not an indictable offence at common law" (at p. 146). There was, in short, no such offence known to the common law.

This principle also demands that the definition of a crime not be so vague that it is unclear whether and in what circumstances it has been infringed. The Criminal Law must, in other words, be certain and specific. In *King v. Attorney General* (1981), Henchy J. observed that it is

> "[a] basic concept inherent in our legal system that a man may walk abroad in the secure knowledge that he will not be singled out from his fellow citizens and branded and punished as a criminal unless it has been established beyond reasonable doubt that he has deviated from a clearly prescribed standard of conduct..." (at p. 257).

In that case, the Supreme Court struck down as unconstitutional legislation that purported to criminalise any "suspected person or reputed thief" who was found loitering in a public place. This definition was so vague and ambiguous, the Court felt, that it could not in law constitute an offence.

20.1.2 The "crime" must have been a crime at the time of its commission

Article 15.5 of the Constitution contains a prohibition against "retroactive penal sanctions". In other words it is not possible to make something a crime "after the fact" if it was not a crime at the time of its commission. Take for instance the following scenario. Helga places a bet on a horse racing on Tuesday. At the time the bet is perfectly legal. The following Friday, however, the Oireachtas outlaws betting. The new ban can only operate prospectively, in other words from the time of its creation and not retrospectively. Thus Helga's bet, having been legally made on Tuesday, cannot subsequently be rendered illegal.

20.1.3 The right to a speedy trial

A person has the right to a speedy or expeditious trial, conducted without unreasonable delay. The rationale behind this may usefully be summarised as "justice delayed is justice diminished". With the passing of time, memories fade and facts become blurred and as such facts may become more difficult to verify. Added to this is the draining effect that a delayed trial has on the accused person. A trial after all affords the accused an opportunity to clear his or name. It would clearly be unfair to deny a person this right indefinitely.

The right to as speedy a trial as possible was affirmed as a constitutional right in the *State (O'Connell) v. Fawsitt* (1986). In that case, for a variety of reasons, none of which was the fault of the accused, a trial on charges, first imposed in January 1981, was adjourned several times until April 1985. At that point, the accused requested an order preventing the trial from proceeding due to this extraordinary delay. The Supreme Court, on appeal, granted the order. Finlay C.J. ruled that if a trial is so unreasonably delayed to the point where the accused's prospects of obtaining a fair trial have been prejudiced, the trial should not be allowed to proceed. In this case, the delay was such that an important defence witness was no longer available to the defence, thereby seriously prejudicing the accused's chances of a fair trial.

That said, there is no fixed quantum of time after which a trial cannot proceed. Unlike civil cases, there is no "statute of limitations" in criminal cases determining specifically the time beyond which a trial cannot proceed. Whether a delay has been so extensive to the point of being "excessive and prejudicial" is a matter to be considered in each individual case by reference to the facts in that case. Particular problems arise in the context of accusations of sexual assault upon children, some of which are first reported as many as 30 or 40 years after the crimes in question were allegedly committed. In *B. v. D.P.P.* (1997), for instance, a man had been accused of having sexually abused his three daughters, over a period some 20-30 years before the case came to trial. This was not due to any fault on the part of either the daughters or the State. While the Supreme Court felt that there was no real risk that the accused in this case would not obtain a fair trial, Denham J. noted that the trial judge would have to give "appropriate directions" where it was felt that the passage of time may have diminished the reliability of evidence or other matters.

20.1.4 The right to be presumed innocent until proven guilty

A cardinal right of the accused person is the "presumption of innocence". A person who is accused of an offence is entitled to be treated as innocent of the offence until such time as he is duly convicted in a court of law. In *King v. Attorney General* (1981), the Supreme Court ruled that a provision making it a crime for a "suspected person or reputed thief" to "loiter with intent" was unconstitutional. A person could not be treated less favourably by the law on account of his having a criminal record (or simply being suspected of a crime).

The presumption of innocence, furthermore, casts a special burden on the prosecution in every case. It must prove, beyond a reasonable doubt, that the accused is guilty of the crime alleged to have been committed. If a jury or judge has any reasonable doubt concerning the accused's guilt, the accused must be found not guilty. In *Hardy v. Ireland* (1994) and *O'Leary v. Attorney General* (1994), the Supreme Court acknowledged that this common law right was also a right protected by Article 38.1 of the Constitution.

The flip-side of the presumption of innocence is that the accused generally cannot be obliged to prove his innocence. Sometimes, however, the "evidential burden" of disproving particular matters is cast onto the accused. This places on the accused the onus of having to disprove, for instance, certain inferences that might otherwise be drawn from evidence. In *O'Leary v. Attorney General* (1993), for instance, the accused had been convicted of membership of an illegal organisation. When arrested, Mr. O'Leary had been found in possession of 37 posters depicting a man brandishing a rifle and the words "IRA call the shots". The law under which he was convicted stated that the possession of such "incriminating documents" would constitute "evidence until the contrary is proved" that the person belonged to an illegal organisation. The plaintiff alleged that this infringed the presumption of innocence.

The Supreme Court rejected this allegation. It noted that throughout the plaintiff's trial, the overall onus of proving membership of an illegal organisation was on the prosecution. The provision in question simply provided evidence (and not proof) of such membership. Thus, while this may have made it substantially easier to convict the accused, it did not shift the overall burden of proving the guilt of the accused.

Similar provisions were also unsuccessfully challenged in *Hardy v. Ireland* (1994). The legislation in question in that case stated that a person found in possession of an explosive substance would be guilty of an offence, unless that person could show that the explosives were to be used for a lawful purpose. This "reverse-onus" provision, however, was again upheld. The Court noted that it simply moved the evidential burden (and not the overall burden of proof) onto the accused. It rendered such possession *evidence but not proof* of the accused's guilt, evidence that could be contradicted by evidence of a lawful purpose.

20.1.5 The right to be present at one's trial

A person cannot, as a general rule, be convicted in his or her absence. This is simply a corollary of the right to defend oneself at trial. In *People (A.G.) v. Messitt* (1972), a conviction was quashed on the grounds that evidence highly prejudicial to the accused had been heard in his absence. The accused had been removed from the trial for disorderly conduct, allegedly the result of a mental illness. His lawyer had also withdrawn from the case. Thus, evidence of a highly prejudicial nature had been heard, which the accused had no opportunity to contradict.

Every person, then, has a right to be present at his or her trial. That said, a person can be tried and convicted where he or she has deliberately and consciously chosen not to attend at trial, as in *People (D.P.P.) v. Kelly* (1982), where the accused escaped at a late stage in his trial. If certain essential procedures require the attendance of the accused (such as his or her formal identification in Court) he or she must obviously be present. Otherwise, the deliberate failure of an accused to show up for trial will not prevent that trial from proceeding, provided always that the rights of the accused are observed.

20.1.6 *The ability to comprehend the proceedings*

An accused person must be able to understand the proceedings of a trial. If necessary, then, an accused person has a right to an interpreter. In the *State (Buchan) v. Coyne* (1936), a Scotsman had been convicted in the District Court during proceedings that were conducted entirely through Irish. The accused, who spoke no Irish, was not afforded an interpreter and thus, could not understand the proceedings. The High Court quashed the verdict.

This right is obviously crucial also when dealing with accused persons who speak little or no English. Such persons have the right to have an interpreter supplied by the State in the course of criminal proceedings. Similar considerations apply when dealing with persons with a hearing impairment.

On a related note, an accused cannot be tried where it is established that the person, for physical or mental reasons, is not fit for trial. A person who is not mentally or physically well enough to face court proceedings, should clearly not be subjected to a criminal trial.

20.1.7 *The right not to be pre-judged*

A person is entitled to a fair trial in front of a judge (or where relevant a jury) that is impartial and independent. In *People (A.G.) v. Singer* (1975), for instance, a jury conviction was quashed on the grounds that the foreman of the jury had a material interest in the result of the case. The accused, who had been convicted of fraud, successfully argued that as the foreman was a shareholder in one of the companies that the accused was alleged to have defrauded, he could not be regarded as "independent and impartial".

That impartiality may also be undermined when allegations of wrongdoing are made prior to or during the trial in a forum other than a court. This pre-trial publicity may have the effect of prejudicing jurors. In some cases, then, it may be impossible to guarantee the accused a fair trial. For instance, in 2000, criminal proceedings were taken against the former Taoiseach Charles Haughey, who was accused of having misled a tribunal of inquiry in the course of its investigations. These proceedings, however, were discontinued after certain comments were made in the media, which allegedly tended to suggest that Mr. Haughey was guilty of the alleged offence. Under the circumstances, the judge ruled, the former Taoiseach could not, at that time, be guaranteed a fair trial (RTÉ News Online, June 26, 2000). Similarly, in *Magee v. O'Dea* (1994) Flood J. refused to extradite the plaintiff to the U.K. on the grounds that his trial had been prejudiced by unfavourable comments in the U.K. media.

20.1.8 The right to prepare and present a defence

A person has the right to defend oneself in court. As a result, an accused person must be afforded an adequate amount of time to prepare his or her defence. (See *Curran v. Attorney General* (1941).) An accused generally has the right, also, to confront his or her accusers and in particular to cross-examine witnesses for the prosecution so that the accuracy of their evidence may be tested (*Re Haughey* (1971)).

In *Donnelly v. Ireland* (1998), however, an accused challenged provisions of the Criminal Evidence Act 1992 that allowed the evidence of a child, alleged to have been a victim of sexual abuse, to be given in a separate room and broadcast into open court via a live video link. This, he alleged, denied him the right to confront his accuser. The Supreme Court, however, ruled that the Act did not breach the accused's rights. The Act still permitted the cross-examination of the alleged victim, during which time the jury could observe the reactions and demeanour of the witness. The Act was, the Court suggested, a fair balance of the rights of the accused with those of the alleged victim, who might be unduly traumatised by an appearance in open court.

20.1.9 The right to legal representation.

An accused person has the right to a lawyer, both following arrest and during trial. This is an essential safeguard of the accused's rights, designed to ensure that the accused has access to a skilled advocate who will assist the accused in his defence. Where a person cannot afford a lawyer, according to the *State (Healy) v. Donoghue* (1976), the State is obliged to grant legal aid for the provision of such a lawyer. This is not to say, however, that an accused cannot be tried where he refuses (for reasons other than lack of funds) the assistance of a lawyer. An accused is perfectly entitled to choose to mount his own defence, unassisted by legal representatives.

20.1.10 The right to silence

Subject to certain notable exceptions, every person charged with an offence is entitled to refuse to answer questions posed by any person relating to that or any other offence. This is sometimes called the "privilege against self-incrimination", but is more commonly known as the "right to silence". An important corollary of this right is that a person cannot be penalised or otherwise prejudiced by the fact that they have remained silent in circumstances of arrest. In particular, the right to silence prevents a court from concluding that because a person did not protest their innocence on being arrested that they must therefore be guilty. In other words, while a person has the right to assert his or her innocence, no inference may be drawn from the fact that a person failed to do so.

Another aspect of the right to silence relates to the trial itself. An accused person has the right to defend himself or herself in a court of law. That said, no accused person can be forced to give evidence in his or her own trial. Furthermore, a court is not entitled to draw any inferences, negative or otherwise, from the fact that a defendant chose not to speak in his own defence. This right is intimately linked to the presumption of innocence. The primary rule in any criminal case is that it is not up to the defendant to prove his innocence. The law requires, rather, that the prosecution prove his guilt.

(1) The constitutional nature (and limits) of this right

Although it is not expressly mentioned in the Constitution, the Irish courts have on a number of occasions acknowledged that the right to silence is a constitutional right. (See *Heaney v. Ireland* (1996), *Rock v. Ireland* (1997)). In *Heaney v. Ireland* (1996) the Supreme Court reasoned that if one has the right to free expression, one must also have, as a corollary, a right to *refrain* from such expression, a right to silence as it were. The cardinal principle here should be that there is no obligation on the accused to supply information on which he or she may be found guilty of a crime.

The right to silence, however, is not absolute, and in fact is subject to certain limitations. In *Heaney v. Ireland* (1996), the Supreme Court had to consider the constitutional validity of section 52 of the Offences Against the State Act 1939. Under that provision, persons charged under the 1939 Act who fails, when asked by a Garda, to provide details of their movements over a particular timeframe, may be found guilty of an offence (punishable by up to six months in prison). The two plaintiffs had been convicted of this offence, effectively for having remained silent in the face of questioning. Both the High Court and Supreme Court ruled that section 52 was nonetheless constitutional. In every case, the Courts ruled, the rights of the accused have to be balanced against the constitutional duty of the State to protect citizens from attack on their person and property. In this case, the Courts held, the balance had been struck by the Legislature in a manner that was both reasonable and proportionate.

The Supreme Court again considered this matter in *Rock v. Ireland* (1997). That case concerned the Criminal Justice Act 1984, sections 18 and 19 of which allow a court to draw certain inferences from an accused's failure to answer questions on arrest. The accused in that case had been arrested in possession of counterfeit U.S. dollars. When asked to account for his possession of the forged notes, the accused refused to answer. The Supreme Court again found that the provisions were constitutional, having struck a reasonable balance between the rights of the accused and the common good of society as a whole. It noted, in particular, that the accused could not be convicted on foot of the inferences alone; other "corroborating" evidence was required to support the inferences that might be drawn from a failure to answer questions posed.

(2) Other incursions upon the right to silence

In recent years, several statutes have extended to the Gardaí the right to question suspects, including those mentioned above. A number of commentators have expressed concern that the right to silence has thus been qualified in a manner that significantly undermines the rights of accused persons.

- Section 18 of the Criminal Justice Act 1984 allows the Gardaí to question a person in relation to any item, substance or mark found on their person, in their possession or in a place where they are arrested. This allows persons to be questioned, for example, when arrested in possession of what turns out to be an illegal drug, or any drug paraphernalia, or with a needle mark on their body. Section 19 of the same Act permits inferences to be drawn from an accused's failure to account for his presence at the scene of a crime. Meanwhile, sections 15 and 16 make it an offence to withhold information on firearms/ammunition and stolen property respectively.

- Section 10 of the Companies Act 1990 requires officials of a company in respect of which an inspector has been appointed to answer questions put to them by the inspector. In *re National Irish Bank Ltd.* (1999), this provision was unsuccessfully challenged, the Supreme Court finding that this restriction on the right to silence was proportionate, that is, no more than was necessary to promote the public interest.

- The Offences Against the State (Amendment) Act 1998 also contains provisions that restrict the right to silence. Where an accused fails to give the Gardaí information that is later relied on in the accused's defence, certain inferences may be drawn from this failure (sections 2 and 5). Where an accused fails to give the Gardaí information that may be of material assistance in the investigation, moreover, he or she will be guilty of an offence under section 9 of the Act.

The tendency of these provisions, then, has been to erode in a most dramatic fashion the right to silence. To date the Courts have yet to call a halt to this seemingly relentless incursion upon an important right.

20.1.11 The right not to be tried on foot of unconstitutionally obtained evidence

Where the State collects or obtains evidence by means that are illegal, though not unconstitutional, the courts generally have a discretion as to whether such evidence should be available to the court during the trial of the alleged offender. Matters are radically different, however, where evidence is collected in a manner that infringes the Constitution. Where such evidence has been collected in deliberate and conscious breach of the Constitution, such evidence cannot be "admitted" (introduced) as evidence before the Court. A simple example of this would be where evidence is collected from the dwelling of an individual without either the consent of that person or the existence of a search warrant in respect of the premises. Except in circumstances where the law exempts the Gardaí from the requirement to obtain a search warrant, such a search would be in violation of Article 40.5, which guarantees the "inviolability of the dwelling place". As such, any evidence collected during such a search would generally have to be ignored by the court.

The breach must however, be deliberate and conscious. Evidence collected where there has been an accidental breach of the Constitution may be admitted, as in *People (A.G.) v. O'Brien* (1965). In that case, a search warrant was issued in respect of the defendant's house. The listed address however was incorrect, with the result that the Gardaí did not technically have the right to search the defendant's dwelling place. This being an accidental error, however, the evidence so obtained could be admitted. That said, one must be careful to distinguish between cases in which rights are breached by accident and where rights are breached in ignorance of the requirements of the Constitution. The fact that a garda is simply not aware that what he is doing is in breach of the Constitution is no defence.

(1) "Extraordinary Excusing Circumstances"

In certain exceptional circumstances, evidence can be admitted in court, even where it has been obtained "in deliberate and conscious" breach of the Constitution. A good example is where a house is raided (contrary to Article 40.5) with a view to preventing the imminent destruction of evidence. In *People (D.P.P.) v. Lawless* (1985), the Gardaí entered a house on what turned out to be a defective search warrant. There they found seventeen packets of heroin, which the defendant had been attempting to dispose of at the time of the Gardaí's entrance. This evidence was admissible, notwithstanding the illegal entry, on the grounds that had the Gardaí not entered at that point, the evidence would almost certainly have been destroyed.

A somewhat starker example is provided by the case of *People (D.P.P.) v Shaw* (1982). In that case, the defendant was taken into custody for the alleged kidnap of two women. These women were still missing at the time of arrest, and the Gardaí, believing that at least one of them might still be alive but fearing for her continued safety, were anxious to discover her whereabouts. To this end, they detained the defendant without bringing him before the District Court, for longer than was permitted by law. 30 hours into his detention the defendant finally made a statement to the Gardaí and brought them to where her body was located. Despite the fact that such evidence had been collected in deliberate and conscious breach of the defendant's rights (*i.e.* while he was being illegally detained), the Supreme Court ruled that this infraction of the Constitution was justified and that the evidence could thus be admitted. The police had acted in the genuine hope that the woman might still be found alive. Their action, then, was calculated to protect and vindicate the superior right to life of the victim, and as such excused the breach of the defendant's right to liberty.

20.1.12 *The right to a certain and proportionate sentence*

A convicted person has a right to receive a sentence that is certain and proportionate. In *State (Keating) v. Ó hUadaigh* (1985), for instance, a sentence was quashed on the ground that it was not certain when it was to begin. Nor can a person be detained indefinitely, as in the *State (O.) v. O'Brien* (1973). In that case, provisions allowing a convicted person to be detained until a Minister considered that he should be released were struck down as being unconstitutional. The courts have also made it abundantly clear that sentences should be proportionate and fair, in other words, that "the punishment should fit the crime". (See for instance *Cox v. Ireland* (1992)).

20.1.13 *The privilege against double jeopardy*

At common law, a person has the right not to be tried for an offence for which he has already been acquitted. This is called the principle of "double jeopardy" or *"autrefois acquit"*. It is not especially clear, however, to what extent Article 38.1 recognises this principle. Indeed, in *People (D.P.P.) v. O'Shea* (1982), the Supreme Court ruled that it was possible for the D.P.P. to appeal an acquittal, the principle of double jeopardy notwithstanding. This was because of the explicit right, in Article 34.4.3, to appeal any decision of the High Court to the Supreme Court, an acquittal being such a "decision".

This only applies, however, where a person has been acquitted before the High Court. In other cases, the law is less certain. It is clear that a person can be retried after an acquittal due to the lack of jurisdiction of a court, the person not having been in "jeopardy" during such trial, (*i.e.* because the court lacked jurisdiction to convict). It appears also that a person can be retried after a conviction has been quashed. (See section 5 of the Courts of Justice Act 1928). It would seem, however, that if a person has been properly acquitted before a fully competent court, he or she cannot be retried in respect of the same offence.

21. TRIAL BY JURY

Except in three specified cases, a person charged with having committed a criminal offence can be tried only before a jury of his or her peers. (Article 38.5) The determination of the guilt or innocence of a person, in other words, is left to a group of laypersons selected as representative of the public at large. Juries, however, are not exclusively a feature of criminal trials. Historically, juries were quite commonly found in civil cases too, their function being to determine certain facts upon which the court would give its legal ruling. There is, however, nothing in the Constitution requiring that juries be present in such civil cases. Indeed, nowadays, juries are required only in certain limited types of civil proceedings: defamation (libel and slander), the tort of false imprisonment and that of malicious prosecution being the most notable. (See the Courts Act 1988.)

21.1 Jury trial matters

21.1.1 Can a person waive the right to a trial by jury?

The wording of Article 38.5 seems to suggest that the requirement of a trial by jury in criminal cases is something more than simply a right of the accused. Unless the offence falls within the exceptions outlined in Article 38.2-4, the Constitution requires that "no person shall be tried on any criminal charge without a jury". Thus, it would seem that even if the accused wanted to forego a trial by jury in favour of a trial before a judge alone, the accused would not be able to do so. As Ó Dálaigh C.J. observed in *Re Haughey* (1971), "Trial by jury of non-minor offences is mandatory, it is not simply a right to be adopted or waived at the option of the accused". In a similar vein, Henchy J., in *Holohan v. Donohue* (1986), observed that trial by jury in criminal cases is "not only preferred but made mandatory" by the Constitution.

21.1.2 A jury must be independent and impartial

A jury can be no less impartial or independent than a judge. Obviously then, when a particular person has a vested interest in the determination of guilt or innocence in a particular trial, that person should not be selected as a juror. A notable example of this can be found in the facts of the *People (Attorney General) v. Singer* (1975). In that case, the accused had been tried and convicted by a jury that included (as fore-man of the jury!) one of the victims of the crimes for which the accused was being prosecuted in that case. The Court of Criminal Appeal quashed the verdict on the grounds that the jury could not have been regarded as impartial.

21.1.3 A jury should be representative of society at large

According to the Supreme Court in *de Burca v. Attorney General* (1976), "the jury must be drawn from a pool broadly representative of the community". If then a particular class of persons is excluded for reasons that are not based on capacity or social function "it cannot be said that a resulting jury will be representative of the community". In *de Burca* itself, the complainants were accused of a crime the prosecu-tion of which required a jury. The Juries Act 1927 (which prescribed the method of selecting juries at that time) effectively limited jury membership in two specific ways:

- Although an individual woman could apply to be selected as a juror, women as a class were automatically exempted from the require-ment to be available for jury service. This meant that, in practice, juries almost invariably consisted only of male jurors.

- In addition, only persons owning property of a particular value were entitled to serve on juries.

The net effect of these provisions was to confine jury service to land-owning males, a situation that the Supreme Court determined was plainly unconstitutional. In the words of Henchy J. "a jury which is so selective and exclusionary is not stamped with the genuine community representativeness necessary to classify it as the jury guaranteed by [Article 38.5]". In other words, these restrictions meant that the accused was not being tried before a group of persons representing a "fair cross-section" of society. The method of selection required by the Juries Act 1927 was, thus, unconstitutional. As such, it had not been carried over in 1937 so as to become a law of this State and could not thus be used for the selection of juries.

The Juries Act 1976 attempted to address the fallout from the *de Burca* judgment. It stipulates that any citizen between the age of 18 and 70 may be selected as a juror. Panels of potential jurors are selected at random from the Register of Electors. Specific jurors are then selected from these panels to serve in particular cases. Certain persons are however legally precluded from serving as jurors. These include gardaí, barristers and solicitors, officials in the D.P.P.'s office and former judges. Persons under the age of 18 and over 70 are also legally barred from serving on a jury. In addition, the Juries Act 1976 provides that certain persons may be excused from jury service, if they so wish: these include doctors, nurses, and others medical professionals, persons over 65 but under 70, priests and other religious ministers, pharmacists and whole time students. It is arguable then that, in practice, a panel from which a jury is selected might be quite unrepresentative of society at large, in that so many classes of persons are effectively excused from selection.

21.2 Basic principles of jury trials

A jury (by virtue of the Criminal Justice Act 1984) consists of twelve persons, although there is nothing in Article 38 requiring that this number always be present. A jury can, indeed, legally act with 11 jurors but no fewer. In *O'Callaghan v. Attorney General* (1993) the Supreme Court rejected the proposition that the Constitution does not permit majority verdicts. Nor does the law require that a jury act unanimously. A jury can convict a person by a majority of its members, although by law that majority cannot be attained without the support of at least 10 members of the jury. (Criminal Justice Act 1984, section 25).

21.3 Criminal trials where juries are not constitutionally required

There are three types of offence that do not require a trial by jury;

- **Minor offences**. These may be tried before a court of summary jurisdiction, in other words before a judge alone and without a jury. The precise meaning of this term is considered further below.

- Crimes tried before **Special Courts** established under Article 38.3.

- Crimes tried before **Military Courts** established under Article 38.4.

Each of these will be examined in turn:

21.3.1 Minor offences

This is, far and away, the most significant exception to the requirement of a trial by jury in criminal cases. The Constitution itself does not define what is meant by the term "minor" in this context. It has, thus, largely been left to the Legislature to determine what types of offence do not require a jury. That said, the courts have more and more frequently intervened to inquire whether an offence allocated to a court of summary jurisdiction is truly a "minor" offence.

The key criterion in this regard is the severity of the highest potential punishment that the accused might be given if he is found guilty of the offence of which he is accused.

In *Melling v. Ó Mathghamhna* (1962), the Supreme Court had to consider whether certain smuggling offences required a trial by jury. The maximum penalty for each offence, at that time, was a fine of £100 (€126) or three times the value of the goods illegally imported. In the course of their judgments the Supreme Court agreed that the primary consideration in deciding whether an offence was minor or not was the severity of the maximum punishment prescribed. Other matters to be taken into account included:

- The moral quality of the act – an offence of some considerable seriousness (such as manslaughter or rape) might still be a "non-minor" offence even if the maximum penalty for such an offence was comparatively small.

- The state of the law (and to a lesser extent public opinion) at the time that the Constitution was enacted – whether an offence was regarded as minor in 1937, the Court suggested, was relevant in determining whether it should be so regarded today.

The generally accepted view is that the nature of an offence is considered by reference not to the actual punishment handed down in any one case but to the maximum penalty that the law allows a judge to impose (*In re Haughey* (1971)). While some doubts have been expressed on this point, the better view appears to be that this is correct. After all if the test referred to the punishment actually handed down, how could one decide whether a jury was needed until *after* the case had been heard?!

There is no one fixed term of imprisonment or fine that definitively marks the line between a "minor" and a "non-minor offence". The maximum penalty falling within the definition of a minor offence would, nonetheless, appear to be one year. An offence attracting a potential maximum penalty of two years is clearly non-minor (see *Mallon v. Minister of Agriculture* (1996)). By contrast, a crime that has been ascribed a maximum sentence of six months clearly falls on the other side of the line, and can safely be said to be a "minor offence" (*Conroy v. Attorney General* (1965)).

Greater difficulty attends the question of whether a fine is of sufficient severity. Obviously, in this context, the severity of a fine will vary depending on the rate of inflation. A fine of £1,000 (€1,260) might have been regarded as very severe in 1951, considering that you could have bought a sizeable house with such a sum. Fifty years later one would be lucky to buy a car for the same price!

In *Kostan v. Ireland* (1978), the penalty involved the forfeiture of a fishing boat worth £102,040 (€128,570), a penalty that clearly made the offence non-minor. Nor can a penalty of nearly £10,000 (€12,600) be regarded as minor according to *O'Sullivan v. Hartnett* (1983) where it was suggested that even a fine of £1,825 (€2,300) would have been "non-minor". The best view perhaps is that an offence attracting significantly more than £1,000 (€1,260) as a fine and/or one year in prison would fall outside the category of "minor offences".

(1) Primary and secondary punishment

In determining the severity of the punishment in any case, the court is required only to take account of the punishment that the offence might attract in law (in other words, the penalties that the court itself may impose), which is called the "primary" punishment. The court is not required to have regard to any secondary consequential side-effects that the determination of guilt might cause (the "secondary" punishment). In *Conroy v. Attorney General* (1965), for example, the plaintiff had been tried and convicted without a jury on charges of drunk-driving. The maximum penalty for this offence being six months, the Supreme Court ruled that this was a minor offence. The fact that the law required that a person convicted of drink-driving also be disqualified from driving for a minimum of one year was held to be irrelevant in assessing the severity of a sentence, notwithstanding the fact that such disqualification might have very serious consequences. Such disqualification, the Court ruled was not a punishment but merely an *executive decision* that the convicted person was no longer fit to drive a vehicle.

Similar sentiments were expressed in the *State (Pheasantry) v. Donnelly* (1982). In that case, the plaintiff, as a result of having committed a third successive licensing offence, lost its right to sell alcohol. Notwithstanding the undoubted seriousness of this loss (the value of the premises dropped to a sixth of its previous value), this consequence was deemed to be irrelevant in considering the severity of the offence. Likewise, the loss of a bookmaker's licence was deemed to be merely a "secondary" (and thus irrelevant) punishment in both *State (Rollinson) v. Kelly* (1982) and in *Charlton v. Ireland* (1984).

21.3.2 Special courts

Where the ordinary courts are not considered to be adequate to secure the effective administration of justice, a person may be tried before a special court established by Parliament. These special courts are not required to have a jury. In fact, one of the main reasons for the establishment of such courts was the fear that juries in cases involving alleged terrorists might feel too intimidated to fulfil in a proper manner their constitutional role.

Provision was made for a Special Criminal Court by Part V of the Offences Against the State Act 1939 (O.A.S.A. 1939). Section 35 of that Act allows the Government to establish such a Court whenever it feels that "the ordinary courts are inadequate to secure the effective administration of justice and the preservation of public peace and order". The Government's power to do so is not subject to challenge in a court of law. In *Kavanagh v. Ireland* (1996), the Supreme Court ruled that the determination that a Special Criminal Court was needed was a matter for the Government alone. The Court could not look behind the decision to see if it was justified or not. A second challenge to the Court's jurisdiction in *Gilligan v. Ireland* (2001) was again rejected. The Supreme Court in that case, moreover, rejected the proposition that the Special Criminal Court, having been established primarily to deal with the fallout from the Northern Irish "troubles", could not be used against a person not involved in those troubles.

Two types of crime can be tried before the Special Criminal Court. The Government is entitled to require that certain offences generally be tried before the Court. These are called "scheduled" offences and must be tried before the Special Criminal Court if the D.P.P. so requires. Yet even where an offence is not scheduled, the D.P.P. is empowered by section 46 of the O.A.S.A. 1939 to require that a person be tried before the Special Criminal Court. This he may do on the grounds that the ordinary courts are inadequate to secure the effective administration of justice and the preservation of public peace and order. The decision of the D.P.P. in either case is not subject to review or challenge in a court of law, except where it can be shown that the D.P.P. acted in bad faith or with improper motives (*Savage v. D.P.P.* (1982)).

21.3.3 Military courts

In certain circumstances, an offence may be tried before a military court or "court martial". Generally, it is only serving members of the armed forces who may be so tried and only for offences committed on active service. These courts are permitted to operate by Article 38.4, and are largely governed by the provisions of the Defence Act 1954.

22. EQUALITY (ARTICLE 40.1)

The Constitution contains a general guarantee of legal equality in Article 40.1:

> "All citizens shall, as human persons, be held equal before the law".

This does not, however, import a requirement of absolute equality in every conceivable situation. Article 40.1 requires no more than that the State should not *unfairly* or *arbitrarily* discriminate between persons in the same position. The State is always entitled (indeed sometimes required) to have regard to relevant differences between citizens. In this regard the proviso to Article 40.1 is important. It says that the equality guarantee:

> "shall not be held to mean that the State shall not, in its enactments, have due regard to differences of capacity, physical and moral, and of social function".

In other words, the State can differentiate between individuals on the ground that there is some good reason based in fact that justifies such differentiation. Article 40.1 simply requires, in the words of Walsh J. in *O'B. v. S.* (1984). that "the distinctions or discriminations which the legislation creates not be unjust, unreasonable or arbitrary ...". In *MhicMhathúna v. Ireland* (1995), for instance, certain social welfare provisions that discriminated in favour of lone parent households were upheld, partly on the basis that the situation of a lone parent could legitimately be regarded as financially more pressing than that of a two-parent household.

By and large, the equality guarantee has been of limited aid to litigants. The courts, as we will see, have tended to interpret Article 40.1 quite restrictively. In fact, even where inequality could possibly be proved, the courts have often preferred to rely on other rights (such as the personal rights guaranteed by Article 40.3) as a source of relief.

22.1 Inequality established

That said, there are several cases in which inequality contrary to Article 40.1 has clearly been established. In *McMahon v. Leahy* (1984), for instance, the plaintiff, who had escaped from prison in Northern Ireland in 1975, was resisting extradition back to that jurisdiction. Four other prisoners, who had escaped with him at the same time, had previously succeeded in avoiding extradition on the grounds that the offences with which they were charged were "political offences" preventing extradition. The plaintiff, however, because of intervening changes in the interpretation of the "political offence" doctrine, was initially told that he could not avoid extradition. The Supreme Court, nonetheless, ruled that as all five prisoners had been in exactly the same position at the time of their escape, the plaintiff could not now be denied the same treatment as his four counterparts.

The Court took a similar approach in *McKenna v. An Taoiseach (No. 2)* (1995). In that case, the Supreme Court, by a majority, ruled that the spending of £500,000 (€630,000) of State money to support a "Yes" vote in the divorce referendum of 1995 was unconstitutional. One of the primary grounds was that the State, in its funding of only one side of the campaign, was unfairly prejudicing those voters who opposed the referendum in question. In the words of O'Flaherty J.:

> "To spend money in this way breaches the equality rights of the citizen...as well as having the effect of putting the voting rights of one class of citizen (those in favour of the change) above those of another class of citizen (those against)".

That case and *An Blascaod Mór v. Commissioner for Public Works* (2000) may exhibit a greater willingness of late to use the equality guarantee as a source of relief. In the latter case, the High Court (and Supreme Court on appeal) struck down legislation relating to the Blasket Islands on the grounds that it infringed the equality guarantee. The relevant legislation purported to allow the compulsory purchase by the State of land on the island. For these purposes, however, the legislation exempted persons who had been resident on the island before 1953 in respect of any land that they owned or occupied. Relatives of such persons were similarly exempted. These provisions according to Barrington J. (in the Supreme Court) introduced "an unusual and dubious classification with ethnic and racial overtones", a distinction which had "no place ... in a democratic society committed to the principle of equality". There having been, in the Courts' opinion, no legitimate legislative purpose for such differentiation, the Act was deemed unconstitutional.

22.2 Sex discrimination

Many of the cases on unequal treatment centre on discrimination on the grounds of sex. In *de Burca v. Attorney General* (1976), for instance, the Supreme Court struck down legislation that had the net effect of exempting all women from jury service, with the result that juries in criminal trials consisted almost exclusively of men. While most of the judges in that case based their judgments on the requirement that a jury be "representative" of society as a whole, at least one (Walsh J.) ruled that the restrictions were in breach of the guarantee of equality. In his view the State was not entitled "to discriminate in its enactments between the persons who are subject to its laws solely on the grounds of the sex of those persons".

Thus, in *T.O'G. v. Attorney General* (1985), McMahon J. declared unconstitutional certain provisions of the Adoption Acts that discriminated between widows and widowers. In that case, a child had been placed for adoption with the plaintiff and his wife. Sadly, the wife died before the adoption had been formalised. In such a case, the legislation allowed a widower to continue with the adoption only where he already had another child legally in his custody. No such condition was applied in the case of similarly placed widows. There having been no good reason for such arbitrary differentiation between similarly placed men and women, the Court found that Article 40.1 had been breached.

Several common law presumptions and principles that treated women differently from men have met a similar fate. In *State (D.P.P.) v. Walsh and Conneely* (1981), the Supreme Court declared unconstitutional a presumption that a wife who committed a crime in the presence of her husband did so under "marital coercion". Likewise, in *C.M. v. T.M.* (1991) and *W. v. W.* (1993), the common law requirement that a wife's domicile on marriage would be the same as her husband's was deemed repugnant to the Constitution. The reasoning in each case was similar: each rule presupposed that wives were "subservient" to their husbands and thus offended the constitutional guarantee of equality.

In each of these cases the inequality was remedied through the abolition of the offending rule, but in *McKinley v. Minister for Defence* (1993), such inequality resulted in the *extension* of a common law rule to include women as well as men. In that case, a majority of the Supreme Court ruled that the common law right to damages for loss of consortium (the ability to engage in sexual relations with one's spouse) was no longer to be confined to husbands but could also be availed of by wives.

22.3 Cases in which a breach was not established

Where it can be shown, however, that the Legislature had some good reason for treating persons unequally, the equality guarantee will not have been breached. In such cases, the courts have tended to lean in favour of assuming that the Legislature was not acting unreasonably, sometimes by invoking "hypothetical reasons" for legislative discrimination, reasons which may or may not have motivated the Parliament but which nonetheless appear to the court to justify the discrimination.

In *Norris v. Attorney General* (1984), for instance, the plaintiff complained that while legislation enacted in the nineteenth century penalised homosexual sexual conduct between males, no corresponding legislation applied to sexual conduct between females. The Supreme Court however, rejected the proposition that this amounted to unfair discrimination, reasoning that the legislature was "perfectly entitled" to consider that female homosexual behaviour did not create the same "social problems" supposedly prompted by sexual conduct between males. In *Murphy v. Attorney General* (1982), the Supreme Court reasoned that taxation provisions that treated married couples less favourably than their unmarried counterparts (while contrary to Article 41), did not an infringe Article 40.1. The rather curious reason for this, according to Kenny J., was that this unfavourable treatment of married couples was offset by other measures that discriminated in *favour* of such married persons. The most remarkable example of these hypothetical justifications for unequal treatment, however, is to be found in *Draper v. Attorney General* (1984). There the Supreme Court ruled that the failure to extend a right to vote by post to a physically disabled woman, a right afforded to army and police officers and diplomats serving abroad, was not unfairly discriminatory. The Court referred to the costs involved and the supposed risks of electoral fraud that might flow if the vote were to be extended as the plaintiff demanded. The fact that legislation has since extended the postal vote to persons confined to the home is, in itself, proof of how weak these justifications were!

In some cases, discriminatory provisions have been upheld on the basis that they are justified by other provisions of the Constitution. In *O'B. v. S.* (1984), for instance, the Supreme Court ruled that the State could (although it no longer does) discriminate between children born to unmarried and married parents, such discrimination being justified by the constitutional preference for marriage contained in Article 41 of the Constitution. In a similar vein, Barron J., in *Dennehy v. Minister for Social Welfare* (1984), ruled that measures that afforded an allowance to deserted wives, but not deserted husbands, did not violate the equality guarantee. The measures were justified, the judge reasoned, by the pledge in Article 41.2 that the State would "endeavour to ensure that mothers shall not be obliged by economic necessity to engage in labour to the neglect of their duties in the home".

22.4 Discrimination must be based on human characteristics

One of the most controversial aspects of the equality guarantee is the suggestion that it can only be invoked where the discrimination is based on aspects of one's human personality. This is based on the wording of Article 40.1 itself, and in particular on the use of the term "as human persons" therein. On this ground, not unsurprisingly, the Supreme Court held in *Quinn's Supermarket v. Attorney General* (1972) that a legal person (such as a company) would not be entitled to rely on the equality guarantee. The Court, however, went further, noting that even a natural person could only rely on the equality guarantee where the inequality related to an essential aspect of one's human nature, such as colour or gender, and not to social differences such as one's profession or trade, or one's place of residence. The right to be treated equally, the Court said "refers to human persons for what they are in themselves rather than to any lawful activities, trades or pursuits which they engage in or follow". Thus, as a hypothetical example, it would seem that a female farmer could complain that she was being unequally treated on the grounds of her gender but not her profession. In *Madigan v. Attorney General* (1986), the plaintiff complained about allegedly unequal treatment in the operation of a residential property tax. The Supreme Court, however, rejected the contentions based on the equality guarantee on the basis that the plaintiff was alleging discrimination based on his status as a property owner, rather than his essential characteristics as a human being.

With respect, this seems excessively restrictive. It is worth noting, however, that in many of these cases, persons denied relief under Article 40.1 may be able to avail of relief under, other broader constitutional guarantees. In *Madigan* for instance, the Supreme Court, while ruling that the plaintiff could not rely on Article 40.1, found that the plaintiff's property rights had been the subject of an unjust attack, entitling the plaintiff to relief under Article 40.3.

22.5 The failure to take into account relevant differences

Just as it is unfair to treat equally placed persons differently, so too is it unfair to treat substantially different situations as if that difference was absent. In *Cassidy v. Minister for Industry and Commerce* (1978), an order setting a maximum price for drinks was struck down on the grounds that it failed to distinguish between drinks served in lounges as opposed to bars. The service expected in lounges being of a higher quality than that in bars, it was unreasonable not to make provision for higher prices in lounges.

22.6 Other legal provisions requiring equality of treatment

It is important to note, in this regard, that other provisions of the Constitution, as well as in legislation, prohibit discrimination on certain stated grounds. In Article 44, for instance, the State is precluded from differentiating between persons on the basis of their religious profession, status or belief. Articles 9 and 16 contain express prohibitions on sex discrimination in matters concerning citizenship and the right to vote respectively.

More general restrictions are imposed by the Employment Equality Act 1998 and the Equal Status Act 2000. Each prohibits discrimination in the areas of employment and the provision of goods and services respectively, on a variety of grounds, being gender, religion, race, colour, ethnic origin, nationality, parental status, marital status, age, membership of the travelling community, sexual orientation and disability.

European Union Law also contains multiple provisions requiring equal treatment. Article 12 EC, for instance, prohibits discrimination between nationals of different member states on the grounds of their nationality. More specific prohibitions relate to measures that impede the free movement of workers between member states (Article 39 EC) and persons wishing to practise a trade or profession outside their member state (Article 43 EC), all of which broadly encapsulate the concept of non-discrimination between citizens of different member states.

23. PERSONAL RIGHTS (ARTICLE 40.3)

The Constitution explicitly lists certain rights that it purports to guarantee — these are dealt with elsewhere but include, for instance, the right to life, (Article 40.3), the right to personal liberty, (Article 40.4), freedom of expression (Article 40.6.1.i) and the free practice of religion (Article 44). The rights that are protected by the Constitution, however, extend beyond those expressly mentioned in the text itself. In other words, the Constitution is not confined to protecting those rights that it enumerates, those to which it explicitly refers. Certain "unenumerated" rights, though not expressly listed in the Constitution, are nonetheless protected by its provisions.

In *Ryan v. Attorney General* (1965), Kenny J. first identified the existence of such unlisted rights. That case involved a challenge to laws that require the flouridation of water. The plaintiff alleged that such mandatory flouridation was a danger to her health and to that of her family, and was thus a breach of the right to bodily integrity. Although the Constitution does not expressly mention such a right, Kenny J. acknowledged that it was indeed the subject of constitutional protection. Article 40.3.2 guarantees to protect the personal rights of the citizen including, "in particular", four enumerated rights, the right to life amongst them. The use of the words "in particular", he noted, indicated that the rights listed in the Constitution were not the only ones protected by that Article. This complements the theory that the constitution does not create rights but, rather, seeks to recognise those that already exist, by virtue of our human personality.

23.1 The source of unenumerated rights

It is, of course, one thing to suggest that such rights exist. It is another matter entirely to determine what the content of those rights might be. A particularly important issue in this regard is the identification of the source of these rights. If, as Kenny J. suggests is true, there are rights not mentioned in but protected by the Constitution, where do they come from? One sensible suggestion is that certain parts of the Constitution "imply" the existence of other rights. It could be suggested, for instance, that the "inviolability" of the dwelling place of the citizen in Article 40.5 implies a wider constitutional right to privacy. Certain rights, moreover, necessarily imply as a corollary the right not to do that thing. Thus, in *Educational Company v. Fitzpatrick (No. 2)* (1961), the Supreme Court ruled that the right to associate with others implied a right not to do so, *i.e.* a right to dissociate. Thus, just as the State cannot prevent membership of a trade union, so too can it not *force* one to join such a union against one's will. In a similar manner one might say that the right to practise a religion implies a corollary right to reject religion and live as an atheist or humanist.

The courts have also used the non-binding "Directives of Social Policy" contained in Article 45 to imply the existence of certain rights protected by Article 40.3. The right to earn a livelihood (see below) is one of those rights. Although the directives themselves are intended only as guidelines and are not binding on the State as such, they can be used in the interpretation of other Articles not subject to such limitations.

Another, if arguably more nebulous, method of determining the rights protected by Article 40.3, is the idea of the existence of natural rights. (See further, the discussion below in Chap. 3). Articles 41 to 43 all refer to rights that exist independently of law, rights that exist by virtue of a higher universal law superior to the State. Article 43, for instance, mentions a "natural right, antecedent to positive law, to the private ownership of external goods". Kenny J. in *Ryan* asserted that such rights include all rights arising from "the Christian and Democratic nature of the State" although it is hard to see how this clarifies matters. A cynic might suggest that such a formula is loose enough to support whatever personal view the judge himself might have. Indeed the formula seems nonsensical — how can it be said that human rights derive from the nature of the State if human rights *precede* the very existence of the State? This formula has been used, nonetheless to establish several rights, including the right to individual privacy in *Kennedy v. Ireland (1987)* and the right to communicate in *Attorney General v. Paperlink* (1984).

The better view, it is suggested, is that of Henchy J. in *McGee v. Attorney General* (1974), that the rights protected by the Constitution are those that are "fundamental to the personal standing of the individual in question in the context of the social order envisaged by the Constitution." In other words, these are rights that are essential if human beings are to live in dignity.

Let us take a look at some of the rights that have been recognised, notwithstanding the absence of express mention in the Constitution:

23.2 The content of unenumerated rights

23.2.1 The right to bodily integrity

The earliest unenumerated right to be recognised was the right to bodily integrity, in other words the right not to have one's health endangered by the State. In *Ryan v. Attorney General* (1965), the plaintiff had
alleged that the State's flouridation of water (the addition of flouride to
water) endangered her health and that of her family. On the facts, the
High Court and Supreme Court on appeal found that the evidence was
not sufficiently conclusive to establish that flouridation was dangerous.
Nevertheless, both Courts acknowledged that had the State action been
shown to be "dangerous or harmful to the life or health of any of the
citizens" the right to bodily integrity would have been infringed. In
State (Richardson) v. Governor of Mountjoy Prison (1980), for
instance, the insanitary condition of a women's prison in which the
plaintiff was incarcerated amounted to a failure by the State "to protect
the applicant's health". The fact that the plaintiff's presence in the
prison was involuntary was particularly relevant.

This issue arose also in the famous case of *McGee v. Attorney General* (1974). In that case, a married woman who had already borne four
children, was told by her doctor that she risked serious health complications (including the possibility of coronary thrombosis, a serious
heart disease) if she had any more children. In order to prevent a further pregnancy, she attempted to import contraceptives for her own personal use. At the time, however, the sale, importation, manufacture and
distribution of artificial contraceptive devices were all deemed illegal
by section 17 of the Criminal Law Amendment Act 1935. As a result,
the customs authorities intercepted and impounded the contraceptives,
preventing Mrs. McGee from using them. On appeal, the Supreme
Court held that this constituted an infringement of the plaintiff's right
to bodily integrity. The State by its actions had endangered the plaintiff's health, by preventing her from having access (in Walsh J.'s
words) to "the means whereby a conception which was likely to put her
life in jeopardy might be avoided" (page 313).

One aspect of the right to bodily integrity involves the right to refuse
intrusive medical treatment. Otherwise than in exceptional circumstances, no person can be forced to undergo surgery against his or her
will. In *Re a Ward of Court (Withdrawal of Medical Treatment)* (1995),
the Supreme Court acknowledged that a person can refuse such treatment even if such refusal will result in the likely death of that person. A

medical practitioner who carries out a medical procedure otherwise than with the consent of the patient may face proceedings for trespass to the person or even assault.

The right to bodily integrity may also include, however, a positive right to have the State *supply* or fund medical treatment in an appropriate case. This right however, is not absolute. In *State (C.) v. Frawley* (1976), the High Court rejected the proposition that the plaintiff was entitled to highly specialised and expensive medical treatment not at the time available in this State. The plaintiff, a prisoner suffering from a severe sociopathic disorder, claimed that this equipment would radically redress his situation. Be that as it may have been, Finlay P. ruled that, in the circumstances of the case, the State was not obliged to fund such expensive treatment.

23.2.2 The right not to be treated inhumanely

A right closely related to the right of bodily integrity is the right not to be subjected to torture, and inhumane or degrading treatment. In *People (A.G.) v. O'Brien* (1965), the Supreme Court noted (although it was not strictly relevant to the case before it) that the infliction of torture, especially to extract evidence, would be "a moral defilement", and a clear breach of the Constitution.

In the *State (C.) v. Frawley* (1976), a prisoner with a serious sociopathic disorder had been subjected to a series of restraints to prevent him from doing an injury to either himself or others. In particular, the prisoner had been handcuffed and kept in solitary confinement without access to any implements that he might use to cause injury. The prisoner complained that this infringed his personal rights. The High Court, however, ruled that such measures were permissible. The plaintiff was prone to violent aggression and recklessly dangerous acts and as such the prison authorities were entitled to take whatever steps were necessary to prevent him from harming himself or others. The Constitution did, Finlay P. agreed, prohibit the use of torture or the inhumane and degrading treatment of citizens. The Courts, however, did not regard as torture that which was designed to prevent "self-injury or self-destruction".

23.2.3 The right to privacy

The Constitution, as interpreted by the Courts, envisages that all persons are entitled to make certain decisions and take certain actions

without fear of State intervention. In other words, each person is entitled to enjoy a degree of privacy, free from external scrutiny or supervision. This right first arose (albeit in a qualified form) in *McGee v.
Attorney General* (1974), already discussed above in the context of the
right to bodily integrity. In that case, we recall, the Supreme Court
ruled that a ban on the importation of contraception infringed the constitutional rights of the plaintiff, a married woman with four children.
Part of the rationale of the Court in this specific case was that the lack
of access to contraception put the plaintiff at risk of serious health
complications. The Court, however, also ruled that the ban offended
the right to marital privacy of the plaintiff and her husband. One of the
rights of the married couple, it was argued, was to determine whether
to have children and, if so, how many children they might have. For
this purpose, a married couple was entitled to access contraception in
order to limit the size of its family, and any attempt by the State to prevent it from doing so would involve an infringement of the couple's
right to marital privacy.

The question that immediately arises, however, is whether this is a
general right of privacy to be enjoyed by all or whether the right was
strictly confined to its marital origins. In *Kennedy v. Ireland* (1987), the
High Court affirmed that there was indeed an individual right to privacy that could be enjoyed regardless of marital status. In that case,
Hamilton P. ruled that the tapping of two journalists' phones without
lawful reason (on Government instructions, and without the consent or
knowledge of the journalists) constituted an unwarranted breach of the
right to privacy. This individual right to privacy was affirmed again in
Re a Ward of Court (1995) where the Supreme Court noted that the
right to refuse medical treatment flowed logically from (amongst other
rights) the right to privacy and the related right to self-determination.

The right to privacy is not, however, absolute. In *Kearney v. Minister
for Justice* (1986), Costello J. observed that while a prisoner may enjoy
the right to privacy, this right may validly be restricted in order to
maintain prison security. The right to privacy, thus, is subject to restrictions. A most striking example of such restrictions is to be found in
Norris v. Attorney General (1984). In that case, the plaintiff had complained that nineteenth century laws that penalised male homosexual
sexual conduct infringed, amongst other things, his right to privacy.
The legislation in question was quite wide-ranging, and applied even
where the parties involved were consenting adults engaging in sexual
relations in private. The majority of the Supreme Court, however,
decided that such restrictions did not infringe the plaintiff's constitu-

tional rights. The right to privacy, according to O'Higgins C.J. for the majority, was not absolute but was subject, as were all other rights, to the requirements of the common good. O'Higgins C.J. laid heavy emphasis on the fact that the State was (in his opinion) a "Christian" State, noting that homosexual activity had consistently been regarded as "gravely sinful" by most Christian denominations. Considering this and the opinion that homosexuality was "morally wrong and harmful to a way of life and to values which the State wishes to protect" the Chief Justice concluded that the restrictions on the plaintiff's right to privacy were not unconstitutional.

Two judges, McCarthy and Henchy JJ. dissented. While they agreed that the right to privacy was not absolute, they believed that the State had not discharged the onus on it of showing that the impugned laws were necessary to protect public order and morality. The right to privacy, in other words, could only be curtailed where the State could clearly establish that a higher interest so required. In this case, the dissenters believed, the State had not proved that the laws in question were required to protect the common good.

23.2.4 *The right to marry*

While the Constitution explicitly guarantees to protect the institution of marriage, there is no explicit mention of a right to marry. Arguably, however, it is implicit in Article 41 that persons have the right to marry. Indeed, in *Ryan v. Attorney General* (1965) Kenny J. mentions this right as one of the unenumerated rights that he claimed arose from "the Christian and Democratic nature of the State". In *McGee v. Attorney General* (1974), moreover, Fitzgerald C.J. refers to the right to marry in terms that suggested it would be protected by the Constitution. Neither case, however, concerned this matter directly and, as yet, there is no clear pronouncement on the exact confines of this right.

When the matter arose in *Donovan v. Minister for Justice* (1951) the Courts seem to have fudged the issue. In that case, Kingsmill Moore J. ruled that garda rules that required that a garda seek the permission of superior officer if he wished to marry were not unconstitutional. A garda could be (and in this case was) denied certain privileges if he married without such consent. This, however, did not, according to the Court infringe the plaintiff's right to marry. While the Court ruled in the plaintiff's favour on other grounds, its ruling on the matter of the right to marry seems excessively narrow.

The right to marry has been much more vigorously pursued as a legal issue in the United States. The Federal Supreme Court, for example, has struck down laws that prevent people of different races from marrying each other (*Loving v. Virginia* (1967)) as well as laws that purport to prevent prisoners from being wed (*Skinner v. Oklahoma* (1942)). A similar approach was taken in *Zablocki v. Redhail* (1978) where the Supreme Court struck down a Wisconsin law that prevented a parent from marrying unless he or she could satisfy the Court that his or her already existing children would not become a financial burden on the State.

Of course there must, of necessity, be certain restrictions on the right to marry. Provided there exist sound reasons for such restrictions, no one can successfully complain that they infringe the constitutional right to marry. For instance, only persons aged 18 or over may marry in this State, the State quite reasonably considering persons under that age too immature to do so.

A somewhat more controversial issue, which has not yet arisen in the courts of this jurisdiction, is whether the requirement that the parties to a marriage be respectively male and female (i.e. of opposite sex) contravenes the right to marry. The consensus from U.S. jurisprudence is that it does not, marriage being, it is said, traditionally a union of man and woman. (See, *e.g.*, the Minnesota case of *Baker v. Nelson* (1973)). That said, in *Baehr v. Lewin* (1993), the Supreme Court of Hawaii ruled that the ban on same-sex marriage infringed, without good reason, their constitutional prohibition on sex discrimination. Though this decision was overturned by constitutional referendum, the issue is far from dead.

23.2.5 *The right to bear children*

Murray v. Ireland (1985) established as a basic principle the right to bear (or "beget") children. It had already been established (in *McGee v. Attorney General*) that a married couple has the right to limit its family size through the use of contraception. As a corollary, it must be accepted that married persons (at the very least) have the right to bear children. Thus any policy or rule that attempted to limit family size (such as the penalties imposed in China on couples with more than one child) would be impermissible in this State.

In *Murray* (1985), a husband and wife were both serving life sentences in different prisons for the murder of a garda. As a married couple, they asserted what they claimed was a constitutional right to beget children, and effectively requested that the State provide them with facilities for engaging in sexual intercourse for that purpose. The Court agreed that they had a right to bear children but concluded that the State was entitled, in this case, to restrict this right in order to maintain prison security. It was noted that if every spouse in prison was to be afforded such facilities, prison security would be greatly compromised.

Nonetheless, this case established an important general principle, that subject to the requirements of the common good, a married couple have a right to bear children. Whether this is a right confined to married persons or that can be enjoyed also by unmarried persons is not yet clear. It is suggested however that there is no reason, this being a personal right under Article 40.3, that the State should be more entitled to interfere in the private decision-making of unmarried persons than would be the case with a married couple.

While on the topic of children, it is worth noting the decision of the Supreme Court in *I. O'T. v. B.* (1998) that an adopted child has the right to know the identity of his or her mother. This right had to be balanced, however, with the competing rights of the mother to her privacy. As such the decision in that case is largely one of principle. The prospect of an adopted child accessing information in a particular case will depend largely on the facts of each individual case.

23.2.6 The rights of non-marital families

Article 41 purports to protect the "Family". The "Family" of which it speaks, however, is exclusively that based on marriage. Article 41 cannot be invoked by family units that exist outside the legal framework of marriage. Nonetheless, the courts have acknowledged that certain members of non-marital families may enjoy personal rights that are protected by Article 40.3.2. This is dealt with further below in Chap. 28. The key point to note at this juncture, however, is that while both a non-marital mother and her child enjoy constitutional rights under Article 40.3.2, the courts have consistently refused to acknowledge that an unmarried father has any constitutional rights in respect of his child.

23.2.7 The right to die a natural death

Death is an inevitable part of life, and as such, the courts have recognised a constitutional right to die a natural death. An individual, as a result, is entitled to reject life-saving medical treatment even if such

rejection results (in the natural course) in death. No person, in short, is
obliged to agree to stay alive at any cost. The right to die a natural
death flows from two other related rights. One is the right to privacy,
which implies a right to autonomy in determining one's own destiny.
The other is the right to bodily integrity, which presupposes that a person is entitled to exercise informed choice as regards what is done to
his or her body. The right to die does not however entail or imply a
right to take active steps to end one's life or that of another, for whatever reasons. The right to die is limited in the sense that it presupposes
that one dies by natural causes and not by human intervention.

The issue of the right to die was considered by the Supreme Court in
Re a Ward of Court (withdrawal of medical treatment) (1995). This
exceptionally tragic case involved a woman who, as a result of complications arising during a routine operation, suffered severe brain damage. As a result, she had been left in a near-persistent vegetative state.
She was unable to control her bodily movements or to communicate,
although there was some evidence that she recognised members of her
family and the regular nursing staff at the hospital in which she was a
patient. Being unable to feed herself, the woman (who was made a
ward of court in 1975) had to be fed through a tube inserted in her
stomach. Despite initial hopes of improvement, the woman remained
in such a state for some 23 years. In 1995 members of her family
applied to have her treatment terminated, and in particular to remove
the gastric tube from her stomach.

Both Lynch J. in the High Court and the Supreme Court on appeal
agreed that a person has the right to refuse any form of medical intervention, even where the inevitable result of such refusal would be the
death of that person. Where a person is not mentally competent to do
so, however, it falls to the guardian of that person (in this case the High
Court, as the woman was a ward of court) to decide what should be
done. In making this decision, the Court said, one must look only to the
best interests of the person involved. The Court should act as a "prudent and loving parent" would act under the circumstances. Given the
severe condition of the woman and the likelihood that she would not
improve in the future, the High Court decided that it was in her best
interests that treatment be withdrawn.

23.2.8 The right to earn a livelihood

While the State cannot be expected to guarantee every citizen a job, it
can be restrained in circumstances where it attempts unfairly to restrict

a person's right to earn a living from a particular profession or vocation. In *Murtagh Properties v. Cleary* (1972), Kenny J. ruled that a picket protesting at the employment of non-union staff was illegal as it was an attempt to deny the non-union staff of their right to earn a livelihood. The union had objected to the employment of female bar staff, who were not members of a union, at a particular public house. The female bar staff were not members of a union, ironically, because the relevant union, at that time, barred these women from membership on the grounds of their gender. Kenny J. looked to the (non-binding) Directive Principles of Social Policy in Article 45. One of these principles was the right of "men and women equally" to an adequate means of livelihood. Although Article 45 did not itself confer any binding legal rights on persons, it could be read, Kenny J. believed, as implying in Article 40.3.2 a right to earn a livelihood without discrimination on the basis of gender.

That said, the right to earn a livelihood is, as with all other rights, subject to certain limitations. It could hardly be denied, for instance, that the State is entitled to place restrictions on the working hours or conditions of underage workers. In *Landers v. Attorney General* (1973), for instance, Finlay J. held that legislation preventing an eight-year-old singer from giving performances in public houses was not unconstitutional. Such limitations are not however, confined to child labour laws. The State is entitled generally to regulate the practice of certain professions with a view to promoting the overall common good. In *Shanley v. Galway Corporation* (1995), McCracken J. ruled that casual trading rules restricting the sale of food from mobile units in a particular part of Galway City did not infringe the plaintiff's right to earn a livelihood.

It is clear also that persons convicted of offences connected to a particular trade, may lawfully be prevented from continuing in that trade, should the seriousness of the offences so demand. In *Hand v. Dublin Corporation* (1991), for instance, the Supreme Court refused to strike down legislation that prevented a person twice convicted of casual trading without a licence from subsequently obtaining such a licence. That said, the penalty imposed must be proportionate having regard to the seriousness of the offence. In *Cox v. Ireland* (1992), measures that precluded a person convicted of an offence under the Offences Against the State Act 1939 from holding employment from the State for seven years thereafter, were struck down. The reason given by the Supreme Court was that while some offences prosecuted under that Act might merit such treatment, other more minor offences would not. The punishment in this case did not fit the crime.

23.2.9 The right to communicate

In *Attorney General v. Paperlink* (1984), Costello J. affirmed that Article 40.3. protected a right to communicate. In that case, Paperlink challenged the postal monopoly of the Department of Post and Telegraphs (now *An Post*), claiming that it infringed the right to communicate. Costello J., while affirming that such a right existed, refused to accept that the exclusive right of the Post Office undermined this right. If anything, he said, it *facilitated* communication between people. In *Kearney v. Minister for Justice* (1987), however, the High Court held that a prisoner's right to communicate had been breached by the failure of the prison authorities to forward mail addressed to the prisoner.

23.2.10 The right to travel outside the State

In *State (M.) v. Attorney General* (1979) Finlay P. acknowledged that the Constitution protected the right to travel outside the State. That case concerned an infant whose unmarried parents wished to send her to stay with her paternal grandparents in Nigeria. The Adoption Act 1952, however, prevented the removal from the State of a child who was an Irish citizen of unmarried parents. Such removal could only occur if the child was being removed with the consent of her mother and would be residing with relatives outside the State. As her father's parents were not regarded as her "relatives" (the father not being married to the mother) the State refused to give the girl a passport. This infringed the girl's right to travel, with the consent of her parents, outside the State. In a similar vein, an attempt to prevent Irish rugby players from describing themselves as an "Irish team" on their tour of apartheid-ridden South Africa was rejected by O'Hanlon J. in *Lennon v. Ganly* (1981) partly on the grounds of the right to travel.

Of course the right to travel is not unlimited. It could quite feasibly be restricted for the purpose of upholding the common good, as in the case of an accused person prevented from leaving the State pending a trial. Indeed, it was once thought that the right to travel might validly be restricted in cases where a person proposed to travel abroad to obtain an abortion (see for instance the decision of the High Court in *Attorney General v. X.* (1992)). Article 40.3.3 (as amended in 1992) however, expressly prevents that Article from being used to restrict the right to travel for such purposes.

23.2.11 The right of access to the courts

Every person has a right of access to the Courts. Where a person alleges that their legal rights have been breached, he or she is entitled to seek relief in a legal forum. In *Macauley v. Minister for Post and Telegraphs* (1966), Kenny J. struck down a measure on this very ground. The relevant law prevented a person from suing a Minister of Government without the Attorney General's approval. This being a restriction of the personal rights of citizens to have access to the courts, the measure was struck down as unconstitutional. In a similar vein, the Supreme Court in *Byrne v. Ireland* (1972) rejected the proposition that the State was immune from being sued, again partly on the grounds that such steps would fetter free access to the courts.

Of course there are limitations upon such access. A person must have the appropriate standing to take a case (*locus standi*). This is discussed above in Chap. 4. A case must, moreover, be taken within a reasonable amount of time. The Statute of Limitations 1957 (as amended) prevents a case in tort from being taken more than three years after the relevant injury arises (or in the case of a personal injury, three years from the date on which the injury was, or ought reasonably to have been discovered). A case for breach of contract cannot be taken more than six years after the relevant breach of contract has occurred. Such limitations are constitutionally permissible according to the Supreme Court in *Tuohy v. Courtney* (1994) provided that they are not unreasonably short. In creating these limitations, the Oireachtas "is essentially engaged in a balancing of constitutional rights and duties". The right to litigate, in other words, has to be balanced against the rights of the persons against whom such cases are taken. The latter have a right to certainty and finality, and in particular the right not to have the possibility of court action hanging over them for all time.

It is not for the courts to determine what the appropriate balance is; that job is reserved to the Legislature. If however, the Legislature choose a limitation period that "is so contrary to reason and fairness as to constitute an unjust attack" on constitutional rights the courts may step in. The courts however seem largely unwilling to do so. In *Brady v. Donegal County Council* (1989), for instance, the Supreme Court upheld a two-month limitation period, with no provision for exceptions. This was despite the fact that Costello J. in the High Court had struck it down as being unduly short and thus as an infringement of the right to litigate. Costello J., in that case, was particularly concerned by the fact that the court had no discretion to exempt those who had not been at fault in failing to take a case on time.

It is worth noting that persons incarcerated in a mental hospital are precluded by section 260 of the Mental Treatment Act 1945 from taking civil proceedings without the consent of the High Court. The reason for this restriction is apparently to prevent delusional persons from clogging the courts with vexatious claims.

The key barrier to court access, however, is arguably not legal but financial. Court proceedings can be prohibitively expensive and as such many persons would not be able to take legal action without significant financial backing. The Constitution does recognise, according to the Supreme Court in *State (Healy) v. Donoghue* (1976), a right to free legal aid, but only in criminal cases. In that case, the Supreme Court quashed the conviction of the accused, a poorly-educated, and relatively needy young man on the grounds that he had been effectively denied his right to free legal aid. The accused, furthermore, was not properly informed of his right, under legislation, to free legal aid in criminal trials. Although he was initially approved for legal aid, and supplied with a solicitor, that solicitor subsequently left the legal aid scheme, leaving the accused without a lawyer at his trial. This effectively infringed the accused's right to legal representation at trial. This right, according to O'Higgins C.J., implied that a person who could not afford such representation would be given a lawyer at the State's expense. A person had the right, moreover, to be informed about the availability of such aid.

From a constitutional viewpoint, however, there is no constitutional right to legal aid in civil cases. The courts have rejected the proposition that there is such a right (see *O'Shaughnessy v. Attorney General* (1971)). In *M.C. v. Legal Aid Board* (1991), furthermore, Gannon J., rejected a complaint that under-funding of the civil legal aid system, which had led to a delay in the plaintiff's nullity of marriage case, was in breach of her right to litigate. The State had no obligation, he asserted, to fund what were effectively private matrimonial proceedings between two spouses. The Courts have also rejected the rather creative suggestion that the right to litigate implies a right to be supplied with a law library by the State (*MacGairbhíth v. Attorney General* (1991)).

23.2.12 The right to fair procedures

There is an implied right to have fair procedures used when decisions are being made that affect one's individual interests. In *Garvey v. Ireland* (1981) the Supreme Court affirmed that this right to fair procedures was a constitutional right protected by Article 40.3.

These fair procedures usually entail the following:

- That the decision-maker be impartial and unbiased ("you cannot be a judge in your own cause");

- That the decision-maker acts in a manner that is fair and reasonable;

- That the decision-maker takes into account all that is relevant to the inquiry and ignores that which is irrelevant;

- That the parties are given equal rights to put their case and to challenge that of their opponents. (The decision-maker should "hear both sides".)

23.3 Summary

The Constitution protects rights other than those expressly mentioned in the text. The most notable are the "personal rights" mentioned in Article 40.3.2. The use of the term "in particular" in that clause suggested to Kenny J., in *Ryan v. Attorney General* (1965), that the Constitution protected a category of unlisted or "unenumerated rights". The underlying theory behind this is that the Constitution does not "create" rights, it simply pledges to protect rights that humans already have by virtue of their human personality.

24. THE RIGHT TO LIFE

The Constitution has always expressly guaranteed the right to life of the individual. This right is amongst the most precious and sacred of rights. Indeed it has been acknowledged that the right to life can take precedence over other constitutional rights where a conflict of rights arises. In *People (D.P.P.) v. Shaw* (1982), the Supreme Court excused a breach of the right to liberty on the grounds that it was necessary to protect the superior right to life of other individuals. The defendant in this case had been kept under arrest for longer than permitted under law. The Gardaí had done this, however, in good faith, believing that his continued incarceration was necessary if one of the defendant's victims was to be found alive. Although the defendant's liberty was thereby unlawfully curtailed, this was considered necessary in order to increase the chances of finding this woman alive.

Of course no person's right to life is absolute. In times of war and rebellion, after all, lives may be taken in order to protect the lives and liberties of other people. On a smaller scale, Irish criminal law acknowledges that some deaths may be justified as having been a product of self-defence. In *People (AG) v. Dwyer* (1972), Walsh J. acknowledged that

> "a homicide is not unlawful if it is committed in the execution or advancement of justice, or in reasonable self-defence of person or property, or in order to prevent the commission of an atrocious crime, or by misadventure. In the case of self-defence, the homicide is justifiable and is therefore not unlawful".

The Constitution itself formerly acknowledged (albeit implicitly) that certain crimes may merit a sentence of death. Article 13.6 made express mention of the President's right to commute or remit a sentence of death, a clause that would not have been inserted had the framers of the Constitution regarded the right to life as unlimited. As a result of the Twenty-First Amendment of the Constitution, 2001, however, Article 15.5.2 now expressly prohibits the Oireachtas from enacting a law prescribing a death penalty. Article 13.6 has been amended accordingly. Indeed, Article 28.3 of the Constitution prevents such legislation *even* under the constitutional exemption available in times of emergency.

24.1 The right to life of the unborn child

Towards the end of the 1970s, the question arose whether the right to life was enjoyed not just by persons already born, but also by "the unborn child", a child conceived though not yet born. The corollary of this question is whether or not a woman has a right to terminate a pregnancy, in other words to have an abortion, and if so in what circumstances. This is a controversial and sensitive topic and should be approached with care.

Though several judges had previously asserted that the general right to life guaranteed by Article 40.3.2 was extensive enough to protect the unborn child, (see for instance Walsh J. in *McGee v. Attorney General* (1974)), a specific amendment explicitly guaranteeing the latter's right to life was proposed in 1983. As a result of a divisive and bitter referendum, the Eighth Amendment was passed and the following clause inserted as Article 40.3.3:

> "The State acknowledges the right to life of the unborn and, with due regard to the equal right to life of the mother, guarantees in its laws to respect, and, as far as practicable, by its laws to defend and vindicate that right".

24.1.1 The "substantive" question — Attorney General v. X

It was widely assumed that Article 40.3.3 created a comprehensive ban on abortion in this State. The Supreme Court, in *Attorney General v. X* (1992) held, by contrast, that an abortion could legally be carried out in Ireland, although only in certain very limited circumstances. That case involved a fourteen and a half-year old girl, who had become pregnant following an alleged incident of rape. The pregnancy greatly disturbed the girl in question, to such an extent that she had threatened that unless she had an abortion she would commit suicide. When the situation was brought to the attention of the then Attorney General, he sought to prevent the abortion from taking place. In the High Court, Costello P. granted an injunction to the Attorney General, preventing the girl from travelling to the United Kingdom for the purposes of terminating the pregnancy. The judge maintained that this was necessary in order to vindicate the superior right to life of the unborn child.

On appeal, the Supreme Court lifted the injunction. It did so on the basis that the abortion was legal in Ireland, and that therefore there could be no legal objection to the girl travelling to the UK in this case. The Court noted that the right to life of the child was subject to the equal right to life of the mother. The right to life of the child, then, was not unlimited. It could be curtailed where necessary to vindicate the right to life of the mother. In this case, there was a "real and substantive risk" to the life of the mother arising from her suicidal state: if she did not have the abortion, the majority concluded, there was a real risk that she would kill herself.

The Government subsequently attempted, by referendum, to prevent persons who were suicidal as a result of their pregnancy, from being entitled to obtain an abortion in Ireland. (The Twelfth Amendment of the Constitution Bill, 1992.) This referendum, however, was defeated. In October 2001, the Government proposed a new referendum to be held in early 2002. The proposed amendment again attempts to fore-close the possibility of an abortion where a mother is suicidal as a result of her pregnancy. The law as it stands at the moment may be summarised as follows:

> Any medical procedure (be it an abortion or otherwise) that results directly or indirectly in the death of an unborn child may legally be carried out in this jurisdiction where there exists a "real and substantive risk to the life of the mother" *necessitating* that such procedure be carried out. (At the moment this includes the risk of suicide).

24.1.2 *The freedom to travel to avail of an abortion*

While the *X* Case largely centred on the legality of the proposed abortion had it been carried out in Ireland, the young woman in the *X* Case was in fact seeking to travel to the U.K. to have an abortion. The Supreme Court's reasoning on the substantive issue, thus, is probably more accurately described as incidental to the issue of the right to travel. If *X* was entitled to have an abortion in Ireland, the Court held, she could not be prevented from travelling to England for the same purpose.

The question remained however, as to whether or not a woman had the right to leave the State in order to avail of an abortion that could *not* have been legally carried out in Ireland. On this point, the various Supreme Court judges differed, some asserting that had the proposed abortion been illegal in Ireland, the State could lawfully have prevented the girl from travelling.

This conflict has now been resolved in favour of the right to travel. With the passing of the Thirteenth Amendment to the Constitution, Article 40.3.3 can no longer be used to prevent a woman from travelling outside the State for the purpose of availing of an abortion lawfully available in another State. The Thirteenth Amendment, however, is specifically confined to attempts to invoke Article 40.3.3 to prevent such freedom of travel. It remains to be seen, then, whether *any other* provision of the Constitution may be invoked for this purpose.

24.1.3 Freedom of information on abortion

A particularly controversial aspect of this debate, though ancillary to the substantive question on the legality of abortion in Ireland, relates to the right to distribute information that advertises abortion services lawfully available abroad. From a very early stage in this clause's history, the Supreme Court displayed its willingness to interpret the Eighth Amendment in a very broad fashion so as to prevent the distribution of such information. In *Attorney General (S.P.U.C.) v. Open Door Counselling* (1988), the Supreme Court held that Article 40.3.3 prohibited the giving of information that might facilitate an abortion. The defendant provided a non-directive counselling service for pregnant women, part of which service involved distributing information on the availability of abortions in the U.K. The Supreme Court granted an injunction preventing the giving of such information. In *S.P.U.C. v. Coogan* (1989) and *S.P.U.C. v. Grogan* (1989), moreover, similar injunctions were granted against Students Unions who were giving advice regarding the availability of abortions in the U.K.

The reasoning of the courts in these cases was that by providing such information, the persons involved were assisting in (as the courts saw it) the "destruction of the life of the unborn child". They were, the courts considered, helping to facilitate such abortions. It might of course be argued that even without such information thousands of women were travelling abroad each year for the purpose of obtaining an abortion. Practically speaking, it is hard to see how the State could prevent any such information from being made available to persons in Ireland.

The rulings in *Grogan* and *Coogan* brought up the question of whether Article 40.3.3 was consistent with the Treaty of the European Community. In *S.P.U.C. v. Grogan* (1991), the European Court of Justice ruled that there was a right to advertise abortion services lawfully available in other E.U. States provided that the advertisement was for economic profit. This meant that assuming that there was an economic connection between the advertiser and service provider, any restrictions upon the advertisement of abortion services would infringe E.U. law.

The conflict was finally resolved in 1992 by an amendment to the Constitution, guaranteeing the right to distribute information on abortion under certain conditions (the Fourteenth Amendment, 1992). The conditions under which such information can be distributed are laid down in the Regulation of Information Act (Services outside the State for termination of pregnancies) 1995. This Act is quite detailed but it broadly provides that information on abortion may be given out only under the following conditions:

- Such information must relate only to abortions which are legal in the state in which they are carried out.

- Those providing information on abortion cannot do so in a manner that promotes or advocates abortion.

- The advice given by the information-provider should be non-directive. When information on abortion is given, the person providing the information is obliged to advise the woman involved on all the options available to her (including, for instance, the prospect of placing the child for adoption, or in foster care).

- The information provider is precluded from making any appointment or other arrangements with an abortion clinic on behalf of the woman involved.

Further reading: Kingston and Whelan (with Bacik), *Abortion and the Law* (Dublin: Round Hall, 1996)

25. PERSONAL LIBERTY: RIGHTS ON ARREST AND IN DETENTION

Articles 40.4 and 40.5 deal broadly with the issue of personal liberty. The key principle in this context is that contained in Article 40.4.1, that "no citizen shall be deprived of his liberty save in accordance with law". This entails, in other words, that a person shall not be incarcerated except after specific pre-ordained procedures have been followed.

25.1 The power to arrest

At common law, a person may be arrested for the sole purpose of their being charged, before the courts, with an offence. An arrest, in short, involves the seizure and detention of a person for the purpose of being charged. Such an arrest may proceed under a warrant granted by a judge although the Gardaí also have legal authority to arrest persons suspected, with reasonable cause, of having committed certain specified types of offence. Unless a person is arrested pursuant to a warrant, he or she must be told why the arrest is taking place (*Christie v. Leachinsky* (1947), *Re Ó Laighléis,* (1970)). The Gardaí need not cite the precise legislation under which the accused is being arrested, but must be able broadly to explain the reasons for the arrest.

A person once arrested must generally be brought before a District Court and charged with an offence at the *earliest practicable opportunity.* This may in some cases necessitate a special sitting of the District Court, outside normal office hours. If, however, a person is arrested at night after 10 p.m., section 15(3) of the Criminal Justice Act 1957 allows that person to be detained without charge until the court sits first thing the following morning.

25.1.1 No arrest without reasonable suspicion

A person cannot be arrested unless there is a reasonable suspicion, supported by evidence, that he or she has committed a crime. In the *State (Trimbole) v. Governor of Mountjoy Prison* (1986), for instance, a person had been arrested in circumstances where the police did not believe that he had committed any offence. The Gardaí at the time were awaiting the delivery of a warrant for the extradition of Mr. Trimbole. Fearing that he would abscond before the warrant arrived, they arrested him purely with a view to detaining him pending the arrival of the warrant. There having been no reasonable belief that the accused had committed the crime for which he was arrested, the arrest was declared illegal.

25.1.2 Rights on arrest

A person has various constitutional rights on arrest:

- The right to be informed of the reasons for his arrest (*People (D.P.P.) v. Walsh* (1980)).

- The right to silence and the right to be informed of that right. (See above in Chap. 20.)

- The right to a lawyer. A person, on arrest, has the right to legal advice and reasonable access to a lawyer for the purpose of obtaining such advice. In *People (D.P.P.) v. Doyle* (1982), the Court of Criminal Appeal observed that any attempt to prevent access to a lawyer would render the accused's detention illegal. (Affirmed by the Supreme Court in *People (D.P.P.) v. Healy* (1990).) The accused, moreover, is entitled to consult with his legal adviser in private (*State (Harrington) v. Garvey* (1976)). Strangely, though, a person does not appear to have a constitutional right to be *told* of his right to a lawyer (*People (D.P.P.) v Farrell* (1978)) nor to have a lawyer present while being questioned (*People (D.P.P.) v. Pringle* (1981)).

- The right to legal aid where one has not the means to afford a lawyer (*State (Healy) v. Donoghue* (1976)).

- The right to medical treatment, when needed.

- A right to privacy (in particular in one's dealings with a lawyer).

- The right of access to the courts, in particular under the *habeas corpus* provisions of Article 40.4. These provisions allow the court, when asked, to order the release of a person being illegally detained.

Where these rights are denied to an arrested person, such denial may render the detention illegal (*People (D.P.P.) v. Healy* (1990)). As such, it may be impossible to secure a conviction of that person on the charges upon which he was arrested. It is worth noting that, in addition to the constitutional rights mentioned above, a person has certain legal rights granted by legislation. For instance, while there appears to be no constitutional right to be informed about ones right to a lawyer, section 5 of the Criminal Justice Act 1984 requires that all persons arrested under that Act be informed of this right.

25.1.3 Detention for questioning

At common law a person cannot be detained against his will for questioning. The Gardaí may not, in other words, arrest someone for the purpose of asking them questions relating to an alleged crime. This largely accords with the right to silence discussed above in the context of the trial of offences. A person cannot generally be made to respond to questions posed by the police, nor can he be penalised for failing to answer such questions. A person can only be arrested, furthermore, with a view to bringing that person before a court so that he or she may be formally charged with having committed a crime. In *People (D.P.P.) v. Higgins* (1985), the Supreme Court ruled that statements made by the accused in this case could not be admitted in evidence. The defendant in this case was arrested and taken to a Garda station for questioning in relation to offences *other than those* for which he had been arrested. No attempt had been made to bring the accused before the District Court. The evidence obtained during this "detention for questioning" could not, thus, be used in Court.

It is worth reiterating that ordinarily the purpose of arrest is solely to allow a person to be charged with an offence before a judge. There are however, important legislative exceptions to the principle that rules out detention for questioning. These exceptions are contained in:

- Section 30, Offences Against the State Act 1939.

- Section 4, Criminal Justice Act 1984.

- Criminal Justice (Drug Trafficking) Act 1996.

(1) Section 30 of the Offences Against the State Act 1939

A person arrested on suspicion of an offence that is "scheduled" under the 1939 Act can be detained for the purposes of investigating that offence. Such detention may continue for an initial 24 hours, which may be extended by a further 24 hours with the consent of a Garda Chief Superintendent or an officer of higher rank. Since 1998, moreover, a District Judge may extend the period of detention by another 24 hours (bringing the total detention period without charge to 72 hours).

(2) Section 4 of the Criminal Justice Act 1984

This Act applies to all offences "for which a person of full capacity and not previously convicted may be punished by a term of imprisonment for a term of at least five years". On arrest for such an offence, the Gardaí have authority to question a suspect for up to six hours, which initial period may be extended by a further six hours (but no more) by a superintendent or officer of higher rank.

(3) Drug Trafficking Act 1996

Persons arrested on suspicion of drug trafficking may be detained for questioning under this Act initially for up to six hours, but this period of detention may be extended quite considerably to allow further investigations to proceed. With the consent of a chief superintendent, the period of detention may be extended by a further 18 hours and then again by an additional 24 hours. With the consent of a District or Circuit Court judge, moreover, the detention may be extended by another 72 hours, and thereafter by another 48 hours. In total then, a person may be detained for questioning under the legislation for no less than *seven days!*

25.1.4 *Is detention for questioning under these Acts constitutional?*

In *People (D.P.P.) v. Quilligan (No. 3)* (1993), the defendant argued that section 30 of the Offences Against the State Act 1939 infringed his right to personal liberty by allowing him to be detained for questioning. The Supreme Court ruled that this was not the case. It noted, however, that the accused retained all of the rights noted above such as the right to a lawyer, the right not to be interrogated oppressively and so on. It appears, then, that provided certain safeguards are maintained, a person can quite constitutionally be arrested for questioning under these Acts.

25.1.5 *Freedom from oppressive interrogation*

Even where the Gardaí are allowed to question a person, however, they cannot interrogate him or her in a manner that is oppressive. In particular, the Constitution prohibits the tactic of "exhausting" a confession out of accused persons by lengthy questioning without a break. In *People (D.P.P.) v. McNally* (1981), for instance, convictions based on confessions made after 40 continuous hours of questioning were quashed by reason of such oppression.

Any confession that is obtained from an accused, furthermore, must be voluntary. In particular, as Griffin J. pointed out in *People (D.P.P.) v. Shaw* (1982), a statement that is the product of physical or psychological pressures, threats or inducements, or that is made while intoxicated, drugged or hypnotised will be not be admitted into evidence in Court.

25.1.6 The right to bail

When a person has been accused of a crime, he or she may be "remanded in custody" to await trial. If one assumes, however, that a person accused but not convicted of an offence is presumed innocent until proven guilty, there is a strong argument that such a person, if possible, should remain free until found guilty by a court. There are of course, risks involved in freeing an accused person, not least the possibility that he or she may abscond before trial or seek to intimidate witnesses. For these reasons and others, a system of bail operates whereby an accused person may be released on condition that he or she return to the court on a specific date or dates to be tried. In order to induce such appearance, the accused (or a person acting on his behalf) might be asked to place a deposit of money which will be forfeited if the accused fails to turn up for trial.

The grounds upon which bail could be refused were, up until recently, quite narrow. The theory being that a person is innocent until proven guilty, it was not possible, before 1996, to refuse a person bail due to a fear (however well-founded) that the person would commit further offences while on bail. In both *People (A.G). v. O'Callaghan* (1966) and *Ryan v. D.P.P.* (1989), the Supreme Court stressed that a person could only be denied bail if there was a well-founded fear that the accused would be likely either:

- To abscond while on bail and not face trial; or

- To interfere with or intimidate witnesses to the alleged crime.

The opinion of some law-enforcement officials, however, was that some accused persons were allegedly using their time on bail to commit offences, sometimes to build up a "nest-egg" prior to their likely imprisonment. As a result of such fears, the Constitution was altered in 1996 by the Sixteenth Amendment to allow bail to be refused to a person charged with a serious offence "where it is reasonably considered necessary to prevent the commission of a serious offence by that person" (Article 40.4.7).

The new Bail Act 1997 thus expanded the range of circumstances in which bail could be refused to include the likelihood that offences might be committed while on bail. The Act applies only where a person is charged with a "serious offence". To be a "serious offence" the offence must be listed in the Schedule to the Act. The Schedule includes a series of different types of offence, including murder, manslaughter, rape, several types of sexual offence, wounding with intent, offences involving firearms, explosives or weapons, and certain grave road traffic offences. To constitute a serious offence, the offence must also be one "for which a person of full capacity and not previously convicted may be punished by a term of imprisonment for a term of at least five years".

In deciding whether to refuse bail, the court must consider several matters, including the degree of seriousness of the offence with which the accused is charged, the strength of the evidence against the accused and the likely sentence the accused might receive if found guilty. The court may also consider past convictions of the accused, including in particular any past convictions for offences committed while on bail. In addition, the fact that the accused is addicted to an illegal substance may be taken into account.

25.2 Detention for other reasons

The State does have certain rights to detain a person, other than for the purpose of charging him or her with an offence.

25.2.1 Preventative detention

A person cannot ordinarily be detained for "preventative" purposes, that is, with a view to preventing the commission of a crime not already committed. In *People (A.G.) v. O'Callaghan* (1966), the Supreme Court ruled out such detention (sometimes called "internment") except in emergency situations. That said, Part II of the Offence Against the State (Amendment) Act 1940 provides for internment without trial in certain limited cases. The Bill upon which this was based was found to be constitutional by the Supreme Court in an Article 26 reference, with the result that the Act can never be challenged again on the basis of its constitutionality. The Government may bring Part II into operation whenever it feels that this is necessary to secure the preservation of public peace and order. During its operation, any person conducting himself in a manner that is "prejudicial to the public peace and order or to the security of the State" may be detained without trial on the orders of a Government Minister.

25.2.2 Detention for a person's own welfare

A person may, it seems, be incarcerated for their own welfare, as, for instance, under the Mental Treatment Acts 1945-1961. These allow the reception into a mental institution of a person found to be mentally ill. A somewhat alarming aspect of this legislation concerns the ease with which a person may be detained. On the recommendation of a relative, a doctor may order the detention of that person against his will. The lack of any judicial safeguards in this process was unsuccessfully challenged in *Re Philip Clarke* (1950).

Normally such persons will be detained in specialised psychiatric institutions although the lack of adequate facilities has led the courts to take some rather drastic steps to secure the welfare of individuals. In *D.G. v. Eastern Health Board* (1998), a seriously disturbed young person, who had committed no crime, was placed in a penal institution for his own welfare. The Supreme Court endorsed this rather extreme step on the grounds that the State, to its shame, had no alternative secure facility. The young person's right to liberty had to give way to the very pressing need to seek secure and safe accommodation for this troubled youth.

25.2.3 Extradition

A person, resident in this State, having committed an offence in the jurisdiction of another State may be removed to that other State for trial. This process is called "extradition". The exact workings of an extradition depend on the particulars of the relevant extradition treaty although certain general points may be made:

- A person cannot be arrested for extradition without a valid warrant issued by the extraditing state.

- The Attorney General must have endorsed such warrant. He is obliged to refuse to do unless he believes that the foreign power intends to prosecute the extraditee for the offences listed in the warrant and that there is sufficient evidence for such a prosecution to proceed.

- A person cannot be extradited unless the alleged offence would, if committed in this State, also have been illegal. This is called the rule of "reciprocity".

- A person cannot be extradited for a politically motivated offence. The scope of this exemption has been considerably narrowed, however, since the enactment of the Extradition (Amendment) Act 1987.

- A person cannot be extradited on allegations of tax evasion.

- An extraditee has the right to contest the extradition warrant on the grounds either that the extradition or the proposed prosecution following extradition would infringe any of his constitutional rights.

25.2.4 Stop and search powers

The Gardaí may generally stop and interview drivers of motor vehicles with a view to stamping out drinking and driving. In *D.P.P. (Stratford) v. Fegan* (1994), a majority of the Supreme Court agreed that the Gardaí had the authority under common law to establish road blocks to catch motorists driving under the influence of alcohol. This is a common law right, but legislative provisions also grant stop and search powers in respect of vehicles and their occupants where the latter is suspected of having committed various crimes, including murder, manslaughter, burglary, malicious damage or various crimes involving firearms and explosives.

Specific legislative provisions, for instance, allow a person to be stopped and searched where a Garda reasonably suspects that that person is in possession of illegal drugs (Misuse of Drugs Act 1977). No warrant is required to do so. This power was found to be constitutional in *O'Callaghan v. Ireland* (1994), the Supreme Court ruling that such measures were necessary and proportionate in combating the social menace of illegal drugs. Persons may also be stopped and searched where a Garda suspects, on reasonable grounds, that a person has committed a crime under the Offences Against the State Act 1939.

25.2.5 Surveillance

The Gardaí may also keep a person under surveillance for the purposes of detecting or preventing the commission of a crime. Even very persistent surveillance, such as that experienced by the plaintiff in *Kane v. Governor of Mountjoy Prison* (1988) is permissible. The Gardaí, in that case, were awaiting extradition warrants in respect of the plaintiff. Pending their arrival, the Gardaí undertook to follow the plaintiff everywhere he went. The Supreme Court found that, under the circumstances, such obvious surveillance was justified, although at least one judge warned that absent a reasonable suspicion that an offence had been or was about to be committed, the Garda action would have been illegal.

26. FREEDOM OF EXPRESSION (ARTICLE 40.6.1.i)

The freedom to express one's opinion is a precious right, but one that is nonetheless fraught with dilemmas. The Constitution, while protecting the right of citizens "to express freely their convictions and opinions", is careful to qualify this right in several respects. In an ordered society, after all, not every type of speech can be privileged. Here again, a delicate balance must be struck between the benefits of free speech and the need to curtail the expression of opinions and ideas that are perceived to endanger the stability and wellbeing of society. Thus, the Constitution expressly permits (and in some cases mandates) restrictions on free speech, in particular those required to uphold public order and morality. The State, for instance, may validly censor material that is prejudicial to the security interests of the State or that it is likely to encourage violence.

It was once thought that freedom of expression was confined to the expression of opinions as opposed to the dissemination of facts, that is the right to give information or to communicate *per se*. These latter rights were, it was said, more properly treated as part of the category of "personal rights" protected by Art. 40.3. (See for instance, Costello J. in *Attorney General v. Paperlink* (1984)). In recent times, however, the courts have taken a more expansive view. In *Murphy v. Independent Radio and Television Commission* (1998), the Supreme Court acknowledged that freedom of expression embraces both the expression of opinions and the dissemination of information and facts in the broader sense. This approach reflects the reasoning of the Supreme Court in *Heaney v. Ireland* (1994). In that case, the Supreme Court extrapolated from the right to free expression a corresponding (implicit) right to silence where a person has been arrested or is being tried on criminal charges. It is difficult to see how this would be so unless one accepts that Article 40.6.1.i. covers facts as well as opinions. After all, it is not the opinions of the accused that the State is primarily concerned to discern in a criminal investigation but the facts of the alleged crime.

In the United States, the courts have taken this expansive approach one step further by ruling that the guarantee of free expression in the U.S. Constitution is wide enough to include actions and gestures as well as words. (The protection of "symbolic speech"). In several cases, for instance, the U.S. Supreme Court has upheld the right to burn the

U.S. flag as a sign of protest, arguing that this is an aspect of free expression protected by their Constitution. (Most recently in *U.S. v. Eichman* (1990)). As yet, the Irish courts have not considered this issue, although it is likely that considering the more limited nature of the right to free speech under the Irish Constitution, the courts might not be willing to follow the U.S. lead in this area.

26.0.1 Freedom of the press

In the *Irish Times v. Ireland* (1998), the Court expressly noted that Article 40.6.1.i guarantees what is broadly termed the "freedom of the press". To this end the Constitution explicitly refers to the "rightful liberty of expression" of the "organs of public opinion, such as the radio, the press, the cinema". Such liberty should not, of course, be used to endanger public order, morality or the authority of the State. In this regard, however, the Constitution is careful to distinguish between speech that undermines the authority of the State and the expression of opinions that are critical of government policy. The organs of media cannot be restrained simply because they criticise the actions and policies of the Government of the day. Indeed the Constitution seems expressly to recognise such a right to criticise government policy.

26.1 Restrictions on freedom of expression

Most of the commentary in this area, however, must inevitably focus on the various restrictions on free expression imposed by the common law and legislation. The Irish Constitutional safeguards for free speech are indeed largely characterised by the many restrictions and conditions that attend its exercise. Such restrictions can broadly be categorised under the following five headings:

- Public morality
- Public order
- The security of the State
- Respect for the court process
- Respect for individual rights

26.1.1 Public morality

The most obvious, although perhaps the vaguest restrictions, relate to the need to protect public morality. The Constitution explicitly deems

illegal "the publication or utterance of blasphemous, seditious or indecent matter" rendering each "punishable by law". The State, then, may
validly prohibit the publication and distribution of such material. Here
again a delicate balance must be struck between promoting free expression and the need to protect persons from offensive and degrading
material. Images of famine-ravaged peoples, for instance, may offend
and upset us: this is *precisely* their merit. The whole point of certain
types of expression is, after all, to provoke people into thinking by
offending and upsetting them, in order to encourage them to reconsider
preconceived notions of the world around them. It is worth noting that
under the U.S. Constitution material will not be regarded as obscene,
(and thus will continue to be deserving of constitutional protection),
unless it is shown to be "without serious literary, artistic, political or
scientific value" (*Miller v. California* (1973)).

(1) Indecency

In Ireland it is possible to restrict access to or ban outright certain publications and films on the grounds that they are considered indecent,
obscene or blasphemous. (Censorship of Publications Acts 1929-1967,
Censorship of Films Acts 1923-1992, and Video Recordings Act
1989). The question of what is obscene or indecent is not defined and
is regularly left to the determination of the various Censorship Boards,
which have often erred on the side of caution. The precise criteria differ depending on the relevant legislation. The Censorship of Films
Acts, for instance, requires that any motion picture shown in public
must first obtain a certificate that it is fit for public viewing from the
Official Censor of Films. (Although no certificate is required for a private viewing of a film.) The Censor is allowed to refuse such a certificate if the film or any part thereof "is unfit for public exhibition by
reason of its being indecent, obscene or blasphemous" or if its showing
"would tend to inculcate principles contrary to public morality" or otherwise undermine public morality.

The Video Recordings Act 1989 similarly requires that a permit be
obtained for the distribution to the public of video recordings. The criteria for refusing such a permit however, are subtly different from those
applying to films exhibited in public. A video may be restricted on
grounds of indecency or obscenity only if the relevant material would
tend "to deprave or corrupt persons who might view it" (1989 Act,
section 3(3)(a)(iii)). At first glance, this is a slightly more rigorous test
than that applied to films intended for public exhibition, although it is
worth noting that the 1989 Act expressly prohibits videos that depict

"acts of gross violence or cruelty (including mutilation and torture) towards humans and animals" (1989 Act, section 3(3)(b)).

In each case, of course, certificates may be granted subject to conditions. The best examples of these are the age-sensitive certificates that prohibit the viewing of a film by persons under a particular age (12, 15 and 18) or by children unless accompanied by their parents ("PG"). Films may also be approved subject to certain scenes being cut or otherwise altered.

Publications, such as books and magazines, differ from films and videos in that they ordinarily do not require State permission prior to their being sold in public. That said, a publication may be banned by the Censorship of Publications Board if it is found to be "indecent or obscene" (1946 Act, section 6). The Board, in making such a decision, is required to consider, amongst other things, the likely audience for the publication and whether the publication has any literary, artistic, scientific or historic merit or importance. If a ban is ultimately imposed, however, the Censorship of Publications Act 1967 limits its duration to twelve years, after which the ban expires.

(2) Control of information on abortion

Section 16 of the Censorship of Publication Act 1929 (as amended) generally prohibits the publication of information that "advocates" the "procurement of an abortion or miscarriage" or any method, treatment or appliance used for the purpose of procuring an abortion. As a result, however, of the Fourteenth Amendment to the Constitution (1992) and the Regulation of Information Act 1995, information that facilitates an abortion legally available abroad may now be legally given to a woman contemplating such a step, but only under certain conditions. In particular, where such information is offered, it must be accompanied by non-directive counselling outlining the alternatives to abortion.

(3) Blasphemy

The Constitution expressly refers to material that is "blasphemous" and explicitly states that such "blasphemy" is a crime punishable by law. Section 13 of the Defamation Act 1961, furthermore, prohibits (though it refrains from defining) the publication of a "blasphemous libel". Blasphemy broadly entails expression that is considered offensive to God or to religion. The Law Reform Commission reported that the protection afforded by this law, however, extends only to religions in the Jewish and Christian traditions (although it is hard to see how this is consistent with the prohibition on religious discrimination in Article 44). Beyond this, however, the definition of "blasphemy" is uncertain to say the least.

Indeed, in *Corway v. Independent Newspapers* (2000), the Supreme Court effectively ruled that, in the absence of specific legislative definition, it could not determine what blasphemy entailed. The net effect of this judgment seems to be that the crime of blasphemy cannot, without further legislative definition, be prosecuted in this State. The plaintiff in that case complained about a cartoon in a newspaper published in the wake of the 1995 divorce referendum. It depicted a caricature of a priest distributing Holy Communion, with the leaders of the then coalition government walking away in apparent rejection of the offer made by the priest. The caption over the cartoon "Hello Progress, 'Bye Bye' Father" was apparently designed to reflect the then Government's rejection of Roman Catholic teaching on divorce. The plaintiff alleged that the cartoon was calculated to show "contempt ... towards the sacrament of the Eucharist". As a result, he wanted the newspaper and its editor prosecuted for blasphemous libel. The Supreme Court, however, ruled that no such prosecution could ensue in the absence of a clear definition of blasphemy. The task of defining that crime, Barrington J. asserted, was one for the Legislature, not for the courts. Considering the vague and uncertain state of the law, the Court "could not see its way to authorising the institution of a criminal prosecution for blasphemy against the respondents".

26.1.2 Public order

(1) Inflammatory material

Under the common law, a person could be arrested for intentionally making comments in public that are likely to lead to a breach of the peace. A good example of such conduct is the old English case of *Wise v. Dunning* (1902). In that case, a Protestant preacher was successfully charged under local legislation of having conducted himself in a manner likely to cause a breach of the peace. The evidence showed that the defendant had made various speeches in the streets of Liverpool denouncing (by the use, in several cases, of the word "red-necks") Roman Catholics and their religion. His speeches were accompanied by offensive gestures made using a rosary beads and crucifix. This conduct led to riots between the preacher's supporters and local Roman Catholics. On appeal, the English Court of Appeal upheld the preacher's conviction.

The relevant common law provisions have largely been superseded by the Criminal Justice (Public Order) Act 1994. Various sections of that Act allow the State to curtail free speech with a view to preventing public disorder. Section 6 of the Act, for example, renders it an offence to use "any threatening, abusive or insulting words" in a public place with intent to cause a breach of the peace (or being reckless as to whether such a breach results). Section 7, moreover, makes it

> "an offence for any person in a public place to distribute or display any writing, sign or visible representation which is threatening, abusive, insulting or obscene with intent to provoke a breach of the peace or being reckless as to whether a breach of the peace may be occasioned".

These measures are largely designed to prevent incitement to violence. Similar measures, however, more generally prohibit public comment that is likely to incite persons to hatred against a particular group of persons. The Prohibition on Incitement to Hatred Act 1989 criminalises, amongst other things, the use of words or the publication of written material in public that is likely to stir up hatred against a group of persons on various grounds including the race, colour, religion, or sexual orientation of such persons.

(2) Incitement to commit a crime

It is an offence, at common law, to encourage other persons to break the law. This again is a restriction on free expression but one designed to protect the common good by preventing the encouragement of crime. It is worth noting that the Video Recordings Act 1989, (section 3(3)(a)(i)) expressly permits the banning of videos that "would be likely to cause persons to commit crimes". Such incitement might include for instance, advice on the best way to commit a crime and how to avoid detection for such crimes once committed.

26.1.3 Security of the State

(1) Sedition

Sedition involves the publication or utterance of words and gestures that tend to undermine the public order or authority of the State. Thus while it is not seditious to criticise the Government and suggest to voters that it be replaced, a suggestion that the Government be overthrown by armed and potentially violent rebellion would be. Thus, section 10 of the Offences Against the State Act 1939 (as amended) bans the publication of treasonable, seditious or "incriminating" documents. An

"incriminating" document is a document published by an illegal organisation.

(2) Official secrets

The Official Secrets Act 1963 prevents persons generally from revealing certain official information relating to the State. The general principle in the Act is contained in section 4, which precludes a person from
communicating any official information, unless he or she has been duly
authorised to do so. Section 9, in particular, prevents persons from
endangering the interests of the State by revealing certain information
regarding the internal operation of the Defence Forces or Gardaí. This
includes any information regarding the movement of troops, army ves-
sels and aircraft, strategies for the defence of the State, the use of
weapons and any other information the publication of which would be
prejudicial to the safety and preservation of the State.

   This culture of official secrecy, however, has been undermined considerably by the Freedom of Information Act 1997. This allows a person to access information in the possession of the State or any State-
run body and creates mechanisms for ensuring that such access will be
available. Nevertheless the Act does preclude access to various types of
sensitive material, including documents relating to the security of the
State and the prosecution of crime.

(3) Undermining the authority of the State

Section 31 of the Broadcasting Act 1960 allows a Minister to prevent
the broadcast of material which is considered likely to promote or
incite to crime or otherwise undermine the authority of the State. For
some time, for instance, members of the Sinn Féin party could not be
interviewed on certain sensitive political matters on national television
or radio, although this ban was lifted in 1995. In *State (Lynch) v.
Cooney* (1982), this ban was challenged on the grounds that it undermined the freedom of speech of the persons to whom it applied. The
Supreme Court ruled, however, that section 31 was simply reflecting
the mandate in Article 40.6.1.i to protect the order and authority of the
State. The State was, thus, not only entitled but obliged to prevent the
use of the airwaves by organisations which (as the Court saw it) sought
to overthrow the State by violence, to "replace law and order by force
and anarchy".

26.1.4 *Respect for the court process*

(1) Contempt of court

Persons are generally entitled to criticise the result of court decisions. Indeed this has been recognised by several judges as an aspect of the citizen's right to free expression. That said, certain comments may lead to prosecutions for contempt of court. It is illegal generally to make comments that "scandalise" the court, that is to suggest that a court has acted in some way inappropriately. Scandalisation, in short, involves bringing the court into disrepute, and thus lowering public confidence in the administration of justice. In *Kennedy and McCann* (1976), for example, a newspaper editor and journalist were charged with contempt of court. They had suggested that, in relation to a specific custody case, the court had been motivated more by the relative wealth and prestige of the family members than by the best interests of the child. This, the Supreme Court agreed, brought the administration of justice into disrepute and the editor and journalist were thus fined.

Similarly, in the *State (D.P.P.) v. Walsh (No. 3)* (1976), two persons were convicted of contempt and thus given suspended prison sentences. In a published interview, the persons involved had alleged that the Special Criminal Court, in trying and convicting persons accused of the murder of a garda, had been motivated by bias and had thus not afforded the accused persons a fair trial. This was, according to the Supreme Court a "wild and baseless" allegation that tended to bring judges into "public odium". As a result the convictions were upheld.

(2) Sub judice restrictions

Comments made in the course of legal proceedings may undermine the prospect that those proceedings will be fair and unbiased. As such, certain *"sub judice"* restrictions apply which prevent persons generally from commenting on the proceedings of a pending court case in a manner that may obstruct or otherwise influence the course of the proceedings. Of particular note, in this regard are statements that may undermine the possibility of a fair trial of an accused person, comments, for instance that suggest that a person is guilty before any conviction has been handed down. Where such comments are published, a trial may be suspended (or in rare cases actually cancelled) if a judge feels that the comments undermine a person's right to a fair trial The fact that a case is to be heard by a judge and not a jury, however, may render it less likely that such comments will prejudice the trial (*Attorney General v. Cooke* (1924)).

26.1.5 *Respect for individual rights*

Various restrictions on free speech are designed to protect individual rights, in particular the right to privacy and the right to one's good name, both of which rights are "personal rights" protected by the Constitution. The legislature, thus, has the unenviable task of creating provisions that achieve a workable balance between these competing interests.

Looking first at privacy, one may consider the Freedom of Information Act 1997. This Act gave members of the public the right to access official documents held by the State or by public bodies. Certain types of information, however, are exempted on privacy grounds. Section 26 for instance excludes information obtained in confidence. Section 28, furthermore, prohibits access to personal information concerning persons other than the applicant. In a similar vein the Data Protection Act 1988 prevents the dissemination of personal information stored in a computer or other information retrieval system, without the consent of the person to whom it relates.

The Constitution also specifically protects the right to one's good name (Article 40.3.2), a matter dealt with more explicitly by the law of defamation. A comment is "defamatory" if it cannot be shown to be true and it tends to bring the person of whom it was made into "public odium and contempt". Such comments are termed "libel" when recorded or put into print, and "slander" when delivered orally. Several defences are, however, open to the person accused of defamation, the most obvious being that of justification (that the comments were true). A person may also claim privilege on the grounds for instance that the comments were made in parliament (thus attracting parliamentary privilege) or in court.

In summary, the constitutional right to freedom of expression is subject to many limits and restrictions. While is has not yet been established that all of the restrictions are constitutionally permissible, the language and tone of Article 40.6.1.i tends to lean in favour of such restrictions.

27. FREEDOM OF ASSOCIATION

The right freely to associate is an enumerated constitutional right but one that gives rise, nonetheless, to some confusion. It is effectively best described as a freedom or privilege from state interference or restrictions on the formation of organisations and unions. The State, in short, cannot normally stop you from or, as a corollary, compel you to join an organisation or more generally associate with a particular person or persons.

27.1 Limits

27.1.1 This right is not, of course, unlimited

As we saw with freedom of expression, freedom of association is subject to public order and morality and as such, can be curtailed in certain circumstances. Here again one encounters the delicate balance between the need to protect individual liberties and the overall concern to protect society at large. Terrorist organisations, for instance, can be and regularly are outlawed. Such organisations may be declared illegal if their activities are considered prejudicial to the security and authority of the State. Membership of such illegal organisations, furthermore, is a crime punishable by up to seven years imprisonment. (See sections 18, 19 and 21, Offences against the State Act 1939 and section 2 of the Criminal Law Act 1976.)

In *Norris v. Attorney General* (1984), the plaintiff claimed that laws banning male homosexual sexual conduct inhibited his freedom to associate with whomsoever he wished. O'Higgins C.J. rejected this argument noting that "freedom of expression and freedom of association are not guaranteed as absolute rights" but were, rather, subject to restrictions in the interests of public order and morality. Even legitimate trade unions and associations face the prospect of "regulation and control" at the hands of the State.

27.1.2 Is there a right to join an association?

Article 40.6.1.iii is carefully worded such that though one may have a constitutional right to form an association, there is no constitutional right to *join* such an organisation. While the State, for example, cannot force you to join or preclude you from joining a union, the union itself is under no obligation to accept you as a member (subject to certain exceptions discussed below). In *Tierney v. Amalgamated Society of Woodworkers* (1957), the plaintiff, a carpenter, was refused membership of the defendant organisation on the grounds that he was under-qualified. The High Court rejected his contention that this infringed his constitutional rights. As a voluntary organisation the defendant was under no obligation to accept his application for membership. While the State could not prevent him from joining the union, the union was perfectly within its rights to refuse him membership.

In *Murphy v Stewart* (1977), the plaintiff wanted to change union membership. The rules of the Irish Congress of Trade Unions, however, precluded his joining a new union without the consent of his old union. The court found that this was constitutionally acceptable — neither union being obliged to accept him as a member, there could be no objection to internal union rules that prevented persons from transferring from one union to another without obtaining certain consents.

Take two individuals A and B. While the State ordinarily can neither force this pair to associate nor preclude them from doing so, A and B are entirely free to decide whether or not to do so. They may decide to associate, but there is nothing stopping A from refusing to associate with B.

There are, however, some notable exceptions:

(1) Equality legislation

While an association may generally choose with whom it associates or interacts, equality legislation precludes various organisations from refusing to transact for certain reasons. The Employment Equality Act 1998 (section 13) specifically bans trade unions and other voluntary organisations from discriminating in matters of membership on the grounds of race, gender, religion, national or ethnic origin, sexual orientation, marital status, (whether you are married, single, separated or divorced), parental status, (whether you are a parent), membership of the travelling community or disability, colour or age.

(2) Abuse of a monopoly position

In *Murphy v. Stewart* (1973), Walsh J. suggested a possible restriction on a trade union's right to refuse a person membership of that union. While the issue did not arise in that case, his Honour noted that where the right to work in a particular place or sector was reserved to members of one union alone, an unjustifiable refusal might constitute a breach of the constitutional right to earn a livelihood. In such a case, the union might be forced to accept the applicant as a member in order to vindicate his or her right to work.

27.2 Right to dissociate

The right to associate implies, as a necessary corollary, the right not to associate, in other words the freedom from being forced by the State to join an organisation. In *Meskell v. CIÉ* (1973), the employer, a semi-state body, had sacked all its workers but agreed to re-employ them, provided that they joined one of four prescribed unions. This was held to constitute an unconstitutional breach of right to dissociate, a breach for which the defendant was held liable to pay damages.

Some unions seek to create a "closed shop" in certain places of employment, where all workers are required to be members of (sometimes specified) unions. Several of the cases in this area derive from situations in which unions have striked and/or picketed with a view to forcing employers to employ only union members. Trade Union Legislation generally grants immunity from suit where strike action or picketing occurs in furtherance of a "lawful" trade dispute. The union cannot, thus, be sued for losses incurred through industrial action (*e.g.* loss of revenue, breach of employment contracts, inducement to breach commercial contracts, etc.). The State cannot, however, grant immunity where a union attempts to deny persons their constitutional right not to be a member of the union. To do so would be to endorse the breach of a constitutional right.

In the *Educational Co. v. Fitzpatrick (No. 2)* (1961), union members were picketing with a view to forcing the plaintiff company to employ only union staff. This picket was held to be illegal on the ground that it sought to infringe the constitutional right of employees to dissociate from these unions. The picketing of a pub in *Murtagh Properties v. Cleary (1972)* was declared illegal on similar grounds. The defendants had objected to the employment of non-union barmaids at the plaintiff's pub, a situation that, ironically, had arisen from the union's own refusal to allow women to join its ranks. The picket was declared illegal on the ground that the union by its actions was attempting to undermine the right of the pub employees to dissociate from it.

These cases are interesting in that constitutional duties tend normally to be placed only on the State and not on private individuals.

Murtagh and especially the *Educational Co.* seem to suggest, by contrast, that private individuals and organisations can be subject to constitutional duties. Indeed in the *Educational Co.,* Budd J. went so far as to
indicate that employers had a "positive duty not to interfere with their
employees' constitutional rights". In *Cotter v. Ahern* (1976-7), the
management of a school was found liable for having conspired to
coerce the plaintiff into abandoning his constitutional right to dissociate. The plaintiff had been appointed principal to a school. A teacher's
union, the I.N.T.O., objected to this appointment on the grounds that
the plaintiff was no longer a member of that union and thus persuaded
the school manager to sack him. The plaintiff was awarded damages
against both the union and the school on the grounds that these parties
had, by their actions, infringed the plaintiff's right not to be forced to
be a member of a particular organisation.

27.3 Trade union recognition

Notwithstanding the freedom of association, no individual employer is
obliged to recognise a union for the purposes of employer-employee
negotiations. There is no obligation on an employer to "recognise" or
alternatively negotiate with a union. Even where a workplace is union-
ised, employers may be anxious to discourage a proliferation of unions
and may thus negotiate only with certain unions and not others. An
employer is constitutionally entitled to do so and may not be forced to
enter into negotiations with any particular union. See *Abbott and Whelan v. IT & GWU and Southern Health Board* (1980), *Dublin Colleges
Academic Staff Association v. CDVEC* (1981), and *Association of General Practitioners v. Minister for Health* (1995).

28. THE FAMILY AND EDUCATION (ARTICLES 41-42)

Articles 41 and 42 are relatively unique aspects of Ireland's Constitution. They reflect the prominence of marriage and the family in Irish social, cultural and religious life and are heavily influenced by the tenets of Roman Catholic theology. The Constitution sees the family as the "natural primary and fundamental unit group of Society", a "moral institution that possesses inalienable and imprescriptible rights". Indeed, Article 41.4.2 goes so far as to suggest that the family is "the necessary basis of social order, ... indispensable to the welfare of the Nation and the State".

While Article 41 recognises in general the special position of the family, Article 42 acknowledges the privileges and rights of the family specifically in relation to the education of children. The cardinal principle here is that, subject to certain conditions, parents are recognised as having the primary responsibility and right to make decisions regarding the education of their children.

28.1 The "Constitutional Family" is the family based on marriage

Yet not every family grouping can enjoy the protections laid out in these Articles. The family that is envisaged by the Constitution is exclusively that based on marriage. Attempts to establish that these provisions protect non-marital family units have largely failed. In the *State (Nicolaou) v. An Bord Uchtála* (1966), the Supreme Court ruled that a father who was not married to the mother of his child could not invoke the provisions of Article 41. This was because the provisions of Articles 41 and 42 were restricted to marital families only. Even as late as 1996 the Supreme Court reaffirmed that families not based on marriage enjoy no protection under these Articles (*K. v. W.* (1990), *W.O'R. v. E.H.* (1996)).

This limitation has been the subject of much criticism. In a state where over one-third of children are born outside marriage, it is unrealistic, to say the least, to suggest that marriage is the only basis on which a family may be formed. Some argue that the Constitution should look to the substance of the relationships involved rather than the form that they take. Others argue that marriage is a valuable institution promoting certainty and stability, and that the Constitution is justified in seeking to give preferential treatment to marital families in order to promote what it sees as a valuable institution. Be that as it may, one cannot deny the proliferation of less orthodox forms of family in the latter half of the twentieth century. The reality is that many couples, heterosexual and homosexual, with or without children, live together outside marriage, and that a significant portion of Irish households, moreover, consist of single-parent families. The Irish Constitution cannot continue to deny these modern realities.

Some limited diversity is, however, allowed. A married couple without children, for instance, enjoys rights under Article 41 notwithstanding the absence of children. In *Murray v. Ireland* (1985 and 1990), both the High Court and the Supreme Court acknowledged that a married couple without children had the right to beget children (although considering the facts of that case, they held that it was a limited right that could be curtailed if the common good so required).

28.2 Individual rights and family rights

The rights that are enjoyed by the family are collective rather than individual rights. In other words, the rights of the family are to be enjoyed by the family as a unit. (See the comments of Costello J. in *Murray v. Ireland* (1985).) The individual rights of family members, on the other hand, are said to be personal rights protected under Article 40.3 rather than Article 41. That is not to say, however, that an individual member of a family cannot invoke Article 41, simply that those rights can only be pleaded for the benefit of the family as a whole rather than any individual member thereof.

That said, in *D.P.P. v. J.T.* (1988), the Court of Criminal Appeal suggested that the sexual abuse of a mentally disabled woman by her father also constituted a breach of the family's rights under Article 41. The logic appears to be that to injure one member of the family in that manner, undermined the family as a unit.

28.3 Family right to autonomy

The family based on marriage enjoys certain privileges that prevent the State from interfering in its activities. In *McGee v. Attorney General* (1974), for instance, the Supreme Court held that the State could not prevent a married woman and her husband from deciding for themselves how many children they would have. To this end, a prohibition on the importation or sale of artificial contraception was struck down as infringing the right of married couples to determine the size of their families by whatever means they considered preferable. The Constitutional family, in other words, is free to make decisions as regards the number of children that it will have. That said, Walsh J. was careful to note that this freedom was not unlimited. A family could not, he warned, limit its size by resorting to abortion as a means of birth control.

Family autonomy was also at issue in *Murray v. Ireland* (1985), although again the courts noted that it was subject to certain limitations. In that case, both the High Court and the Supreme Court acknowledged that a husband and wife could not generally be prevented from bearing as many children as they wished. The plaintiffs in that case were a childless married couple, both of whom were serving prison sentences for the murder of a garda. By the time they would have been due for release, the couple argued, they would have been too old to bear children. Thus they asserted that the prison authorities were obliged to provide facilities so that they could start a family. The courts agreed that a married couple ordinarily had an unfettered right to bear children. In the circumstances of this case, however, both the High Court and Supreme Court ruled that the State was justified in curtailing this right with a view to maintaining prison security.

The autonomy of the family unit was a prominent feature in the Article 26 reference of the *Matrimonial Home Bill 1993* (1994). That Bill purported to change the law so that every family home, regardless of the arrangements that families themselves had made, would be deemed to be jointly owned by both spouses. According to the Supreme Court, this threatened to undermine the authority of the family to make decisions regarding the ownership of family property. Families which had made decisions regarding the disposition of family property were entitled to remain free of state interference in such decisions.

28.3.1 Even family rights can be curtailed

It is difficult then, but by no means impossible to interfere in the workings of a family unit. In *Murray v. Ireland* (1985), Costello J. observed that notwithstanding the very strong language in Article 41, the rights of the family were not absolute and could be curtailed with a view to upholding the common good. This was despite the fact that those rights are described in Article 41 as being "inalienable" (cannot be given away) and "imprescriptible" (cannot be taken away or lost) and deemed, furthermore, to be "antecedent and superior to positive law". In the *Matrimonial Home Bill* reference the Supreme Court noted that the State is entitled lawfully to impose certain rules on the family, provided such intervention is shown to be reasonable and proportionate, that is, no more than is necessary to achieve certain legitimate purposes.

28.4 The constitutional preference for marriage

Article 41.3.1 expresses what might best be described as a constitutional preference for marriage. That sub-clause pledges the State to safeguard the institution of marriage (on which, it claims, the "Family is founded") and to guard it against unjust attack. One of the unfortunate consequences of this measure is that it grants constitutional permission to discriminate against unmarried couples and the children of such unions. In *O'B. v. S.* (1984), for instance, the Supreme Court held that a child born outside wedlock could be treated less favourably than a child born to married parents. In that case, the father of the plaintiff, who was not married to the mother of the plaintiff, had died without making a will. The Succession Act 1965 at that time allowed only children born within wedlock to succeed to their parents in such circumstances. The Court held that while such treatment was clearly discriminatory it was justified by the preference for marriage expressed in Article 41. It is worth noting, however, that such unequal treatment of children is no longer permitted by law, the Status of Children Act 1987 having outlawed discrimination against non-marital children. (See also the Employment Equality Act 1998 and the Equal Status Act 2000).

By the same reasoning, measures that threaten to undermine the status of marriage will generally be deemed unconstitutional. In *Murphy v. Attorney General* (1982), the plaintiffs, a married couple, challenged certain provisions of the income tax code on the ground that they penalised married persons. In short, the relevant legislation gave rise to the possibility that two persons married to each other, both of whom were working outside the home, would pay more tax than a similarly placed unmarried couple. The Supreme Court ruled that this amounted to an attack on the special position of marriage. It was not necessary, it noted, to establish that these measures discouraged people from marrying. It was enough to show simply that the measures unduly penalised persons on the grounds that they were married.

A similar result was reached in *Greene v. Minister for Agriculture* (1990). That case concerned certain rules for determining the eligibility of farmers for EU farm incomes support. In order to determine whether farmers were eligible, a means test was put forward. For this purpose, however, farmers' incomes were aggregated with the incomes of their spouses. Where a farmer, however, was not married to but cohabiting with a person no such aggregation occurred. This can be better explained by a hypothetical example. Ms. Farmer earns £10,000 net per annum from her farm. She is dating Mr. Teacher who earns £15,000 a year. If the threshold for farm aid is £12,000, Ms. Farmer would be eligible for farm aid only if she remained unmarried. If she married Mr. Teacher his income, combined with hers, would have made her ineligible for income support. Again, the Court found that this amounted to an unjust attack on the institution of marriage.

It is possible, however, to treat single parents preferentially in certain circumstances. In *MhicMhathúna v. Ireland* (1995), the plaintiffs, a married couple, complained that the provision of a special social welfare allowance to lone parents was an attack on the status of marriage. The Supreme Court rejected this proposition. The allowance it said, simply recognised the significantly more difficult plight of the single parent (who may well be married but separated) when compared with that of a couple with children. The State was perfectly justified, it concluded, in giving additional support to a single parent for the benefit of the child.

28.5 The rights of unmarried parents and their children

Nowadays, almost one-third of children are born outside marriage. In the face of such statistics, the State's continued reluctance to recognise non-marital unions seems, to say the least, rather short-sighted. Nevertheless, in the *State (Nicolaou) v. An Bord Úchtala* (1966), the Supreme Court affirmed that Article 41 can only be invoked on behalf of the marital family. This is not to say, however, that persons in non-marital family units have no constitutional rights. *In Re M., an infant* (1946), Gavan Duffy J., ruled that a non-marital child, enjoyed (as part of his or her personal rights under Article 40.3) rights similar to those enjoyed by a marital child under Article 42. These included the right to the care and custody of his mother, and the right to an adequate education and upbringing.

In *G. v. An Bord Uchtála* (1980), the Supreme Court finally laid to rest any doubts that the mother of such a child independently enjoyed a right to care for and have custody of her child. These again were acknowledged as part of the personal rights protected by Article 40.3.2. In the *Nicolaou* case, however, the Supreme Court rejected the proposition that an unmarried *father* had similar constitutional rights. Indeed, the Courts have consistently ruled (see *K. v. W.,* (1991), *W.O'R. v. E.H.* (1996)), that whatever rights an unmarried father may have at common law or in legislation, he does not have any *constitutional* right to the care and custody of his child. This rather patent gender discrimination, the courts have said, is justified by the "different nature" of the relationship between the mother and the child and the father and the child. While it is inescapably true that the mother, by virtue of her pregnancy, has a closer biological and thus emotional link to her child, it seems unfair in the extreme to say that this means that the unmarried father has *no* constitutional rights at all in respect of his child. It is especially unfair considering that a married father has full constitutional rights equal to those of the mother in respect of their marital children.

28.6 The guardianship, custody and adoption of children

Where a child is born to married parents, both of those parents are deemed to be joint guardians of the child. The mother and father, where married, enjoy equal rights in respect of the upbringing of a child (*Re Tilson* (1951)). By contrast, in the case of a child born to unmarried parents, the law generally regards its mother as the primary care-giver. Although an unmarried father can be made a guardian of his child, (under, for instance, Section 6A of the Guardianship of Infants Act 1964), only the mother of the child enjoys *automatic* guardianship rights.

In making an order relating to the care and upbringing of a child, the general rule is that the court should act primarily by reference to the best interests of the child. The child's welfare, in other words, is the predominant issue for the court. The Constitution however places significant limitations on the extent to which these interests can be promoted. In particular, the constitutional preference for the married family means that it must be assumed, unless there is strong evidence to the contrary, that a child's best interests lie with its remaining with its constitutional family.

28.6.1 Adoption

As a general rule a child born within marriage cannot be adopted unless its parents have completely abandoned their parental rights and duties in respect of the child. This is because Article 42 describes the rights and duties of married parents as "inalienable". These rights and duties in other words cannot be waived. The Adoption Act 1988, however, allows for the adoption of marital children in extreme circumstances, basically only where their parents have failed comprehensively in their duties toward the child and where such failure is likely to last until at least the child's eighteenth birthday. Such failure must amount, in short, to an abandonment of all parental rights in respect of the child.

A child of unmarried parents, by contrast, can more easily be adopted, but only where the mother of that child gives a full, free and informed consent to such adoption (*G. v. An Bord Uchtála* (1980)). Such consent will be lacking where, for instance, a mother is not fully informed of the consequences of placement and of adoption, and of any rights she may have pending an adoption (*M. v. An Bord Uchtála* (1977)). Recently enacted legislation has also allowed an unmarried father to be heard in relation to a proposed adoption, although, unless that father has been appointed a guardian of the child, he has no outright veto in respect of the adoption. (Adoption Act 1998).

28.6.2 Custody

In *Re J.H.; K.C. v. An Bord Uchtála* (1985), a child had been placed with potential adoptive parents for some time. After that placement had commenced, however, the child's natural parents married and applied to have the child returned to them. Where a child's parents marry after its birth the adoption can only proceed if the child has not been re-registered and if the father consents to the adoption. In this case the adoption could not proceed because of the father's refusal to consent thereto.

The question then arose as to who would have custody of the child, its natural parents, or the persons with whom the child had been placed. While the Courts had the power to leave the child in the custody of the latter, the Supreme Court ruled that the best interests of the child generally lay with its being part of its original constitutional family. The Constitution, in other words, required that the courts assume that a child's welfare was best served by its being in the custody of its marital parents. This was a presumption that could only be displaced in exceptional cases or for compelling reasons to the effect that the child's best interests required that it be taken from its constitutional family. Thus despite a near three year absence from them, the child was returned to its natural parents. The prospect of significant psychological harm ensuing seems to have been largely glossed over in favour of an ideologically driven preference for the child's marital family.

28.7 Divorce

Prior to 1995, Article 41.3.2 of the Constitution expressly prohibited the Legislature from creating legislation allowing a marriage to be dissolved. This ban remained in place until the passing of the Fifteenth Amendment to the Constitution Act 1995, which now allows for divorce but only in very limited circumstances. A divorce may be granted by a court designated by law only if at least the following three conditions can be satisfied:

- The spouses, at the date of the institutions of the proceedings, must have been "living apart" for at least four of the previous five years.

- The Court must be satisfied that there is no reasonable prospect of reconciliation between the spouses.

- The Court must be satisfied that reasonable provision has been made for both spouses and any children of either spouse.

Article 41.3.2 as amended allows, furthermore, for the addition in legislation of further conditions precedent to the granting of a divorce. The procedures for the granting of a divorce are now laid out in the Family Law (Divorce) Act 1996. That said, the first divorce in the history of the State was granted not under that Act (which was not, at the time, in force) but under the provisions of the Constitution itself. In *R.C. v. C.C.* (1997) the High Court ruled that Article 41.3.2 itself gave the High Court the full jurisdiction to grant a divorce, provided that the relevant conditions had been met.

28.8 Education

Article 42 of the Constitution concerns the education of members of the family. In this context, however, as in Article 41, the family is confined to that based on marriage. As such the rights and responsibilities vested in parents by this Article can be invoked only in respect of a marital family.

"Education" for these purposes, includes the "religious and moral, intellectual, physical and social" education of children. Despite this rather broad sweep of objectives, however, the courts have ruled that the term "education" as used in this Article is confined in meaning to the formal instruction that one would normally receive in a school. *In Ryan v. Attorney General* (1965), the plaintiff had argued that the term "education" in this context included everything that was connected to the overall "upbringing" of children. Kenny J. disagreed. Noting that Article 42 expressly referred to education in schools, he concluded that the meaning of the term education in this context was confined to the formal or "scholastic" aspects of education and did not extend to the practical process of rearing a child. In *Landers v. Attorney General* (1975), the High Court reaffirmed this formal view, noting that a child's singing performances in public houses did not form part of his "education" for the purposes of Article 42. In *Sinnott v. Minister for Education* (2001), however, the High Court took a somewhat broader view. It ruled that education did include instruction for a disabled person with a view to his carrying out elementary tasks, such as dressing himself or eating.

28.8.1 Educational freedom of choice

Article 42 effectively gives the family freedom of choice in respect of the education of family members. In Article 42.1 the parents of a child are acknowledged as the "primary and natural educator of the child". The parents of that child, furthermore, are recognised as possessing "an inalienable right and duty to provide ..." that education. As a result, the extent to which the State can force parents to educate their children in a particular manner is strictly limited. Parents, for instance, have full freedom in respect of the venue for such education. They are, according to Article 42.2 "free to provide this education in their homes or in private schools, or in schools recognised or established by the State". The State cannot, as Article 42.3 makes clear, force parents to send their children to a particular school or type of school against the parents' will. Article 44.2.4 is also worth noting in this context. This allows every child attending a publicly funded school the right to refrain from attending religious instruction at that school. Presumably this is a right to be exercised on the child's behalf by its parents, the religious upbringing of a child being the responsibility of its parents.

28.8.2   The State may set minimum standards for education

That said, the State is obliged to ensure that whatever education children do receive meets certain minimum standards. Article 42.3.2 requires the State to see that children receive a certain minimum education, "moral, intellectual and social". Thus, even though the State cannot stop a parent from educating his child at home, it *can* require that the child be taught certain basic skills such as reading, writing and arithmetic. Failure to provide "suitable elementary education" may lead to a prosecution of parents, as in *D.P.P. v. Best* (1999).

In the Article 26 reference of the *School Attendance Bill 1942* (1943), the Supreme Court had to consider the constitutionality of section 4 of that Act. This allowed the Minister for Education to certify that the education being received by all children (and the manner in which it was being delivered) was "suitable". The Supreme Court considered however that the provision was unconstitutional on three grounds.

- The first was that the section gave the Minister the power potentially to impose a standard higher than the "minimum" standard mandated by the Constitution. The State was only entitled to ensure that children received a "minimum standard of elementary education of general application" and by allowing the Minister to go further, the legislation was in breach of Article 42.

- The second point the Court made was that the standards imposed "might vary from child to child" and not thus be of "general application". The standards imposed by the State had to be equally applied to all children.

- The third point was that the legislation in question allowed the Minister to monitor not only the standard of education received but also the manner in which it was being administered. The Court felt that the Constitution only allowed the State to ensure that the child was receiving a certain "minimum education". It did not, it considered, allow the State to inquire into the manner in which that education was being delivered.

28.8.3   The right to free primary education

The State is obliged by Article 42.4 "to provide for free primary education". The use of language here is quite subtle. Article 42 does not require the State to provide such education itself but to *make provision for* such education, in short, broadly to support the provision of primary education and specifically to fund its delivery. As Kenny J. noted in *Crowley v. Ireland* (1980), the State itself "... is under no obligation to educate". The point behind this Article is largely that the State should support the delivery of primary education by others, mainly the local communities involved usually under the auspices of their Churches. Effectively then the State is required "to provide the buildings, to pay the teachers...to provide the means of transport to the schools if this is necessary to avoid hardship, and to prescribe minimum standards".

The State is not obliged however, to cater to parental choice at any cost. *In O'Shiel v. Minister for Education* (1999), Laffoy J. refused to accept that the State was obliged to fund a school which had failed to meet certain minimum standards as regards the qualifications of teachers and the teaching of Irish. The State was entitled, in other words, to make its funding conditional upon certain standards being met. Laffoy J. did observe, however, that the State could not fund only schools with a denominational ethos and might be required, in appropriate cases, to fund the provision of an alternative non-denominational education with a view to facilitating a maximum of parental choice.

28.8.4 People with disabilities

While disabled children do have a constitutional right to free primary education, disabled adults do not. The constitutional right to free primary education does not extend, according to the Supreme Court to persons who require elementary education beyond their eighteenth birthday. In *Sinnott v. Minister for Education* (2000), the High Court ruled that the State was obliged by the Constitution to provide for continuing primary level education in respect of a severely autistic adult for so long as it was to his benefit. Indeed, in an earlier case it was established that the State was generally obliged to provide for the special educational needs of persons with disabilities (*Comerford v. Minister for Education* (1997)).

On appeal however, the Supreme Court in *Sinnott v. Minister for Education* (2001) ruled that the right to free primary education could only be enjoyed by children, being persons under the age of eighteen. Thus a mentally disabled adult could not rely on the State, as a matter of Constitutional Law at least, for a continuing primary education. This most unadventurous and restrictive approach to the rights of the disabled could so easily have been different. It would not have been impossible for the court to rule that a person with a serious mental disability may, with respect, be treated as the functional equivalent of a child. After all that person may remain largely dependent on his parents well beyond the age of majority. Arguably the State has an especially strong duty to support the family when that family faces the challenge of a family member with a disability. That the Supreme Court in *Sinnott* did not appear to agree is unfortunate in the extreme.

Further reading: Shannon, (ed.) *Family Law Practitioner*, (Dublin, Round Hall, 2000).

29. PROPERTY RIGHTS (ARTICLE 43)

Article 43 of the Constitution concerns the right to own private property. As such, it touches upon a matter of some considerable political and social controversy. The key dilemma in this regard concerns the extent to which the State can interfere with and regulate the actions of property owners in respect of their property. Can the State prevent a landowner from building a particularly ugly house on his own land in an area of great natural beauty? Should the State be entitled compulsorily to purchase a small farmer's only field for the building of a motorway? Questions such as these frequently arise in this context and demand a delicate balance of interests by the State. While the primary responsibility for striking this balance lies with the Legislature, the courts have on occasion stepped in to ensure that the State does not unfairly interfere either with the general right to property or the property rights of specific individuals.

29.1 The scope of Article 43

Article 43 is largely crafted by reference to Roman Catholic teaching on the ownership of property. A key feature of this teaching involves the natural right to own property. Indeed Article 43.1 acknowledges that the human person (the English text uses the term "man" but the Irish text refers to the gender neutral "duine") has "a natural right", "in virtue of his rational being", "to the private ownership of external goods". This right is "antecedent to positive law", in other words, it is a right that does not depend for its effectiveness on man-made laws. The net effect of this is that the State is required generally to recognise the right to own private property. Thus, as Article 43.1.2 explicitly states, the State may "pass no law attempting to abolish the right of private ownership". Furthermore the State is prevented from abolishing the general right to transfer property, or to bequeath it by will. The right to inherit property on the death of another is also clearly protected.

In this regard however, it is important to distinguish between the *general* right to own and transfer property and the *personal* rights of an individual in respect of certain specific property. The latter is protected not by Article 43 (which concerns the general right of all to deal with property) but rather by Article 40.3 under which the State guarantees to protect personal property rights. O'Higgins C.J. explained this distinction in *Blake v. Attorney General* (1982), noting that Article 43 is directed generally to the State's overall attitude to property. Article 43, he observed "… prohibits the abolition of private property as an institution" whereas Article 40.3 concerns "the citizen's right to a particular item of property".

In short, if the State were to attempt to abolish entirely the right to own property, by, for instance, establishing a Marxist state in which the means of production would belong to the public as a group, a breach of Article 43 would clearly have occurred. If, on the other hand, the State wished to deprive a *particular* person of his rights in respect of a specified farm or house, this would more properly concern the personal right to own property, a right guaranteed by Article 40.3.

29.1.1 The limits on the exercise of property rights

Neither guarantee, however, gives a property owner an absolute right to deal with his property without any state regulation. The State is entitled to limit the full exercise of property rights with a view to "reconciling their exercise with the exigencies of the common good". In other words, a person's use of property may be restricted where it is deemed necessary to do so for some higher social purpose. Article 43.2 observes that the exercise of property rights in civil society ought "to be regulated by the principles of social justice". In consequence, the State is permitted to "delimit by law the exercise of such rights" where it considers it necessary for the common good (*i.e.* the good of all) to do so. The State, for instance, may compulsorily purchase land for certain public projects (such as the building of a road) or prevent the construction of certain buildings in areas of great natural beauty. The purpose of such measures being to vindicate the interests of the public at large, the Constitution would permit such regulation.

29.1.2 The meaning of "property"

Property may be "real" or "personal". "Real property" essentially means land and all that is connected thereto. Personal property, on the other hand, includes moveable goods and other items of value not attached to land. The term "property" in Article 43 clearly includes real property such as land and all interests in land but is not confined to such property. In fact, the term has been interpreted quite widely as the following examples show. Tangible items, goods such as the vehicle that was the subject of *Attorney General v. Southern Industrial Trust*

(1960), clearly constitute property for these purposes. Money in a bank account may also be the subject of a property right (*Buckley v. Attorney General* (1950)). Even what are strictly intangible rights such as rights under an employment contract (*Cox v. Ireland* (1992)) or a taxi licence (*Hempenstall v. Minister for Environment* (1994)), have been regarded as "property" for this purpose. In *Lovett v. Minister for Education* (1997), furthermore, Kelly J. ruled that measures that deprived a teacher of his pension rights infringed the latter's property rights. It seems that even the right to take a case (a cause of action) may amount to a property right, although this point is not yet settled.

29.2 Rent restrictions and property rights

In *Blake v. Attorney General* (1982) certain rent control provisions were struck down as constituting an unjust attack on the personal property rights of the plaintiff, a landlord of rent controlled property. The legislation challenged in this case, the Rent Restriction Acts 1960 and 1967, had two broad purposes — to restrict the level of rent collected from tenants of certain properties and to protect those tenants and their families from eviction. The result was that the plaintiff could not without State permission raise rents beyond the level they had reached in 1966. This, the Supreme Court concluded, constituted an unjust attack on the property rights of the landlord of such premises. Rents having been "permanently frozen", landlords were effectively deprived of a reasonable income from these rent controlled premises. This injustice was compounded by the fact that the Acts applied only to properties built before 1941, excluding local authority houses. The exclusion of the latter and of houses built after 1941, the Court felt, was arbitrary and unjust and thus added to the injustice suffered by the plaintiff.

The Oireachtas' subsequent attempt to repair the injustice of the Acts met a similar fate. In the Article 26 reference of the *Housing (Private Rented Dwellings) Bill 1981* (1983), the Supreme Court ruled that the rent restriction provisions contained in that Bill were also unconstitutional. That Bill purported to phase out rent control of certain properties over five years. During that period, however, landlords were to receive substantially less than the market value of the rent, a factor that led the Court to conclude, once again, that the property rights of landlords had been unjustly attacked.

In both cases, however, the Court was careful not to damn entirely the principle of rent control. Indeed, it is arguable, in principle, that setting limits upon the rent that may be collected in respect of a particular property is justified by the need to protect tenants from exploitation. The net point that the Supreme Court was making, however, was that in so acting the State could not place undue and unreasonable burdens upon landlords alone.

There can be no doubt that the State is entitled to collect taxes and rates from its citizens. The method of assessing and collecting such revenue, should, however, be reasonable and not arbitrary or irrational. In *Brennan v. Attorney General* (1984), Barrington J., in the High Court, struck down the collection of rates based on valuations of farm-land that were, in some cases, over one hundred years old. The evidence showed that the valuations did not thus reflect the true modern value of the land to which it applied. In several cases, poor farmland was subjected to rates far in excess of those applied to more valuable land. The system of valuation, furthermore, was found to have varied widely from area to area with little internal consistency being in evidence. Under the circumstances, it was no surprise that this clearly irrational, arbitrary and unfair rating system was deemed "an unjust attack" on the property rights of the farmers involved.

Certain restrictions on property rights have been held to amount to an unjust attack on the grounds that they are disproportionate. A measure is disproportionate where it does more than is necessary to achieve a particular objective, or where it is unduly harsh having regard to the seriousness of a particular situation. In *Cox v. Ireland* (1992), for instance, a teacher convicted of offences under the Offences Against the State Act 1939 was prevented from working for the State for seven years. This, the Court felt, infringed the plaintiff's property rights in his contract of employment with a state-owned school in a manner that was not justified by the seriousness of his offence. This lack of proportionality, thus, constituted an unjust attack on his property rights. Similar provisions were struck down in *Lovett v. Minister for Education* (1997). In that case a teacher convicted of an offence attracting a prison sentence was deemed as a result to have forfeited his pension rights. Although Kelly J. did not expressly rule that the measure was disproportionate, he did find that the provisions were so arbitrary that they amounted to an unjust attack on the teacher's property right in that pension.

29.3 Arbitrarily selective impositions on property rights

The State cannot, without good reason, single out one segment of society, in placing restrictions on the exercise of property rights. In the

Article 26 references of the *Employment Equality Bill 1996* (1997), and *the Equal Status Bill 1997* (1997), the Supreme Court had to consider the legality of provisions that placed on employers and businesspersons, respectively, the obligation to equip their premises for people with disabilities. The Supreme Court, while not denying that this was a worthy aim, ruled that it was unfair to cast the burden of providing for people with disabilities on one segment of society alone. There was no good reason why such persons should be singled out in this manner, the obligation to provide for persons with disabilities being a general duty of society as a whole. This approach was not taken however in another Article 26 reference, that of *Part V of the Planning and Development Bill 1999* (2001). In that case the Supreme Court ruled that provisions requiring builders to set aside up to 20 per cent of their land for the development of affordable housing was constitutional, a judgment that seems to signal a departure from earlier authority.

29.4 The right to compensation

Where property is taken compulsorily by the State, the question arises whether the property owner is entitled to compensation. The only express reference to the right to compensation is in Article 44.2.6, which prevents the property of religious denominations from being diverted "save for necessary works of public utility and on payment of compensation". Nevertheless it is clear that even outside the context of religious-owned land, the right to such compensation will almost invariably exist, the courts having taken the view that the taking of land without compensation may be an unjust attack on property rights. In *Central Dublin Development Association v. Attorney General* (1975), Kenny J. rejected the proposition that compensation was not mandated in cases of compulsory purchase. While some minor restrictions, he observed, might not merit compensation, there was little doubt but that State acquisition of the full ownership rights in a property without compensation "would in all cases be such an attack".

There is little question then that, otherwise than in times of emergency, the State cannot compulsorily acquire the full interest in land without giving compensation. The right to compensation in cases not involving the acquisition of full ownership depends on the circumstances of each case. In *ESB v. Gormley* (1985), the Supreme Court had to consider provisions allowing the plaintiff to route electricity lines through private property without the consent of the owner. The ESB, in this case, proposed the construction of three masts on the defendant's land, the highest of which would have been 40 metres tall. The Supreme Court held that while the power to interfere with the defendant's land was justified by the requirements of the common good, the lack of a firm right to compensation for such interference amounted to an unjust attack on the defendant's property rights.

30. FREEDOM OF RELIGION (ARTICLE 44)

Freedom of religion is a constitutional concept of some considerable vintage on this island. With Catholic emancipation in 1829, the British Parliament first gave legal expression to a growing recognition that religious intolerance could no longer be sanctioned by the State. All three Home Rule Bills as well as the Anglo-Irish Treaty of 1921 included clauses explicitly precluding religious discrimination, a principle now reflected in Article 44 of the 1937 Constitution.

During the discussion leading up to the adoption of the latter document, there was some pressure for a clause recognising the status of the Roman Catholic Church as "the one true church", a wording that was ultimately rejected. In its place, however, the original drafters inserted a clause recognising "the special position" of that Church, being the Church of the majority of the population. Considering the charge that "Home Rule is Rome Rule" this move was arguably ill-advised and led, in 1973, to the enactment of the Fifth Amendment of the Constitution. This removed the "special position" clause.

Article 44, unlike its U.S. counterpart, is not "neutral" about religious belief as a general phenomenon. Article 44.1 is clearly pro-religion in both language and spirit. It acknowledges that "homage of public worship is due to Almighty God" and requires that the State "hold His Name in reverence", hardly a formula for State indifference towards religious belief. The terminology is quite exclusive. There is no room for polytheistic perspectives (a belief in more than one God, *e.g.* Hinduism) or for religions that do not have a God as such (*e.g.* Buddhism). While the State, then, is obliged to "respect and honour religion", the concept of religion upheld in Article 44.1 seems rather limited.

In this context it is worth noting the comments of several judges that, despite the principle of non-discrimination in Article 44, Ireland is a "Christian state". Various references in the Preamble to the Constitution have been used to support this claim, including the reference to "the Most Holy Trinity" and "Our Divine Lord Jesus Christ". For instance, in *Norris v. Attorney General* (1984), (a case challenging the criminal prohibition on primarily homosexual sexual conduct), a majority of the Supreme Court invoked the preamble to support its assertion that the Constitution broadly reflected Christian principles of right and wrong. In a similar vein, Walsh J., in *Quinn's Supermarket v.*

Attorney General (1972), again referred to the Preamble in support of the proposition that the Irish "are a Christian People". (It is worth noting too, that the endnote to the Constitution dedicates the document to "the Glory of God and the Honour of Ireland" ("Do chum Glóire Dé agus Onóra na hÉireann").)

30.1 Free conscience and profession of religion

Article 44 guarantees, subject to public order and morality, the right to profess and practise one's chosen religion. By implication, one is presumably entitled to practise no religion at all. "Freedom of conscience", however, covers only religious conscience and not matters of social conscience. In *McGee v. Attorney General* (1974), the plaintiff alleged that the ban on the importation of contraceptives infringed her conscientious belief that it was appropriate to use a contraceptive device. The Supreme Court rejected this argument, noting that this was a matter of social conscience only and was not, thus, a matter with which Article 44 was concerned. With respect, it might be argued that the line between religious and social or philosophical perspectives is a lot thinner than the Court suggests.

30.1.1 Subject to public order and morality

As with all of the fundamental rights, there are limitations on the free exercise of one's religion. The fact that a particular practice is an integral part of one's religious rights or duties does not of itself render that practice immune from legal sanction. In *Prince v. Massachusetts* (1944), for instance, a U.S. court ruled that Massachusetts child labour laws did not infringe the Constitutional guarantee on free practice of religion, even though it precluded a Jehovah's Witness child from distributing religious pamphlets on the street. In a similar vein, laws banning polygamous marriages have been upheld in the U.S., despite the fact that Mormon men were once required by their religion to take plural wives (*Reynolds v. U.S.* (1878)). It might even be constitutionally possible, it is suggested, to ban a religion outright, if the State could show that its practices were manifestly contrary to the welfare of individuals and the public at large.

30.2 Supporting the practice of religion

An "established" religion is the official religion of a particular state. In Ireland there is no "established" religion. In England and Wales, Episcopalianism (Anglicanism) is designated as the official religion of State: the Queen is, for instance, the Head of the Church of England. Although our Constitution does not directly preclude the possibility of establishment *per se*, it is likely that such favouritism in this jurisdiction would offend the anti-discrimination clause mentioned below.

30.2.1 The non-endowment clause

As a general rule, the State is precluded from funding or otherwise endorsing the propagation of religion. The State, for instance, could not fund the building of a church or of an icon worshipping a particular religious figure. To this, however, there are significant exceptions, not least that the State is entitled to fund the giving of religious instruction in schools. In the *Campaign to Separate Church and State v. Minister for Education* (1998), the Supreme Court ruled that the State was entitled even to pay the salaries of school chaplains. The reasoning of the Court was that the State, in doing so, was simply fulfilling its duty (under Article 42) to support parents in their endeavours to educate their children. The State, by funding a system of chaplains, was supporting parental choice as regards the religious education of their children. In so ruling, the Court seems to have endorsed a general legal trend in favour of supporting the practice of religion even where this *prima facie* might involve the endowment of religion or discrimination between various religious perspectives.

30.2.2 The anti-discrimination clause

The State is precluded from discriminating between persons on the grounds of their religious profession (what they say they believe), belief, or status (what rank they occupy within a religious denomination). In *Mulloy v. Minister for Education* (1975), the last of these grounds was invoked where the Department of Education had refused to grant extra salary increments to a Catholic priest in respect of teaching experience obtained abroad. The Department's attempt to limit these increments to lay teachers who had taught abroad (and not extend them to priests, nuns and religious brothers who had also taught abroad) was held to infringe the anti-discrimination clause.

The State, moreover, is not entitled, according to the decision of Pringle J. in *M. v. An Bord Uchtála* (1975), to penalise married couples of mixed religion. In that case, the High Court struck down provisions of the Adoption Act 1952 that required that both parents adopting a child be of the same religion as the child. This condition being impossible for couples of mixed religion to satisfy, the provision was struck down as infringing the freedom of religion guaranteed by Article 44, (the parties effectively having been penalised for being of different religious persuasions).

In certain cases, however, discrimination may be justified by the requirement that the State support the free practice of religion. In fact, in most of the Constitutional cases on freedom of religion, the courts have tended to favour a result that aids the free practice of religion, even where this seems to involve the infringement of the non-endowment or anti-discrimination clauses. In *Quinn's Supermarket v. Attorney General* (1972), the plaintiff had complained that Jewish kosher shops had been exempted from general shop closing hours regulations. The Supreme Court accepted that some exemption was necessary in order to facilitate those of the Jewish faith in the practice of their religion — even if this was *technically* discriminatory, it was justified by the need to protect the free practice of the Jewish faith. While the Court concluded that the full exemption was more than required to achieve the latter aim, it accepted in principle that where there is a conflict between the requirement of non-discrimination and the need to support the free practice of religion, the Court would generally lean in favour of upholding the latter right.

This inclination was matched by the Supreme Court decision in *McGrath and Ó Ruairc v. Maynooth College* (1979). In that case two lecturers were dismissed from their posts at a State-funded third-level institution, having allegedly breached certain rules of the Roman Catholic Church. The Court ruled that although the institution had discriminated against them on the grounds of religious belief and status, there had been no breach of the Constitution. The State was entitled to support the free practice of religion, even if this involved indirectly endorsing the inherently discriminatory tenets of a particular religion.

With respect, this seems to go further than even the Constitution would require. The State is not required to support religion at any cost. Nonetheless, a religious body may plead its religious ethos in support of discriminatory action proscribed by the Employment Equality Act, 1998 and the Equal Status Act, 2000, even where that religious body is receiving State funding for its activities. In the older case of *Flynn v.*

Power (1985), a teacher who had become pregnant outside marriage was dismissed by her Roman Catholic employer on the ground that her presence in the school might undermine its ethos. The High Court concluded that the order was entitled to rely on its ethos as a defence against a charge of unfair dismissal. With respect, this appears to give too much free rein to the churches, at the expense of personal liberties.

30.3 State aid for schools

In the United States it is not possible for the State to fund a school where that school purports to give instruction in the religious doctrine of any particular religion. This stance of strict neutrality is most clearly evident in the ban on school prayer in state-funded schools (*Abingdon School District v. Schempp* (1963)). Recognising the important contribution of the religious denominations in the Irish education system, the Irish Constitution seems to reject such a rigid approach and thus, does allow state-funding for religious-run schools. (See *Campaign to Separate Church and State v. Minister for Education* (1998) where the plaintiff conceded that the State could fund religious-run schools.) The State may even fund, according to the Supreme Court in the *Campaign to Separate Church and State*, religious instruction in such schools. The State is, however, precluded from discriminating between different religions in the provision of such aid. In addition, every child who attends a state-funded school has the right (presumably exercised on its behalf by its parents) to opt out of religious instruction.

30.4 Autonomy of religious denominations

The State is not generally entitled to interfere in the running of religious denominations. Each denomination has the right to manage its own affairs, to own property (and correspondingly to deal freely with it) and to establish institutions for religious and charitable purposes. The State is explicitly precluded from taking the property of any religious denomination or educational institution except for "necessary works of public utility", in which case compensation must be paid.

Despite the wording of Article 44, the Constitution, as interpreted by the courts, seems to lean very heavily in favour of state support for religion, even where this may involve apparent infringements of the requirements of non-endowment and non-discrimination.

31. AMENDMENTS TO THE CONSTITUTION

Generally, it is open to the electorate alone to amend the Constitution. Between 1938 and 1941, however, the Legislature was entitled to amend the Constitution without recourse to the people. This facility, however, was deliberately limited to a short three year transitional period. Since then, only the people may make amendments and this they do by means of referenda (the plural of "referendum"). The rules for such referendum are set out in Articles 46 and 47.

For a constitutional referendum to take place, a Referendum Bill must be introduced in Dáil Éireann and passed by both Houses of the Oireachtas. Such a Bill may only include proposed amendments to the Constitution — the same Bill should not include any other non-constitutional matter. Once passed the Bill is then put directly to the people. All citizens (but only citizens) being entitled to vote at Dáil elections may vote in a referendum. If a majority of the votes cast support the amendment then the amendment is deemed to have been carried. Once carried the amendment is signed into law and promulgated by the President.

Certain rules apply to the conduct of a referendum. While a government is free to speak its mind on a referendum issue, it is precluded from giving financial support to one side of the argument without also funding the opposing arguments (*McKenna v. An Taoiseach (No. 2)* (1995). To do otherwise would be to infringe the guarantee of equality (Article 40.1) and the personal rights of those voters who disagreed with the proposal, including the right to express one's convictions and opinions. Moreover, the State media is obliged to give equal airtime to both sides of the argument (*Coughlan v. RTÉ* (1998)).

Provided that a Referendum Bill is properly submitted, there is no restriction on the content of a proposed amendment. In *Riordan v. An Taoiseach, (No. 2)* (1998), a concerned citizen challenged the manner in which the nineteenth Amendment proposed to alter the Constitution. This amendment proposed that Articles 2 and 3 could be changed by the Government contingent only on certain conditions being met. The Supreme Court, however, concluded that it is possible to amend the constitution in this conditional manner. This ruling again underlines the fact that the people, as supreme arbiters of national policy, have complete discretion as regards the content of the Constitution (see also

In the Matter of Article 26 and the Regulation of Information Bill, 1995 (1995)).

A referendum, thus, can be passed without any intention to change the Constitution but with a view simply to clarifying the already existing position thereunder. In *Finn v. Attorney General* (1983), the plaintiff had complained that the Eighth Amendment guaranteeing the right to life of the unborn child was not an amendment, as the Constitution already protected that right (see Walsh J. in *McGee v. Attorney General* (1973)). Carroll J. ruled that a constitutional amendment can be passed even if it only clarifies and does not change the constitutional position on a particular issue.

31.1 Requirements of a referendum

A constitutional referendum is deemed to have passed if a majority of votes cast are cast in favour of the proposed Amendment.

31.2 Successful Amendments

No.	Year	Effects	Purpose
First	1939	Art. 28.3 amended	Extended the definition of national emergency to include conflicts in which the State was not a participant.
Second	1941	Miscell.	Miscellaneous amendments, mostly to the Irish text of the Constitution.
Third	1972	Art. 29.4.3 added	Allowed Ireland to join the EEC, Euratom and the ECSC.
Fourth	1973	Art. 16.1.2 amended	Voting age lowered to 18.
Fifth	1973	Art. 44.1 replaced	Removed the "special position" of the Roman Catholic Church from Article 44.
Sixth	1979	Art. 37.2 inserted	Exempted the Adoption Board from the requirement that justice be administered only in courts of law.
Seventh	1979	Art. 18.4.2 added	Extended the franchise for elections to the Seanad.
Eighth	1983	Art. 40.3.3 inserted	New clause purporting to guarantee the right to life of the unborn child, subject to the equal right to life of its mother.

Constitutional Law

No.	Year	Effects	Purpose.
Ninth	1984	Art. 16.1.2 amended	Made provision for non-citizens to vote in Dáil elections.
Tenth	1987	Art. 29 amended	Allowed State to ratify Single European Act.
Eleventh	1992	Art. 29 amended	Allowed State to ratify Maastricht Treaty.
Thirteenth	1992	Art. 40.3.3 amended	Guaranteed the right to travel to obtain an abortion abroad.
Fourteenth	1992	Art. 40.3.3 amended	Guaranteed, subject to statutory conditions, the right to obtain information regarding abortion abroad.
Fifteenth	1995	Art. 41.3.2 amended	Permitted, in limited circumstances, the granting of a decree of divorce.
Sixteenth	1996	Art. 40.4.7 inserted	Allowed for the restriction of the availability of bail for persons accused of a crime.
Seven-teenth	1997	Art. 28.4.3 replaced	Loosened the rules on cabinet confidentiality, allowing the High Court to require the giving of evidence otherwise precluded by the rule.
Eighteenth	1998	Art. 29 amended	Allowed the State to ratify the Amsterdam Treaty.
Nineteenth	1998	Art. 29.7 inserted	Allowed the State to ratify the British-Irish (Good Friday) Agreement, with provision for the amendment of Articles 2 & 3 of the Constitution.
Twentieth	1999	Art. 28 A inserted	Constitutionally recognised Local Government; required that local elections be held at least every five years.
Twenty-first	2001	Art. 15.5.2 added, Arts. 28.3 an d 13.6 amended	Oireachtas prevented (even under exemption in Article 28.3) from legislating for the death penalty.
Twenty-second	2001		Ratification of Treaty concerning International Criminal Court of Justice.

31.3 Defeated referenda

Not every attempt to change the Constitution has been successful. Specifically five proposed amendments have failed to obtain majority support in referenda. Governments have twice attempted (1959 and 1968) and failed to replace the proportional representation system of voting with the "straight vote" system favoured in Britain. An initial attempt to remove the ban on divorce was defeated in 1986. Similarly, a controversial proposal to restrict the application of the X case was defeated in 1992. As a result, one will note, there is no Twelfth Amendment. And most recently, an attempt to allow the adoption of the Nice Treaty failed in 2001.

31.4 Article 27

Certain types of Bills, not intended to amend the Constitution, can be referred to the people under Article 27 of the Constitution. This mechanism, however, is much more limited than a cursory glance might reveal. Only Bills passed as a result of Article 23 can be the subject of such a reference. Article 23 pertains to Bills that have been rejected by the Seanad. After a 90-day delay, and notwithstanding the Seanad's opposition, the Dáil may pass a resolution deeming the Bill to have been passed by both Houses of the Oireachtas. Only in such a case may a Bill be the subject of an Article 27 referendum. The Article 27 procedure, to date, has never been used. It is also worth noting that the majority required for such a referendum is lower than in the case of a constitutional referendum. The proposal will be deemed to have passed unless more than half of the votes (representing at least 1/3 of the total electorate) are cast against the measure. (Article 47.2).

APPENDIX A

Alternative sources of information on the Constitution

Textbooks

Casey, *Constitutional Law in Ireland,* (3rd. ed., Dublin, Round Hall Sweet & Maxwell, 2000)

Kelly, Hogan and Whyte, *The Irish Constitution* (3rd. ed., Dublin, Butterworths, 1994)

Doolan, *Constitutional Law and Constitutional Rights in Ireland* (3 rd. ed., Dublin, Gill and Macmillan, 1994).

Report of the Constitution Review Group 1996 (Dublin, Stationery Office, 1996)

Beytagh, *Constitutionalism in Contemporary Ireland* (Dublin, Round Hall, 1997)

Ó Cearúil, *Bunreacht na hÉireann, a study of the Irish Text*, (Dublin, Government of Ireland, 1999)

On specific aspects of the Constitution:

Morgan, *The Separation of Powers in the Irish Constitution,* (Dublin: Round Hall, Sweet and Maxwell, 1997.)

Farrell (ed.), *DeValera's Constitution and Ours,* (Dublin: Gill and Macmillan, 1988)

Murphy and Twomey, *Ireland's Evolving Constitution, 1937-1997,* (Oxford: Hart, 1998)

O'Reilly, (ed.), *Human Rights and Constitutional Law: Essays in Honour of Brian Walsh,* (Dublin: Round Hall Press, 1992)

Useful websites

Information on the Irish State:	**www.irlgov.ie**
Courts Service:	**www.courts.ie**
RTÉ Guide to the Dáil	**www.rte.ie/news/dailguide/**
Irish Legislation and recent cases	**www.bailii.org and www.irlii.org**
European Commission:	**www.europa.eu.int**

APPENDIX B

Summary of Judicial Review

	Article 34	Article 50	Article 26
What type of legislation does this Article concern?	Measures adopted by the State *after* December 29, 1937	Measures adopted by the State *before* December 29, 1937 (and not repealed before that date	Bills passed (or deemed to have been passed) by both Houses of the Oireachtas but not yet signed into law by the President
Who can make a challenge to such a measure?	Any person adversely affected by the measure	Any person adversely affected by the measure	The President of Ireland
Who decides such cases?	The High Court, or on appeal, the Supreme Court	The High Court, or on appeal, the Supreme Court	The Supreme Court
Does the presumption of constitutionality apply?	Yes	No	Yes
What is the effect of a ruling of unconstitutionality?	The parts of the measure that are unconstitutional, are void and thus have no legal effect	The parts of the measure that are unconstitutional are deemed not to have been "carried forward" in 1937 into the law of this State	The entire Bill can never become law

INDEX

Abortion, 10, 11, 103, 105, *see* **Life, right to**

Adoption, 119, *see also* **Family**

Amendments to Constitution, 218 *et seq.*, *see also* **President**
Article 27 and, 219, 220
referendum,
    defeated, 219
    requirements of, 217
    successful, 217, 218, 219

Arrest, powers of, *see* **Personal Liberty**

Attorney General, 102 *et seq.*
appointment of, 72, 102
defender of public rights, 105, 106
independence of, 102, 103, 105
prosecution of offences by, 104, 105
role of, 72, 102
specific function, 103

Auditor General, 72

Bail, *see* **Personal liberty**

Chief Justice of Ireland, 74, 107

Children, *see* **Family**

Circuit Court, *see* **Courts**

Citizenship,
acquiring of, 50, 51
birth, by, 50
citizens, rights of, 125
definition of, 50
descent, by, 50
fundamental political duties of, 51
marriage, by, 50

Citizenship — *contd.*
naturalisation, by, 50
non-citizens and conditional rights, 123, 124
non-denial of on grounds of sex, 50
obligations of, 51

Comptroller, 72

Constitution, *see also* **Amendments to Constitution, Interpretation of Constitution, and State**
creation of, 1
operation of, came into, 3
purpose of, 5 *et seq.*

Contraception, 11, 156, *see also* **Family**

Council of State, 25, 72, 73, 74, *see also* **President**
membership of, 73, 74

Courts, 107 *et seq.*, *see also* **Separation of Powers**
Article 37, 117
Circuit Court, 108, 110
    criminal jurisdiction of, 108
    members of, 108, 109
court process, respect for, 181, 187 *et seq.*
courts, right of access to, 163, 164
discipline, matters of, 115, 116
District Court, 109
    jurisdiction of, 109
    members of, 109
exclusive powers of, 111, *see also* **Separation of Powers**
    can the Oireachtas reverse effects of a court decision, 112

Courts — *contd.*
  fair procedures, right to, 165
  freedom of expression, *see*
  Freedom of Expression
  High Court, 16, 108, 109
    members of, 108, 109
    President of, 108
  in camera proceedings, 111
  judges,
    appointment of, 71, 109
    retirement of, 110
    salaries of, 110
  judicial function, exercise of,
    111, 113, 114, 116, 117
  jury, *see* **Jury**
  justice to be administered in
    public, 111
  military courts, 141, 145
  special courts, 141, 144, 145
  Supreme Court, 16, 17, 107,
    108, 109
    Chief Justice, 107
    members of, 107
    referral of Bills to, 26
  tribunal, *see* **Tribunals**

Cumann na nGaedhal, *see* **Fine Gael**

Dáil Éireann, 1, 85 *et seq.*, *see also* **Government**, **Oireachtas** and **Seanad Éireann**
  Ceann Comhairle, 74
  chairman of, 74
  conduct of international affairs by, 89, *see also* **International relations**
  debates of, 7
  dissolution of, 72
  election to, 85, 89
    voting for, 86
  legislative powers of, 87
  more powerful than Seanad, 87
  number of members of, 85

Dáil Éireann — *contd.*
  public finances of, 88
  supervisory role of, 89
  voting, 86

De Valera, Eamon, vii, 2, 3, 4

Die, right to, *see* **Personal Rights**

Director of Public Prosecution, 22
  creation of office of, 104
  independence of, 104
  review of decision of, 104
  unfettered discretion of, 104

Divorce, *see* **Family**

Easter Rising, 1

Education, 193 *et seq.*, 200
  freedom of choice of, 201
  minimum standards for, set by State, 202
  people with disabilities, and, 203, 204
  primary, free, right to, 202, 203
  religion, *see* **Religion**

Edward VIII, King, abdication of, 3

Emergency powers, 99 *et seq.*
  actual invasion, 99
  constitutional exemption, 100
  death penalty, 100
  declarations of war, 99
  emergency, ending of, 100
  invocation of Article 28.3, 100, 101

Equality, 146 *et seq.*
  discrimination, basis for, 150
  employment, 151
  inequality, 146, 147
  no breach of, 149, 150
  other legal provisions for, 151
  relevant differences to be taken into account, 151
  sex discrimination, 147, 149

European Union, 76, 57 *et seq.*,
see also **International relations**
Article 29.4.7, 58
direct effect of EU law, 59, 60
European elections, 89
impact of EU law, 44, 80
implementing directives, 60, 61
referendums and EU treaties,
61, 62
supremacy of EU law, 58

Executive Council, 2, 3

Extradition, 53, 177, 178

Fair trial, right to, *see* **Offences, trial of,**

Family, 193 *et seq.*, *see also* **Citizenship** and **Personal rights**
autonomy, right to, of, 194, 195
basis of constitutional family,
193, 194
children, *see also* **Personal rights**
adoption of, 198, 199
born outside marriage, 9
custody of, 198, 199, 200
guardianship of, 198
divorce, 200
education, see **Education**
family rights, curtailment of,
195
individual rights and family
rights, 194
marriage, constitutional preference for, 196
procreation, right of, 126, 158, 159
non-marital, see **Personal rights**
taxation of married couples, 20,
21, 35, 36
unmarried parents and their children, rights of, 197, 198

Fianna Fail, 2

Fine Gael, 2

Freedom of association
right not unlimited, 189
trade union recognition, 192

Freedom of expression, 152, 180 *et seq.*
freedom of press, 181
restrictions on, 181 *et seq.*
court process, respect for,
181, 187
contempt of court, 187
sub judice restrictions,
187, 188
individual rights, respect for,
181, 188
public morality, 181, 182
blasphemy, 183, 184
control on information on
abortion, 183, *see also* **Life, Right to**
indecency ,182
public order, 181, 184
incitement to commit a
crime, 185
inflammatory material,
184
security of State, 181, 185
official secrets, 186
sedition, 185, 186
undermining authority of
State, 186

Freedom of Information, abortion, and, 169, 170

Freedom of Travel, *see also* **Life, Right to**
outside the State, 162
Senators, and, 83
TDs, and, 83

Fundamental Rights, 6, 9, *see* **Personal Rights**

Government, 92 *et seq.*, *see also* **Dáil Éireann**, **Oireachtas**, **Seanad Éireann** and **Separation of Powers**
cabinet confidentiality, 97 *et seq.*
Seventeenth Amendment and, 98
collective responsibility of, 97
eligibility for, 89, 90
executive privilege of, 96
foreign policy and, 52 *et seq.*
membership of, 92
ministers, 95, 96
requested resignation of, 92
termination of post of, 92
voluntary resignation of, 92
Tánaiste, *see* **Tánaiste**
Taoiseach, *see* **Taoiseach**

High Court, *see* **Courts**
Home Rule, 1
Homosexuality, 12, 18, 19, 34, 54, 127, 149
female versus male, 149

Human rights, 123 *et seq.*,
Constitution and, 123 *et seq.*
distributive justice, 127
legal persons and constitutional rights, 125
no right is ever absolute, 126
non-citizens and constitutional rights, 123
universal nature of rights, 123-125

International relations, 52 *et seq.*, 89, *see also* **European Union**
dualism v monism, 53-55
international agreements, approval of by Dáil, 53
extra-territoriality, 55, 56
impact of international law in Irish courts, 55

International relations — *contd.*
party to international agreements, 53
Interpretation of the Constitution, 7 *et seq.*
broad, 8, 9
conflict with Irish text, 7
double construction rule, 15
harmonious, 9, 10
hierarchical, 10, 11
historical approach, 11, 12
literal, 7, 8
natural law approach, 13, 14
presumption of, constitutionality, 14, 24, 26
Irish Free State, 1, 2

Judges, *see* **Courts**
Judicial review, 16 *et seq.*, 25, *see also* **President**
Acts of Oireachtas post 1937, 16
one judgment rule, 16
Article 26, reference of Bills to Supreme Court, 18, 24, 25 *et seq.*, *see also* **President**
Article 50, 17, 24
certain matters beyond, 21, 22, 23
locus standi, 18, 19
retrospectivity of a finding of unconstitutionality, 20, 21
summary of, 24
Jury,
selection of, 21
trial by, 139 *et seq.*
basic principles of, 141
impartiality of jury, 139
independence of jury, 139
jury representative of society at large, 140
trials where juries not constitutionally required, 141 *et seq.*

Jury — *contd.*
  military courts, 141, 145
  minor offences, 141, 142, 143
  primary and secondary punishment, 143, 144
  special courts, 141, 144, 145
  waiver of right to, 139

Language, 48, 49
  right to use Irish in court, 49

Liberty, 126, *see* **Personal Liberty**

Life, right to, 152, 166 *et seq.*, *see also* **Abortion**
  unborn child, of, 167 *et seq.*
  freedom of information on abortion, 169, 183
  freedom to travel to avail of abortion, 168, 169
  substantive question, 167, 168

Local Elections, 90

Minor Offences, 11, *see also* **Jury**

Money Bills, 25, 72

Nation, *see also* **Preamble and State**
  concept of, 38, 39
  Northern Ireland and, *see* **Northern Ireland**
  reunification of, 34

Nice Treaty, 57

Northern Ireland, 2, 38 *et seq.*
  Articles 2 and 3 and, 38 *et seq.*, 41-43
  recognition of, 40
  Good Friday Agreements, 1998, 40, 41

Offences, trial of, 128 *et seq.*, *see also* **Jury**,
  ability to comprehend proceedings, 132
  alleged crime must be known to law, 128
  autrefois acquit, 138
  certain and proportionate sentence, 138
  courts, right of access to, 163, 164
  crime a crime at time of commission, 129
  crime, definition of, 129
  extraordinary excusing circumstances, 137
  fair procedures, right to, 165
  fair trial, principles of, 128 *et seq.*
  innocence, presumption of, 130, 131
  "innocent till proven guilty", 130, 131
  legal representation, right to, 133
  prepare and present a defence, right to, 133
  prejudged, right not to be, 132, 133
  present at one's trial, right to be131
  privilege against double jeopardy, 138
  silence, right to 134-136
  speedy trial, right to, 129, 130
  statute of limitations and, 130
  unconstitutionally obtained evidence, 136, 137

Oireachtas, 14, 76 *et seq.*, *see also* **Dáil Éireann** and **Seanad Éireann**
  cannot delegate right to make policy, 81
  cannot pass certain laws, 77
  change of legislation by, 80

Oireachtas — *contd.*
  delegated legislation, 78-80
  exclusive powers of within Ire-
    land, 77, 78
  emergency powers, *see* emer-
    gency powers
  exclusive right of to legislate, 76
  parliamentary privilege, 82, 83
  repeal of legislation by, 80, 81
  Sheehan principle and, 81, 82
  sole right of to legislate, 76

Partition, 1

Personal liberty, 10, 153, 171 *et
  seq.*
  arrest, power to, 171
    bail, right to, 175, 176
    detention,
        constitutionality of, 174
        extradition and, 177, 178
        person's own welfare, for,
          177
        preventative detention,
          176, 177
        questioning for, 173, 174
    freedom from oppressive
      interrogation, 174, 175
    reasonable suspicion, 171
    rights on arrest, 172, 173
    stop and search powers, 178
    surveillance, 178, 179

Personal rights, 35, 152 *et seq.*,
  see also **Freedom of expression, Life, Right to, Personal
  liberty and Religion**
  bodily integrity, right to, 154,
    155
  children, right to bear, 126, 158,
    159, *see also* Family
  communicate, right to, 162
  courts, right of access to, 163,
    164, *see also* courts
  Directives of Social Policy and
    153

Personal rights — *contd.*
  fair procedures, right to, 165,
    see also **Offences, trial of**
  livelihood, right to earn, 160,
    161, 162
  marry, right to, 157, 158, *see
    also* **Family**
  medical treatment, right to
    refuse, 154
  natural death, right to, 159, 160
  non-marital families, rights of,
    159
  privacy, right to 155, 156, 157
  protection of, 152 *et seq.*
  source of unenumerated rights,
    152, 153
  travel outside State, right to,162
  treated inhumanely, right not to
    be, 155

Preamble, 34 *et seq.*
  goals of, 34
  judicial comment on, 34
    dignity and freedom of the
      individual, and, 35
    prudence, justice and charity
      and, 34, 35
    religious values of state, and
      34
    reunification of nation and,
      34, *see also* **Nation, North-
      ern Ireland**
    true social order and, 35
  language of, 34
  religious tone of, 34

President, 18, 24, 25 *et seq.*, 69 *et
  seq.*
  Council of State and, 25, 73, 74
  discretion of, 73
  dismissal of, 75
  election of, 69, 70, 89
  eligibility requirement of, 69
  nominations for, 70
  powers of, 70-73
  Presidential Commission, 74

President — *contd.*
  reference of Bills by, 25
  advantages of Article 26 procedure, 29, 30
  Bills and part of referred, 28, 29
  can a part of a Bill be referred, 26
  consequences of decision, 27, 28
  no provisions unconstitutional, 27, 28
  part of Bill found unconstitutional, 27
  disadvantages of Article 26 procedure, 29, 30
  one judgment rule, 27
  presumption of constitutionality, 26, 27, *see also* **Interpretation of Constitution**
  to whom is reference sent, 26
  what can be referred, 25
  what happens when reference is made, 26
  term of office of, 70

Prisoners,
  rights of, 126

Privilege,
  double jeopardy, against, 138
  executive, 45, 96
  parliamentary, 82

Procreation, right of, 126, 158, 159, *see also* **Family**

Property (rights to), 205 *et seq.*
  compensation, right to, 209, 210
  impositions on, 208, 209
  limits on exercise of, 206
  property, meaning of, 206, 207
  rent restrictions, 207
  scope of right to, 205 *et seq.*

Referendum, *see* **Amendments to Constitution and President**

Reference of Bills, *see* **President**

Religion, 153, 211 *et seq.*
  anti-discrimination clause and, 213, 214, 215
  autonomy of religious denominations, 215
  discrimination on basis of, 7
  free conscience, 212
  non-endowment clause and, 213
  public order and morality and, 212
  State aid for schools, 215
  support for practice of, 213

Rights, *see* **Freedom of Expression, Life, right to, Offences, trial of, Personal Liberty and Personal Rights**

Rule of Law, 6, *see also* **Interpretation of Constitution**

Separation of Powers, 5, 65 *et seq.,* see also **Courts, Dáil Éireann, Government, Oireachtas and Seanad Éireann**
  blurring lines of, 67
  concept of, 65
    executive power, 65, 66
    legislative power, 65, 66
    judicial power, 65, 66
    exclusivity of roles, 66

Seanad Éireann, 85, 86 *et seq.,* see also **Dáil Éireann, Government, Oireachtas and State**
  legislative powers of, 87
  less powerful than Dáil Éireann, 87
  members, number of, 86, 87
  public finances of, 88
  voting for, 90

Sinn Féin, 1, 111

State, 44 *et seq., see also* **Emergency Powers, European Law,**

International Relations, Government and Oireachtas
citizenship of, *see* **Citizenship**
framework for governing, 5, 6
independence of, 44, 45
jurisdiction of,
definition of, 5
languages of, 48, 49
legal person as, 45
national flag, 47, 48
privilege, *see* **Privilege**
relationship with inhabitants of, 66
right to ratify international agreement, 19
royal prerogatives, 45, 46, 47
security of, *see* **Freedom of expression**
sovereign as, 45-47
treasure trove, 45, 46, 47

Succession, 9

Supreme Court, *see* courts

Tánaiste, 91 *et seq.*
nomination of, 94

Taoiseach, 91, 94, 95, *see also*
Government and Tanaiste
appointment of, 71, 92, 93
powers of appointment of, 67
responsibilities of, 93, 94
resignation of, 94
temporary absence of, 95

Treasure Trove, *see* **State**

Tribunals
Beef, 115
judicial functions, cannot perform, 114, 115

Tricolour (National Flag), 47, 48

Unenumerated rights, *see* **Personal rights**

War of Independence, 1

World War One, 1